Wealth and the Will of God

Philanthropic and Nonprofit Studies
Dwight F. Burlingame and David C. Hammack, editors

Wealth and the Will of God

Discerning the Use of Riches in the
Service of Ultimate Purpose

Paul G. Schervish and Keith Whitaker

INDIANA UNIVERSITY PRESS

BLOOMINGTON & INDIANAPOLIS

This book is a publication of

Indiana University Press
601 North Morton Street
Bloomington, IN 47404-3797 USA

www.iupress.indiana.edu

Telephone orders   800-842-6796
Fax orders   812-855-7931
Orders by e-mail   iuporder@indiana.edu

♾ The paper used in this publication meets the minimum requirements of
the American National Standard for Information Sciences—Permanence
of Paper for Printed Library Materials, ANSI Z39.48-1992.

Manufactured in the United States of America

Library of Congress Cataloging-in-Publication Data

Schervish, Paul G.
  Wealth and the will of God : discerning the use of riches in the
service of ultimate purpose / Paul G. Schervish and Keith Whitaker.
    p. cm. — (Philanthropic and nonprofit studies)
  Includes bibliographical references (p.) and index.
  ISBN 978-0-253-35407-5 (cloth : alk. paper) — ISBN 978-0-253-22148-3
(pbk. : alk. paper) 1. Wealth—Religious aspects—Christianity—History of
doctrines. I. Whitaker, Albert Keith. II. Title.
  BR115.W4S34 2009
  261.8'5—dc22
                      2009022813

1 2 3 4 5 15 14 13 12 11 10

To Jen, for the gift of time
KW

To Terry Chipman, for wisdom better than gold
PS

Contents

Preface

This book is about disposition and doing. It is about vocation—the intersection of thinking, feeling, and acting in regard to the specifics of the will of God for a particular individual, in a particular place, at a particular time. We ask the six teachers from Aristotle to Edwards just what they have to offer to help shape a spiritual vocation of wealth for our time. We seek to guide today's wealth holders (and ultimately all people) and those pastors, counselors, financial professionals, and fundraisers who associate with them. We offer a contemporary lens on the spiritual nourishment provided by Western Christian religious traditions. This fresh approach provides a new reading of these traditional figures. Our aim is not to gather norms to be imposed on wealth holders. We are not engaged in an effort to ferret out and organize the mandates of religious founders on the use of wealth for doing good in the world. Instead, we seek to locate what is unfamiliar in six familiar authors. This is to uncover what these founders can offer those seeking to live a contemporary rather than a conventional religious biography of wealth.

The difference is to look for what the authors would have to say were each writing within the framework of a contemporary theory of agency. Such a theory of agency considers agents as reflective actors. They possess enough everyday working awareness to make conscientious choices about how to move forward with their desires within the hand of enablements and constraints they have been dealt. Today, what makes a biography of wealth religiously grounded is not submission to tenets enunciated by religious figures of the past or their followers in the present. Rather it is approaching religious traditions in a fresh way, one by which religious adherents discover from within their traditions of choice the array of responsibilities that they are called to figure out for their own circumstances, time, and place. In a word, they are reflectively putting together the meanings and practices of a calling particular to them.

There was an ancient tale in the Middle East about a beautiful ring with magic powers. It made the man who wore it rich, for the ring opened to its owner the door of wealth, God's love, and the love of other people. This man wished to pass his good fortune to his descendants. He gave the ring to his oldest son and then told his other children to look to that son for guidance and help. That son did the same when he grew old, and so the family enjoyed happiness and wealth for years and years.

Many generations later, however, one inheritor was in a quandary: he had three virtuous sons whom he loved the same. When it was time to pass on the beautiful ring, he could not choose. So he had a jeweler fabricate two exact copies of the ring. He then took each son aside and secretly gave each of them one of the three rings.

When the father died, each son produced his ring and claimed title as master of the family and its fortune. But no one knew which of the three rings was the authentic one. The sons quarreled and with their own supporters divided into camps. Instead of the love of others they found hatred. And none found the door to wealth, for they were too busy arguing about the beauty and authenticity of their rings.

But others recalled the ring's power and searched for the door of wealth. To their surprise, they found that each of the rings could locate the door. But it could open the door only to him who possessed a certain frame of mind. A seeker of wealth had to view the ring with indifference and refrain from grasping at wealth or quarreling over it. The others found that when they had this attitude, they could find the door merely by tracing the outline of the ring.[1]

Like any good story, this one adds meaning to our experience and suggests inner questions that we have. The dazzling ring is said to bring to its owner love, for example. How many beautiful possessions appear to do just that! People do find this idea tempting. But as the story reminds us, people also hope to use their treasure for "something more" than themselves. Wealth inspires thoughts of legacy, such as an inheritance, which is what the ring symbolizes. But a legacy is not only monetary in nature; it encompasses values and even a way of life. The value of caring for others is seen, for example, in the old man's wish to keep the doors of wealth and love open to his descendents.

While wealth can instruct and inspire union and, in the tale, family happiness, it can also incite discord. Because we are human, ownership of riches can generate claims of privilege, prestige, and power that are at odds with love, as shown by the father with three sons. He wants to take care of his family, but he tries to improvise a solution to his dilemma without making a decision. Chaos ensues. And the sons show that while beauty (here, that of the ring) can elevate us, it can also make us put appearances before reality.

---

1. There are several sources for this story: Lessing's *Nathan the Wise* III.7; Boccaccio's *Decameron* I.3; and the *Gesta Romanorum*, tale 89. We have combined Lessing's version with the version that appears in the Sufi tradition, ascribed to the Suhrawardi School. See Shah, *Tales of the Dervishes*, 153–154.

In the end, none of the rings were truly valuable in themselves. The "other people" found that by adopting a peaceful attitude, they could find the door of wealth by tracing the outline of the ring. True wealth, they learn, depends not on things but on our attitudes toward things, on a stance and not on stuff, inspiration rather than inheritance. Ultimately, the apparently prized possession of the ring was but a sign, a marker, pointing toward the real prize, and available to everyone.

There is also a religious interpretation of the story, which may explain why it was retold for centuries. Recall that the ring was said to bring the love both of other people and of God. In this reading, the first patriarch is God. God gives His seal and "ring," which stands for true religion or a sort of natural faith, to humankind. People preserve this faith through many generations, until we come to the father with three worthy sons. The eldest would symbolize Moses, the middle son Jesus, and the youngest Mohammed. The descendents or followers of each "son" have their virtues, but the religious camps that develop around them fall to squabbling over which is the chosen branch of the family. In doing so, they lose sight of the true worth of the gift.

Confounding orthodox adherents of the three Abrahamic faiths, none of the "sons" in the story can "prove" his ring is the true one. (And perhaps even the original ring is not the true prize.) Its mere outline opens the door to wealth to whoever adopts a mindset of love and faith. Even the ring copies do this, for they have the outline and beauty of the original. The story teaches, then, that each of religious traditions contains truth. To find that truth, one must overcome temptations to ownership and preeminence.

What is wealth, how do we recognize it, and what it is for? How do we understand it in the context of faith, which assigns ultimacy to God alone? These are some of the broader questions the story poses, and they are the focus of this book. To explore answers, we consider six great theologians, philosophers, and spiritual leaders and their thoughts on life and wealth, especially how riches can serve ultimate purposes. We turn first to Aristotle, then to five Christian thinkers: Thomas Aquinas, Ignatius of Loyola, Martin Luther, John Calvin, and Jonathan Edwards. Although the meaning of wealth in Christian thought is our main focus, we include Aristotle because Christians have long found in his ideas a wisdom that illuminates the truth of their tradition. The book does consider the nature of giving and spending money via consuming, tithing, or other means, but its scope goes beyond philanthropy. Those topics are examined as they relate more to the meaning and purpose of life for people of faith.

Our Method

We seek as much as possible, by turning to their texts, to allow each of our thinkers to express his own views. We cite many fine biographies of these thinkers, so that readers, if they wish, can learn more. But our primary desire is to engage our thinkers' ideas. Here we take inspiration from another story, about a college freshman assigned to write a report on Aristotle's *Ethics*. The freshman had no idea who Aristotle was, but plunged in. "In the first page of his *Ethics*, Mr. Aristotle argues," began his report, which he read to the class. He continued in this vein, talking about the opinions of "Mr. Aristotle." He thought Aristotle was a contemporary thinker, and not someone who lived 2,400 years before! No doubt this textual approach can lead to overlooking fine historical points. But this risk is worth it, if we can engage in conversation with these minds with the freshness of this freshman.

To facilitate that conversation and maintain a consistency of approach, each of our six chapters uses similar terms and is organized in three similar sections, covering five topics. Our hope is that with this structure, readers especially interested in certain topics can more easily draw parallels or contrasts between the different chapters.

- The first section of each chapter covers two topics: the nature of ultimate reality and what human practical life best approaches ultimate reality during our earthly life. First we examine what each thinker has to say about the *ultimate purposes* of human life, that is, our goals or highest aspirations, what it is that we live for. These views are often found in the theologians' arguments about their faith. We then turn to discussions about the nature of virtue, since virtue reveals something of one's views about the ultimate purpose of human life as carried out through practical daily living.
- The second part of each chapter also covers two topics: the meaning of capacities and specific directions for use of capacities. We unfold what each thinker has to say about the *capacities* available to us in living our lives. We look to see how each defines wealth, money, and resources. Since, as the tale of the ring reveals, people often mistakenly limit their view of wealth to the category of "stuff," we examine how each writer broadens the definition of resources beyond wealth and money. This section also addresses our fourth topic—the possible forms of action available to us, ways in which we might use wealth, such as lending and tithing.
- Finally, in the third section of each chapter, we examine the fifth topic. We study the process of *deliberation* that connects those resources with ultimate purposes. Deliberation is the process by which we move from consideration of ends and resources to making a choice. One thinker's method may involve more logic; another's may be more intuitive or imaginative. All demand a clear

conception of the goal, some reasoning about the steps, and some inspiration about the whole. In short, this third part connects the other two and offers readers a method they can apply to their lives.

Ultimate purposes, capacities, and *deliberation* are the signposts by which we direct our inquiry into each of these thinkers' ideas.

Our Religious Focus

This book focuses on the Christian tradition, but it does not do so to trump or dispute other traditions. Christianity is simply the language of faith the authors know best and chose to write about. We believe that each of the Abrahamic offspring can learn from the others, as our theologians attempt to discover and explain the truth that resides within and perhaps beyond their own tradition.

The ideas of any religious faith tend to become embedded in an interpretive tradition or formal system of thought that becomes sedimented over time. People turn to these six thinkers first and foremost as teachers and authorities, forgetting that they began as seekers of the truth themselves. In order to break through sedimented thinking, we turn to the thinkers' own words. It is our hope that this book will help illuminate wisdom—truly and broadly considered—not only to interested Christians but to those who have abandoned or even never really known Christianity.

On the exclusivity of religious truth, the tale of the ring suggests much about our purposes and attitudes. The chapters of this book are not offered as summaries of dogma or as proof-texts. Nor are the teachings of these thinkers the "possessions" of one or another person or tradition. Instead, we ask our readers to consider these chapters as rings. We cannot say which thinker holds the "true" ring—if any one does. Their thoughts have a grand, complicated, sparkling beauty. They also say many different things, contradicting one another at times. It may be impossible to say, on the basis of reason alone, that any one of them (or any one of their traditions) stands preeminent above the others.

If these chapters are the rings of the ancient tale, then we are the seekers. Instead of grabbing at these, then, or learning them by rote, we invite you to inspect these chapters for the traces, the outlines, of a way to live with respect to your own purposes and your own resources. These thinkers found the traces that made sense for their circumstances; we must find the traces that work for us. With their examples in mind, we hope that our readers may become seekers, those who discover a stance that suits their own life so that they too may trace in their day and circumstances an outline that opens "the door to wealth."

Acknowledgments

We are grateful to all those who encouraged, supported, and assisted directly with this book. But initially we recall with fondness and respect the special teachers in our past. These mentors schooled us enough that we dared to inquire about the nexus between wealth and ultimate concern expressed by the wise thinkers and religious founders we discuss in this book. In particular one of us owes a happy debt to Aristotle, the other to Ignatius Loyola.

We are grateful to Craig Dykstra and the Lilly Endowment Inc. for entrusting us with a grant to research and write this book. Craig wisely counseled us to expand the breadth of the book, and from there on let us pursue our own lights—never looking over our shoulder and patiently awaiting this publication.

We are grateful to Dwight Burlingame, editor of Indiana University Press's series Philanthropic and Nonprofit Studies, in which our book proudly resides. Dwight saw promise in the book, even from its earliest draft. He shepherded things along as we sent each chapter to an appropriate expert and revised the chapters in light of their comments. We thank these scholars, each of whom poured over a chapter to make the book more faithful to its subjects—Amy Kass, Stephen Pope, Howard Gray, S.J., John Schneider, James Wind, and George Marsden. We, of course, are responsible for all the weaknesses, not to mention errors, in our exposition.

We thank, too, Richard Higgins for his refined editing skills; he did the invaluable task of cutting down the number and sprucing up the comprehension of our words. We are grateful to Michael Bell, an undergraduate research assistant at the Boston College Center on Wealth and Philanthropy, for his careful job in gathering and formatting our long list of references. We wish to thank Jill Thomas and Justine Hyland of Boston College's Bapst Library for so graciously searching out and garnering the permissions for the images displayed on the cover and throughout the book. We are also grateful to Nicholas Redel, Michael Bell, and Lisa Kaloostian at the Center for their gracious editorial assistance.

We warmly thank Thomas Murphy who, for twenty-five years, has helped inspire and support the spiritual horizon of our work at the Center.

We are grateful to our partners at Indiana University Press who brought this book to fruition—editorial director Robert Sloan, managing editor Miki Bird, editorial assistant Anne Clemmer, copyeditor Carrie Jadud, and the design and production team. We are also grateful to Neill Bogan for the index.

Finally and profoundly, we thank the two good souls to whom we have dedicated this book.

Wealth and the Will of God

Introduction

Moral Biography

Before turning to the subject of the will of God and wealth, to Aquinas, Ignatius, Luther, and our other fellow seekers, let us consider the contemporary context of our inquiry. Whether the market is up or down at the moment, overall, improved material conditions have pushed timeless moral questions to the forefront. These can be summarized by the overarching query, "How shall I live?" One may begin to answer it through what we call a *moral biography,* which begins, in turn, with the process of *discernment.* This preliminary survey of these terms will provide a contemporary vocabulary to help us better read and understand these thinkers from the past and also to help readers apply the thinkers' insights to their own lives. Indeed, we hope that this book, as a whole, will set readers on the path of deepening their own moral biographies.

A moral biography is a narrative that examines the integration of two elements in an individual's life, personal capacity and moral compass or bearing, to achieve worthy ends.[1] Individuals from any economic or social position may construct a moral biography. Living one can be as simple as leading a good life—and as profound as following Aristotle's teachings on choice and virtue. Whenever we seek to match our material capacity to our moral character and aspirations (rather than to carelessness and waste), we are living a form of moral biography. Helping our readers see life's ultimate meaning as a dimension of moral biography and our material capacity as a tool in the care of others is the overall task of this book.

---

1. We use the terms *moral compass, moral bearing,* and *moral direction* interchangeably along with the terms *aspiration* and *purpose* to emphasize the dimension of moral biography that charts, mobilizes, motivates, and provides direction to how individuals activate their capacities to achieve a goal.

Like a moral biography in general, a *moral biography of wealth* applies to anyone with a substantial resource or capacity of any kind, not only to those whose capacity is chiefly financial. What are such resources or capacities? They are intellectual, artistic, and psychological skills we may draw on and other personal gifts, such as the ability to love or relate to others. They may also be networks of social connections, such as positions held in a company, organization, government, or church, or other types of social posts. Highly endowed individuals often possess sufficient wherewithal not only to live within but also to shape the organizations and institutions of the day. For such individuals, the question is how to discover and live a responsible and rewarding moral biography.

Stories from history and literature may help to clarify the meaning of a moral biography. Two such examples are Moses, from the book of Exodus, and Luke Skywalker, from *Star Wars*. Born a powerless Hebrew slave, Moses is unwittingly adopted by the royal family and rises to become Pharaoh's heir. He enjoys princely power and anticipates ruling the nation. But in time Moses learns his true bloodline. Realizing that his power lacks moral compass, he abdicates and flees. In the mountains, his resources are only those of a stout and faithful shepherd. Yet Moses receives a new mandate from the Lord through the burning bush. He protests that he lacks the power, the capacity, to accomplish his task, adding that he even stutters. The Lord promises him an arsenal of miraculous powers to defeat Pharaoh and declares that his brother, Aaron, will help him speak. And so it happens. Imbued with God's power and moral purpose, Moses breaks Pharaoh's resolve, parts the waters of the Red Sea, and leads his people through the desert from the chains of slavery to the land of milk and honey. As he nears his goal, Moses falters in faith and obedience, striking the rock for water rather than speaking to it as the Lord commanded. In punishment, Moses is allowed to see but not enter the Promised Land.

With its cosmic overtones, *Star Wars* also exemplifies the elements of a moral biography as often found in tales of fantasy and superheroes. Luke Skywalker, the hero, enters the story as a dutiful orphan farm boy with no special capacity or aspiration other than to help his aunt and uncle tend their farm on a desert planet. But he soon becomes caught up in the galactic confrontation between "the Old Republic," which is led by a diminishing cadre of Jedi knights who honor the cosmic moral law known as the Force, and "the Empire," which is led by former Jedi Darth Vader, who has gone over to the Dark Side. When Vader's agents murder Skywalker's guardians, the boy's capacity and moral bearing are thrown into disarray. He embarks on Jedi training to assist the Old Republic. The more entwined Skywalker becomes in the interstellar struggle, the more he searches for a deeper capacity and wiser purpose with the help of his Jedi mentors. At times, his budding powers exceed his strength of character, imperiling him and others. Other times, Skywalker's moral purpose outstrips his still-growing capacity, and he enters a fray unprepared. Eventually, Skywalker fully acquires a Jedi moral biography, and in a struggle to the death with Vader, ends up helping his foe regain his nobler side.

Despite the larger-than-life quality of these examples, or of, say, a Mother Teresa, ultimately they are only magnified instances of how each of us applies our resources in the service of a moral purpose—be it running a business, raising children well, completing a college degree, buying a house, or making donations to charity. Again, moral biography describes a pattern of life choices by anyone, not just the rich or well-connected. Some people may find the moral biographies of others repulsive or even immoral. But we can call a certain life path a moral biography if it is directed not by impulse or instinct but by beliefs, desires, and purposes about the whole of things and our place within that whole.

The Elements of a Moral Biography

Aristotle's philosophy of the good life offers a convenient starting point to examine the elements of moral biography more closely. Figure 1 diagrams Aristotle's thinking. In the *Nicomachean Ethics,* Aristotle reasons that the goal of life is happiness, and that happiness is "an activity of the soul in accordance with virtue," that is, in accordance with true purpose. For Aristotle, we achieve greater happiness by exercising a wide array of virtues, but especially that of *phronesis,* the virtue of making wise choices or judgments in practical affairs. As Aristotle says, "all virtues [of choice] will be present together when the one virtue, practical judgment, is present." Practical judgment and the other virtues of choice are needed to "govern action." The array of virtues "makes one bring the end into action, and [practical judgment] makes one enact the things related to the end." Along these lines, a moral biography traces a life engaged in making wise choices or exercising practical judgment in line with the proximate and ultimate ends, especially that of wisdom, or *sophia* (2002: VI.13).

Aristotle thus insists three elements are present in the good life: choice, virtue, and *phronesis* or practical wisdom (see VI.7). Choice is the outcome of deliberation about things that could be otherwise if we don't act and are "matters of action." It is "the deliberate desire of things that are up to us, for having decided as a result of deliberating, we desire in accordance with our deliberation" (2002: III.3). There can be no virtue without choice; likewise, there can be no good choices without virtue; and so there can be no good life, or moral biography, without free practical judgment to properly combine choice and virtue in daily life.

Figure 2 elaborates Aristotle's teaching. Starting at the top, it shows that a moral biography is the movement of a choosing agent from genesis to telesis, from history to aspiration. Genesis is our starting condition, the origins

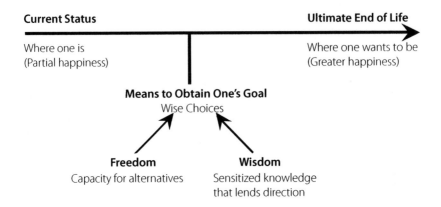

Figure 1

and circumstances of our lives (in both the ultimate and the more immediate sense). It refers to the given physical, metaphysical, and social conditions, those constraints, resources, knowledge sets, and values within which we must make choices. Genesis is our chosen and unchosen past. But these initial conditions do not predetermine our choices. They are simply what we have to work with—a happy or homeless childhood, a prospering or failing business, a confident or hesitant personality, and so forth.

Telesis is our destiny, the outcome toward which we aspire. It can be an intermediate goal or the ultimate goal of life. Telesis is defined by the possibilities, aspirations, needs, desires, and interests to which we are drawn. An ultimate purpose, Aristotle said (2002: I.2.1. and I.7), is that which people determine to be their fundamental goal in life. Through repeated testing, that goal by turns is found complete: it serves no further or additional purpose. An important goal may be to obtain an education or buy a house. But in both cases one can identify a deeper goal such as happiness, which either education or owning a house serves in turn.

Our past choices naturally shape the conditions we have to work with at any point in time. In contrast, aspirations—although ultimately constrained by reality and by our ability to imagine and achieve alternatives—are allied to freedom. They invite us to transcend and transform our given conditions to apprehend and pursue our ultimate end.

If genesis concerns the past (the conditions we receive) and telesis the future (the condition we strive to create), human *agency* is about what we are doing in the present to close the gap between history and aspiration. Agency derives from the Latin *agere*, meaning to lead, do, or act. Agency is the enactment of choice—both weighty and everyday choices. Agency is enacted within given conditions but is oriented to transcending those conditions in line with

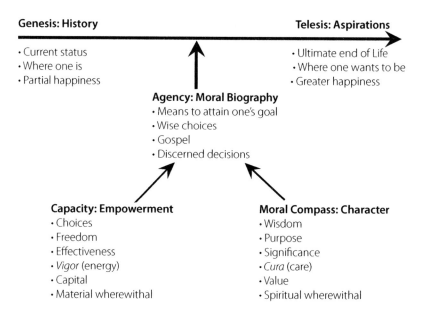

Genesis: History

- Current status
- Where one is
- Partial happiness

Telesis: Aspirations

- Ultimate end of Life
- Where one wants to be
- Greater happiness

Agency: Moral Biography
- Means to attain one's goal
- Wise choices
- Gospel
- Discerned decisions

Capacity: Empowerment
- Choices
- Freedom
- Effectiveness
- *Vigor* (energy)
- Capital
- Material wherewithal

Moral Compass: Character
- Wisdom
- Purpose
- Significance
- *Cura* (care)
- Value
- Spiritual wherewithal

Figure 2

our needs, desires, and objectives. A moral biography bridges where we are and where we want to go, and that bridge is composed of a series of acts of agency.

Figure 2 contains two lists (at bottom of figure) pairing various forms of capacity and moral purpose. Each form of capacity on the left can be paired with a form of moral compass on the right, and vice versa. In addition to speaking about a moral biography as the intersection of capacity and moral purpose, we can also describe it as the place where freedom and purpose meet. In that biographical crossroads, effectiveness intersects with significance, energy with care, and capital with value. The terms we select to describe this confluence of capacity and choice-making form a path to self-knowledge and are themselves an important act of moral agency.

It is worth noting that a moral biography may also be a spiritual or religious biography. While it may not be wise to distinguish too much between moral and spiritual, contemporary studies show that Americans across the economic spectrum speak readily and explicitly about their "spiritual" lives.

A spiritual biography exists when the capacity and moral compass of a moral biography are grounded in a sense of ultimacy about one's origins and purposes. Those who see Maslow's notion of self-actualization as their end might describe their moral biography as spiritual. A moral biography is also a religious one when the genesis and telesis of a human life are explicitly connected to what Rudolf Otto (1923) calls the *numinous,* a being or force to which we bow our heads in worship—or connected, to quote Paul, to that force (God) in whom we live and move and have our being. Those whose telesis is love of God, neighbor, and self and final union with God, to paraphrase Aquinas, would likely understand their moral biography as religious.

Moral Biography and the Moral Citizenship of Care

If a moral biography is the confluence of capacity and moral compass in daily practice, we must explore the outlines of a moral biography in the specific context of philanthropy and the generation of voluntary networks of mutual assistance. We call this the *moral citizenship of care*. Here we are guided first by Aristotle, who, as chapter 1 shows, found the essence of philanthropy in loving friendship, or *philia,* which is in turn the basis for community.

Philia is first encountered at home, where family members love others as themselves. Friends, says Aristotle, are a type of "other self" (2002: VIII.12); thus a person is "related to a friend as he is to himself" (IX.4). The upshot is that friendship occurs in and creates community. It extends beyond family to companions, fellow citizens, and so forth, "wherever the relationship is extended toward something good and superior" (VIII.12). Happiness requires others, Aristotle holds, and thus "it is necessary for a happy person to have friends." He or she "supplies what someone is incapable of supplying by himself." Conversely, "the excellent person will need people for him to benefit" (IX.9). This is why we can refer to philanthropy as strategic friendship, and to strategic friendship as the foundation of the moral citizenship of care.[2]

No moral biography exists in isolation. The capacities and purposes executed through its judgments are developed in connection with, and affect, others. There is an organic link between what is personal and what is social and cultural. To the extent that a moral biography is intentional in the realm of friendship and extends into philanthropy, it is conjoined to and constitutive of a moral citizenship of care. Since capacity and purpose intersect in the conduct of all practical affairs, a moral biography of wealth is implied in economic and political citizenship. When philanthropy is one of those affairs, the moral aspiration takes on a distinctive purpose. It is true that in commercial and political relations, individuals may also aspire to achieve "something good and superior." But this goal is mediated by market relations, in which goods and services are supplied only to the extent that people voice their need or "demand" through purchases in dollars, or in the political realm, through financial contributions and votes.

---

2. See Schervish and Havens (2002) and Schervish (2005) for an elaboration of the notion of the moral citizenship of care.

In the philanthropic realm, the *telos* of a moral biography is tied to the well-being of the other *directly* (even when the other is at a distance). A friend "wishes for and does good things . . . for the sake of the other person," according to Aristotle, and "wants the friend to be and to live for the friend's own sake" (XI.4). The moral imperative of philanthropy draws on his insight that "life is difficult for one who is alone," and that "a human being is meant for a city and is such a nature as to live with others."

A moral biography, then, is inherently communal. The arrow of its moral compass points to others' needs directly, rather than through the market. Thus it is the building block of the moral citizenship of care, that array of intersecting relationships by which individuals respond to the needs of others as an expression of *philia,* or loving friendship, that common bond one wishes to honor effectively and strategically.

The Moral Biography of Wealth

Having introduced moral biography's communal dimension, we will now compare it to moral biography in the context of wealth. Put simply, the difference is that not only can wealth holders choose a substantial and consequential moral purpose, but they also possess a substantial and consequential level of material capacity. As a result they have the capacity to produce alternatives to conditions and to set their hearts on great aspirations and responsibilities. Financial wealth was not the capacity that Moses or Skywalker mobilized, nor is it the only capacity that wealth holders muster in pursuing their purposes. Nevertheless, great wealth is a capacity that allows for great expectations and the realization of them. Consequently, wealth holders, when they so choose, are in their world-shaping ability more akin to the Moses of the Exodus than to Moses of the highlands, to Luke Skywalker the Jedi knight than Skywalker the orphan farmhand.

In order to better understand moral biography in today's world, it helps to examine the changing capacities and aspirations of individuals within our economy. Despite ten recessions in the United States between 1950 and 2008, private wealth in the nation grew at a yearly inflation-adjusted average of over 3 percent. Even from 1998 through 2003—which included September 11 and the bursting of the technology-driven stock bubble—wealth grew at a real annualized rate of 2.6 percent. Twenty-five years ago, the big news was that the nation had one million millionaires. In 2007 ten and a half million households belonged to the club. Even by the dollar's value at that time, there are *five and a half times* as many today. It now takes a net worth of over $1 billion to make *Forbes*'s annual list of the 400 richest Americans! Estimates based on a Federal Reserve survey done in 2007 suggest that 805,500 of the nation's 116 million households had a net worth of at least $10 million. Of these, 752,500 had an estimated net worth of $10 to $50 million, 36,000 controlled from $50 to $100 million, and some 17,000 households had an estimated worth of $100 million or more.

Other indicators come from our own wealth transfer projections at Boston College's Center on Wealth and Philanthropy. We estimate that, in 2007 dollars, $52 to $173 trillion will have been transferred from 1998 to 2052 from estates of final decedents alone, and that this will produce between $2.5 and $10.5 trillion in charitable bequests. (The range reflects alternative assumptions of annual growth in wealth, 2 and 4 percent.) We also estimate that lifetime giving (versus bequests) will provide an additional $19 to $53 trillion in charitable contributions over same period. Between one-half and two-thirds of this total infusion of philanthropic money will come from households with $1 million or more in net worth. Despite the economic crisis of 2007–2009, there is every reason to expect that the total wealth transfer and related charitable giving will be at least as great as the lower estimates.

Hyperagency

These figures indicate not only that are there more wealth holders with greater net worth, but that a growing proportion of them have sufficiently solved their personal "economic problem" so as to make major gifts to charity. In the context of a moral biography of wealth, this point is important because it indicates the growing capacity of wealth holders to make choices. On every dimension of capacity listed in figure 2, the possession of material wealth offers the opportunity for hyperagency. Wealth holders have a broader array of choices, alternatives, capital, energy, and effective action at their disposal. Such capacity provides wealth holders with the opportunity to be what we call *hyperagents*.[3]

Hyperagency refers to the institution-changing capacity of wealth holders—a trait akin to Aristotle's and Aquinas's notion of magnanimity. Most people spend their lives as agents living within established organizational environments. Hyperagents spend a good part of their lives as agents in this sense as well. But when they desire to do so, they are capable of forming rather than just working within institutional settings. While not all hyperagents are wealth holders, all wealth holders are potential hyperagents in the material realm. They can apply their material resources to shape the tangible world.

Hyperagents, then, are world-builders. While most of us are agents who attempt to find the best place for ourselves within existing situations, hyperagents are founders of the institutional framework within which they and others will work. What takes a coalition of social, political, or philanthropic agents to accomplish, hyperagents can accomplish relatively single-handedly. They can

---

3. See Schervish (1997) and Schervish, Coutsoukis, and Lewis (1994).

design their houses from the ground up, create the jobs and businesses within which they work, tailor-make their clothes and vacations, and create new foundations, new philanthropic enterprises, and new directions for existing charities. When we speak about today's donors being entrepreneurial or venture philanthropists, we are pointing to their capacity and disposition to shape and not just participate in the goals and accomplishments of the causes and charities they fund. While most of us participate as supporters of charitable enterprises, wealth holders, when they elect to do so, are producers of them.

Beyond this world-building capacity, hyperagency is also a psychological orientation of moral compass. In the telesis of aspiration, wealth holders harbor great expectations, view them as legitimate, and possess the confidence to achieve them. Liberation from economic necessity seems to change wealth holders' expectations dramatically.

But it is not always easy. Wealth holders find it challenging to read the moral compass that will guide them to use their capacity to serve the moral citizenship of care. They worry over how their riches will shape their own moral biographies and those of their children and the people they affect in business and in philanthropy. Acquiring wealth, it turns out, is the beginning, not the end, of a moral biography of wealth.

The result is a growing need for a deliberate process of self-reflection by which wealth holders discern how to complement growth in material quantity with a commensurate growth in spiritual direction-setting. They need not to own more money but to discern the moral compass that will guide the deployment of their wealth to enlarge the moral citizenship of care.

Discernment and Moral Biography

One method used effectively for this purpose is group conversations among wealth-holding peers and their advisors. These conversations are built on trust and intimacy and may be organized as part of retreats, conferences, and seminars. This book proposes another method for arriving at these choices, a process of self-reflection known as *discernment*. It is related to the former method but is more interior. Discernment is a spiritually attuned, often faith-based process by which individuals review and decide upon the conditions and directions of their decision-making. The term *discernment* derives from the Latin *cernere*, "to sift," and *dis*, "apart." Discernment is a process of interior moral and spiritual dialogue in which the discrete aspects of life are sifted through and ordered into meaningful patterns and purposeful decisions.

Like group conversations, discernment is aided by the questioning and direction of an advisor and by letting individuals clarify and make decisions in an environment of liberty and inspiration. Liberty is material and psychological freedom from unfounded assumptions, fears, and anxieties. Inspiration is the self-understood array of desires that provide the freedom for commitment.

Discernment can be an informal process of decision-making undertaken by a self-reflective individual or a more formal process carried out in a more or less systematic manner aided by an advisor. Discernment is a mediating variable in the model of charitable giving in the sense that it influences the way other variables have their effects. In regard to charitable giving, the discernment process first helps individuals clarify what they have to give (arrow 1, figure 3) and their meanings and motivations for giving (arrow 2, figure 3). By helping individuals combine a clarified sense of financial capacity with a clarified understanding of their meanings and motives, it enables them to decide upon and implement what we call discerned philanthropy (arrows 3 and 4, figure 3).

When discernment is assisted by advisors and counselors hired or chosen by the donor, it takes place on the supply- or donor-side of the philanthropic relationship. When discernment is assisted by fundraisers and charity professionals, it takes place on the demand-side of philanthropy. Neither the supply-side nor the demand-side style of discernment necessarily produces a more propitious charitable decision. However, on the demand-side fundraisers may feel such a need to garner support for their causes that they have to take special care to ensure that liberty and inspiration—and hence the integrity of any decision, including the decision not to make a gift—are preserved throughout the discernment process.

Discerned Philanthropy

Discerned philanthropy is the outcome of the process by which an individual applies a conscientiously decided-upon level of financial resources to implement a conscientiously decided-upon aspiration to care. Discernment can be useful for donors across the economic spectrum, since there are no essential elements of discerned philanthropy other than that it be self-reflective. Nonetheless, in discerned philanthropy, several and sometimes all of the characteristics indicated on figure 2 are manifest.

In general terms, discerned philanthropy tends to result in an increase in the quality and quantity of individual gifts and charitable giving in general. A quantitative increase in giving is not a *defining* element of discerned philanthropy, but it is likely to occur due to the fact that self-reflection provides donors with a better appreciation of their financial capacity and of the importance of charitable needs in relation to their own needs. More likely, however, is that discerned philanthropy is as much a formative activity for the donor as it is for the beneficiary. Such philanthropy is a biographical event of character and vocation. It derives from a personal history of identifications, gratitude, blessings, and troubles, and is destined toward a final end of care for self and others. As such, discerned philanthropy tends to be more explicitly strategic, in that it is a mode of personal engagement that coherently combines a way of thinking, acting, and feeling in order to accomplish a philanthropic purpose.

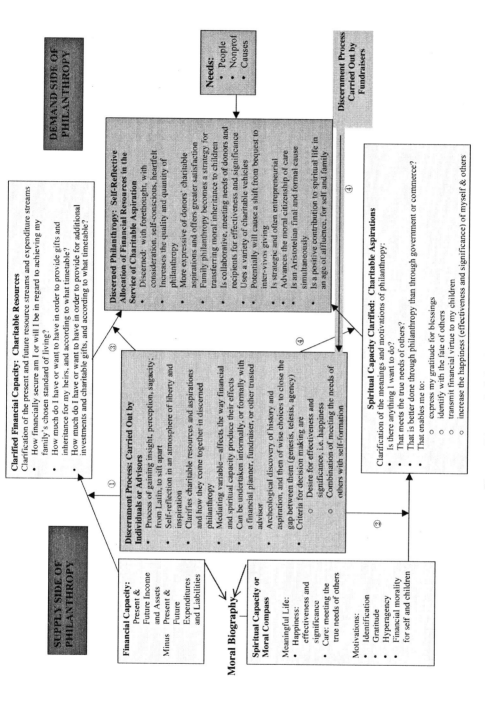

Figure 3. Discerned Philanthropy

Discerned philanthropy also tends to be entrepreneurial, that is, self-directed, at least in disposition if not also in actual practice. This means that it is sufficiently thought through and planned as to result in either new philanthropic initiatives or the setting of new directions for existing ones. But even when it doesn't explicitly produce innovation, it is entrepreneurial in the sense that it is self-consciously expressive of an entrepreneurial disposition of the donor to be a producer of effective outcomes.

Another characteristic of discerned philanthropy is that it is not tied to any particular charitable vehicle or tax outcome; instead the donor's biography orients the financial and moral content and the timing of substantial giving. The element of "planning" in discerned giving is more holistic than the term "planned giving" usually implies. Planned giving usually refers to the charitable vehicles that are connected to trusts, bequests, and other mechanisms related to financial events that occur at the death of the donor. Discerned giving includes such conventional planned giving but also includes giving under a broader definition of "planning." For example, donors may carefully chart and time their giving in light of their life's purpose. Discerned giving includes outright gifts and pledges executed as a self-reflective translation of financial capacity into charitable gifts. Discerned philanthropy, then, is a financial and biographical event that produces a collaborative relationship that meets the needs of both donors and recipients for effectiveness and significance.

Financial gifts flow to fulfill the needs of recipients for happiness and also to close the gap between the beneficiaries' history and aspiration. Moral and spiritual gifts, however, flow to the donors as a result of charitable giving that fulfills their true needs for happiness. These mutual benefits, in turn, advance a more caring society as defined by a moral citizenship of care. Although the latter concept has always been part of an ascetic way of life, it is especially valuable in the spiritual life in an age of affluence. As personal and social wealth expands the horizon of choice for individuals, it becomes increasingly important to develop an intentional spirituality for affluent living and making wise choices amid the obstacles and opportunities affluence poses.

A distinctive trait of wealth holders in all eras is that they possess the fullest range of choice in determining and fulfilling who they want to become and what they want to do for themselves, their families, and the world around them. Today, increasing numbers of individuals are approaching, achieving, or even exceeding their financial goals with respect to providing for their material needs, and doing so at younger and younger ages. A level of affluence that heretofore was the province of a scattering of rulers, generals, merchants, industrialists, and financiers has come to characterize whole cultures. Never before in history has the question of how to align broad material capacity of choice with spiritual capacity of character been placed before so many people.

Nothing about world-building hyperagency requires it to use virtue and wisdom. Today's Pharaohs of financial skullduggery and totalitarianism demonstrate that well enough. An expanded *quantity* of choice does not guarantee a finer *quality* of choice. But quantity of choice always highlights the moral purpose of a moral biography that is released from economic constraint. Making free and wise choices about wealth allocation for the deeper purposes of life, especially for philanthropy, is now and will increasingly become the prominent feature of financial morality and personal fulfillment for high-net-worth individuals. Clarifying the process of a moral biography will help anyone with capacity and choice chart a path of greater happiness for themselves, their families, and others in the world. Indeed, finding a way to clarify and pursue moral aspirations during the quest for significance is not only a pressing need of wealth holders but also the noble need of every person.

A Prescient Observation on Economic Change

We conclude by recalling a great economist's searching insight into wealth and legacy that has stood the test of almost four-score years and bears on the moral citizenship of care. In 1930, John Maynard Keynes wrote "The Economic Possibilities for Our Grandchildren." He reflects in the essay that his generation will witness "the greatest change which has ever occurred in the material environment of life for human beings in the aggregate" (1933: 372). Indeed, he adds, it has begun. "The course of affairs will simply be that there will be ever larger and larger classes and groups of people for whom the problems of economic necessity have been practically removed" (ibid.). As Keynes knew, the standard of living was rising rapidly in industrialized nations, and industrialization was spreading steadily into the rest of the world. The wealth and comforts once reserved for kings were becoming the possibility, the expectation, even the right, of everyone.

The essay foresees a spiritual transformation following the material one: "When the accumulation of wealth is no longer of high social importance, there will be great changes in the code of morals. We shall be able to rid ourselves of many of the pseudo-moral principles . . . by which we have exalted some of the most distasteful of human qualities into the position of the highest virtues" (369). Keynes does not expect the need for money-making to disappear overnight. But he predicts a radical change to gather in attitudes toward wealth acquisition: "The love of money as a possession—as distinguished from the love of money as a means to the enjoyments and realities of life—will be recognized for what it is, a somewhat disgusting morbidity, one of those semi-criminal, semi-pathological propensities which one hands over with a shudder to the specialists in mental disease" (ibid.).

To love money as a means to worthy ends, rather than as an end in itself, focuses attention on those possible ends. Here, Keynes offers a new perception of economic progress. He foresees a change in "the nature of one's duty to one's neighbour. For it will remain reasonable to be economically purposive for others after it has ceased to be reasonable for oneself" (372). This shift from wealth as end to wealth as means involves transforming capacity and character in the light of ultimate purpose. It is a critical move in any moral biography of wealth.

Keynes saw that this altered economic environment spelled huge changes not just for individuals but for humanity as a whole. Thus he predicts that "for the first time since his creation, man will be faced with his real, his permanent problem—how to use his freedom from pressing economic cares, how to occupy the leisure, which science and compound interest will have won for him, to live wisely and agreeably and well" (367).

As with much else in the modern world, this view may put too much weight on material things: Keynes might appear to say that increased GDP leads necessarily and by itself to an increase in national virtue. But the movement he suggests is not so mechanical. The stunning increase in material wealth and thus power could as easily be said to have created a modern crisis. We have so much more power than any age before our own. Do we have so much more wisdom with which to direct that power? If not, is it not our duty to reflect and to discover more thoughtful ways to govern our lives and our choices? This question expresses what Keynes calls the "real" and "permanent" problem of humanity, one that does not belong to rich or poor epochs—or people. Insofar as we all have some resources and must all make choices, this is our problem as well.

To return for a moment to the even farther past, Socrates saw this problem in the Athens of his day, 2,500 years ago. He spent time in the marketplace, he said, asking young Athenians why they spend so much time pursuing money. Do they not know, he asked, that virtue does not come from money, but rather that money comes from virtue? Socrates knew that wicked people might well amass piles of gold coins. But by "money" he means less monetary riches than wealth or wellness. He saw that resources find their meaning in the light of wisdom and capacity finds its definition in the light of ultimate purpose, not the other way around.

This volume, then, is an effort to gather some measures of the wisdom needed to address this permanent problem. We cannot fix this problem with a policy but must face it each in our individual soul. We create stances toward wealth suited to our lives and times. But we need to seek help in this from the thinkers we discuss and from talking with other people in our own life. At times, the philosophers and theologians in this book unite apparently discordant things such as virtue and money, reason and faith, indifference and love. This may seem paradoxical. But following the lead of their ideas is worthwhile as we construct and review our own moral biographies, as we find new ways to combine our capacities and ultimate purposes, our wealth and aspirations. This is also worth doing as we think about what kind of legacy, material and spiritual, we will hand on to those who come after.

1 ～

Aristotle

"Being-in-Action" and Discernment

How can thoughtful people connect their wealth to their spiritual aspirations? Indeed, what is wealth, and what is it for? How may we discern its role in the will of God? One means of exploring this complex, challenging issue is to examine what great thinkers have said about it. We chose six as our worthy guides: Aristotle, Thomas Aquinas, Ignatius of Loyola, Martin Luther, John Calvin, and Jonathan Edwards. In our consideration of the uses of wealth, we focus not on finance, markets, fund scandals, or the estate tax but on these pressing questions of prosperity, which, in turn, lead to other questions: How can people who live in affluent societies care best for others? And even: What constitutes a happy life? Though writing from far-off times and places—maybe even because they are free from today's biases and distractions—our philosopher-theologian guides are ready and willing to answer.

In conversing with each thinker, we will address three main topics: purposes, resources, and discernment. Purposes are ultimate spiritual aspirations, those ends for which we strive and live. Resources include wealth, of course, but also our time and talents and much more. Discernment, this book's special concern, encompasses any process of reflection, thought, deliberation, contemplation, or "mulling over" that seeks to bridge the gap between capacity and aspiration, between here and there, now and the future.

Aristotle (384–322 BC), the first of our interlocutors, was also deeply interested in discernment. But first we should observe that his terms differ from ours. If we were to guess how he might address our stated inquiry in brief, it might be something like this: "What you're searching for, ultimately, is *happiness,* which is the work of virtuous activity. So you must decide how to use your *equipment,* the wealth at your disposal, in a virtuous way. To do that, you must engage in *practical judgment.*" Where we speak of purposes, resources, and discernment, Aristotle speaks of happiness, equipment, and practical judgment. Within purposes, Aristotle directs our attention broadly at happiness, the goal of virtue as a whole, and more narrowly at liberality and magnificence, two virtues related to wealth. From these distinctions follow the three sections of this chapter.

Happiness

For Aristotle, the ultimate purpose of life, and the goal of living virtuously, is happiness. Whatever we are doing, or whomever we do it with, we aspire most of all to happiness. Today we may think of this state as "feeling good" or being contented or satisfied. Passing feelings do play a role in what Aristotle understood as happiness—but only a small one. Nor do other contemporary claims to happiness—owning more stuff, enjoying finer pleasures, or attaining honors—do much to describe Aristotle's meaning. He recognized this. Most people, he wrote in the *Ethics,* seem to think that happiness consists in such things, or they act as if they do (2002: I.5; references in this chapter will be to the book and chapter of Aristotle's *Nicomachean Ethics,* unless otherwise noted). But Aristotle also noted that people say as well that happiness should be lasting, and that no one else should be able to take it away. Possessions, pleasures, and honor often do not last, or they are subject to others' whims. Aristotle never denies that the happy life includes possessions, pleasures, and honors. But ultimately it consists of a quality that these things cannot generate.

Happiness, in Aristotle's view, is not something that simply happens to us. Nor, as we said, can it be merely a transient affective state. Rather it results from human agency or "activity," which, in Aristotle's lexicon, means any conscious exertion of one's being. When we are happy, we are most at work, most active, most alive.

Being-in-Action

Aristotle called this combined excellent activity *energeia.* We may call it agency, or literally, "being-in-action." We can think of it as living out a moral biography—implementing one's inner and material capacities to accomplish the goal of happiness. To know, express, and fulfill one's *energeia* is to follow the royal road to happiness, according to Aristotle. Happiness is our highest activity, our highest energy, our most comprehensive "being-in-action."

This holds whether something is living, inorganic, or artificial. What makes an acorn an acorn is its ability to grow, in its fullness, into an oak tree rather than an aardvark. In Aristotle's view, we can never truly know things by reducing them simply to their materials or structure, their manner of production, or their producer. A car is more than a bunch of metal and plastic; a dog is more than a bundle of cells. Aristotle would say that we know something's capacity or power precisely by knowing its characteristic activity. "What makes something work," in his view, is not simply its parts or attributes but its *energeia.* Indeed,

Aristotle's great insight is that, if you want to discover what a thing is, you must find its being-in-action.

This approach to understanding or classifying particular things may seem obvious, but it can yield surprising results. What about our own selves? Are we our bodies? Inorganic stuff, like atoms? Are we our parents' children—or our children's parents? Particular instances ("accidents," Aristotle might say) of the species *homo sapiens*? Animals? Spartans of Greece—or New York or Illinois? Citizens? Thoughts in the mind of God?

Perhaps, in some way, we are each and all of these things. Aristotle would help us answer by adding a critical question: *What do you do? What is your being-in-action?* Aristotle wrote an entire book, the *Nicomachean Ethics*, on that question. As people, we desire, think, and choose; we pursue money, honors, and friends; we play and seek justice; we laugh and blush, we struggle; we do right and wrong. Above all, we pursue happiness. All these activities are part of our being-in-action.

Specifically human activity involves both thinking and doing. But though Aristotle speaks of a "theoretical life" and an "active life," he does not treat these as completely separate. Both depend on a uniquely human quality that he calls *nous,* or "intellect." Intellect is both a capacity and that capacity's work. Intellect, for Aristotle, is our ability to perceive, and our perceiving. It is the mind in action. As we recognize intellect at work, perceiving well the right and the true, we recognize, according to Aristotle, our specifically human "being-in-action," and so we answer that question, "Who are you?" What makes you one person and your life whole is *nous.* We'll look more closely at *nous* both in what follows and as we examine practical judgment in the third part of this chapter.

Being-in-action then is a form of self-expression and human expression. It takes the human soul and our capacity for reason, reflection, and speech to achieve that expression. Of all possible human activities, Aristotle concludes that happiness must consist above all not in excellent digestion, or a highly refined nose, but in some sort of excellent being-in-action of the soul.

HAPPINESS AND THE VIRTUES

Happiness is the most excellent being-in-action of the soul, and the "excellent" here belongs to the realm of virtue. Aristotle saw virtues as subordinate ends: we pursue them *for the sake* of happiness. They resemble musicians' instruments. Guitarists don't play for the guitar; they play the guitar for the sake of the song. Perhaps the virtues most of all resemble a singer's voice: in that case the artist, the instrument (the voice), and the end (the song) almost become one in the activity, the singing.

The virtues have their own characters. They don't belong to the body or to our senses. Some people may have a "strong stomach," but that doesn't make them brave. Others might have a "good nose," but that doesn't make them wise.

An oak tree might flourish with vegetative virtue. A fox might do very well with excellent senses. But it takes more, better work, to be an excellent human being.

Looking in more detail, Aristotle saw two main activities in particular as forming the core of human happiness: excellent thinking, the highest form of which is wisdom, and excellent practice, the highest form of which is friendship. Gnawing a bone might form part of a dog's happiness; enjoying sunshine and nectar may do for butterflies. But human beings work at different activities and pursue a different sort of happiness. For us, excellent thinking leading to excellent doing would make for perfect happiness.

In a word, since we all care about happiness, and since happiness depends on virtue, we must look more closely at virtue. There are many virtues that move us toward happiness, such as courage, temperance, honor, wit, and justice, and each of these has the two forms of doing and thinking. But Aristotle found that two grand virtues encompass all the subordinate ones: wisdom and friendship. Achieving them is the most worthy penultimate goal—the earthly activity that best corresponds to and brings us to happiness. Understanding wisdom and friendship is necessary if we are to understand anything else, including the contribution of giving to a happy life.

Wisdom

Wisdom, in Aristotle's view, is the greatest of the virtues; next to the goal of happiness, it is the ultimate object of aspiration. Wisdom is required for happiness, for if, as we shall see below, you do not activate the highest part of your soul, you cannot be happy. Like all the other virtues and happiness too, wisdom is an activity, a "being-in-action." That work, of course, may be wholly internal. Wise people may not look like they are doing much, but the highest parts of their soul are fully energized. That said, wisdom underlies all excellent activities. For example, as we shall see in another part of this chapter, magnificence, the virtue of making large gifts or expenditures, closely depends upon wisdom.

Aristotle teaches that wisdom activates the highest part of the human soul, that which knows things. Aristotle divides the soul into a hierarchy of four parts. The first three are the vegetative part that keeps us growing and digesting, the desiring part, through which we feel bodily sensations (including pleasure and pain), and the "reckoning" or "opining" part, by which we number and keep track of all the things in the world. "Reckoning" governs our actions in this ever-changing world. The fourth, the knowing part, stands above all. It perceives and makes true deductions about things that never change, about enduring principles. Wisdom perfects the activity of this knowing part, allowing us to see these true principles most clearly and to deduce conclusions about them most ably.

From these distinctions, one can see that wisdom truly relies on two elements: it perceives enduring principles and it deduces truths from or about them. The part of wisdom that deduces truths Aristotle calls "knowledge." All knowledge for Aristotle is deductive, similar to the proofs used in geometry. But what about the part that perceives principles? We come back to *nous*, intellect. Intellect not only allows two friends to perceive their shared "being-in-action," it allows the solitary wise person to perceive the highest principles of the universe. Intellect plus knowledge equals wisdom. Or, as Aristotle puts it, "Wisdom is knowledge with its head on" (VI.7).

Wisdom is the highest human virtue, and contributes most powerfully to happiness, because it activates the highest part of the soul and brings us closest to the divine. If we are looking for the most satisfying, penultimate goal for our aspirations, we will find it above all in wisdom.

To make this point clearer, in his *Metaphysics* (1995: XII.6–8) Aristotle argues that even God, the most perfect being in all the cosmos, spends his entire existence contemplating his wisdom. Aristotle's God is not a creator; he does not "make" the world out of nothing. Instead, the universe in Aristotle's view has existed for all time, and for all time this most perfect being, God, has engaged and will engage in the most perfect activity: being wise and contemplating his own perfection. Indeed, Aristotle suggests, all the world's motions—the movement of the stars, sun, moon, and earth, and maybe we could add the universe's cycles of contraction and expansion—move in imitation of God's perfect self-reflection. So too, when human beings pursue wisdom, we do the best we can do, imitating God and thereby participating in God's own perfect existence. This imitation does not just mimic God but actively aligns us with the metaphysical activity that is God. In this way, our happiness encompasses a union with the divine.

Intellect underlies wisdom, friendship, and the subordinate virtues of courage, temperance, justice, and practical judgment. Intellect guides the liberal giving of liberal people, and it allows them to perceive the liberal quality of the gift and its friendly consequences. Intellect allows brave people to see the moment to act or to appreciate bravery when others perform it. And so on for the others. Thus our every deed, our every action, provides a possible starting point for wisdom and contemplation. Because intellect is at work in every human act, and every human act takes place within this cosmic whole, every moment opens a door to happiness through the pursuit of wisdom and the imitation of God.

That said, pursuing wisdom and doing the courageous deed are not the same; nor are pursuing wisdom and eating or sleeping well. Every moment offers the opportunity to pursue wisdom, but once you pass through, you may leave other activities temporarily behind.

That's why, Aristotle recognizes, no person, no matter how wise, can spend all day every day pursuing wisdom. Unlike God (see VII.14–15), even wise people need to eat, and they need money to buy food. Likewise, unless they want to live as a hermit—something that would take a lot of time away from contemplating—wise people need to rely upon other people to live. Wise people need to be able to get along with others. Thus wisdom and friendship go hand in hand.

In short, Aristotle would say that our penultimate aspiration should be wisdom. But because life is not simple, happiness depends on more than being wise. We cannot pursue *only* wisdom: we need all the other virtues and especially friendship to provide wisdom a daily home.

Friendship

"A friend is another self." "Friends share one soul in two bodies." "One friend loves the other for the other's own sake." Aristotle coined these well-known phrases, making it easy to see that friendship (or, in Greek, *philia*) forms one of the most important virtues to him.

Aristotle observes that there are several different types of friends. *Philia*, or friendship, begins in the family, in the bonds between parents and children and between siblings. Among our other friends, Aristotle first identifies the category that includes what we call our "acquaintances" or "professional contacts." We get along with such people and probably would say, "I'm friendly with so and so." But when one comes down to it, our "friendship" with them is built on use: I use him and he uses me. There's nothing wrong with mutual use; it makes living and working together possible. But it's hardly complete friendship. Friends through mutual use hardly value each other "for the friend's own sake."

Besides friendships of use, there are friendships of pleasure. Aristotle observes that these friendships crop up readily among young people. They have a good time together. Maybe they tell jokes, or enjoy the same music, or play the same sports. They may not share the same "values," as we would say today, about important things. But those opinions don't get in the way of their enjoying each other's company. Again, there is nothing wrong with such friendship. A good life should involve some pleasure. Who wants to be around dour, boring people? But such friends can come and go easily, and they can be "friends" without really knowing each other. Friendship for pleasure is then not the most complete.

The best friendship, in Aristotle's view, is one that inspires the friends to live well, to be most "in action," to develop and exercise all their virtues. Such friends will be useful and pleasant but they also reveal to each other that which is most worth striving for, and they help each other get there.

Friends who use each other share little: for example, one friend covers the other's shift on Tuesday and the other reciprocates on Wednesday. They needn't even work around each other to be "friends." Friends for pleasure share a certain activity—being pleased—but it's notoriously fleeting. Just look at how unstable friendships among young people can be. Friends for virtue share the most, the best, and for the longest time. Whether they are inciting each other on to honor, justice, or wisdom, their activity may encompass a lifetime. It involves them in seeing and doing the same things. They set their eyes on a truly unified goal. They may even begin to think the same thoughts. They partake in mutual nourishment. It is this kind of friendship that is captured in the saying, "Friends share one soul in two bodies." As we shall see at more length soon, when we examine the virtue of liberality, such friends get the great pleasure of perceiving their own "being-in-action" in one another. That's why a true friend is "another self."

The grand virtue of friendship, then, is an excellent guide for our public and private lives. Friendships "for use" appear in all our dealings with others. Our civic and family lives would grind to a halt if we couldn't trust each other in simple exchanges. Friendships for pleasure sweeten our existence. But friendships of virtue give our lives their true direction. Such friendship, with one other person or among many persons, is a worthy goal to pursue through practical judgment. And friendship to one degree or another appears in all the other virtues.

Many Virtues, One Goal

There are differences between wisdom and friendship, or friendship and liberality, but it is good to remember that, for Aristotle, these activities exist under one rubric—that of virtue. One faculty makes them possible—intellect. And they aim at one end—happiness.

The virtues also complement each other. Though often pursued alone, wisdom inspires and unites friends with each other. Likewise, friendship provides a rich starting point for the contemplation embodied in wisdom; in our friends we see being-in-action in the most concrete and varied display.

While we can discuss and examine these activities separately, we should also see them on another level as one because human life is unified. Everything—the unity and complexity—is present from the first in Aristotle's great insight: being-in-action. These virtuous activities illuminate the first part of our inquiry by showing purposes and ends toward which we seek to connect our wealth and other resources, namely happiness and its two closest sources, wisdom and friendship.

Equipment

External Goods

We have seen how Aristotle defines ultimate purposes. Now let us turn to his discussion of resources, his distinction between natural or unnatural wealth, and his sense of how resources may be put to virtuous use in order to live well. We will explore the two virtues Aristotle connected to the use of wealth: liberality, which we touched upon in the context of friendship, and magnificence.

What we call wealth, money, or material possessions Aristotle called "equipment," but he included in this category wealth of a more subjective nature. Aristotle divides goods into three types: *psychic goods* (wisdom and other virtues), *bodily goods* (strength, beauty, health, etc.), and *external goods,* which include monetary wealth but which also include friends and honors.

Let's focus first on what Aristotle has to say about wealth itself. Though he lived nearly 2,500 years ago in ancient Greece, Aristotle knew quite a bit about the perils and promise of wealth. His teacher Plato's teacher, Socrates, was famous for asking tough questions about money. Besides living much of his life in Athens, the financial and political hub of the world, Aristotle was a tutor and advisor to Alexander the Great, who was a master of conspicuous acquisition and consumption. Aristotle's culture even worshipped wealth as a god—but a blind one who stumbled into some hands for no apparent reason, and who had wings, to fly away when his seeming "possessors" least expected. Aristotle, interestingly, managed to hold onto some of wealth's bounty for himself. When he died, he left an extensive will appointing executors, trustees, and guardians for his family and estate, along with instructions concerning the proper care of his long-term companion, children (biological and adopted), books, artwork, and homes.

Natural and Unnatural Wealth

Aristotle teaches that wealth consists of two main types: natural wealth and money. He identifies "natural wealth" as the crops the farmer grows, the flesh the hunter or fisherman captures, and the milk and meat cultivated by the herdsman. It may also include one's friends, family, and companions. Natural wealth satisfies natural human needs for food, drink, shelter, companionship, and the like. Aristotle recognizes that some "natural wealth" may come through a marketplace exchange rather than directly from the land. Yet exchange, which uses money as its medium, often aims at amassing not natural wealth but money itself, which no one can eat, drink, or find shelter under. So Aristotle notes in his *Politics* (with chagrin) that some people trade in money itself, making money, rather than nature, the source of more money, via interest (I.8–10).

Aristotle recognizes two types of wealth acquisition. We acquire natural wealth through "household management," or *oikonomike,* the root of our word *economics.* Good household managers seek food, drink, shelter, friends, and other forms of natural wealth so that they and their families can enjoy a good life. They may use money in order to attain some of these goods, but they should not properly count money as part of their true "wealth." Were such a household manager to make himself a net worth report, the balance sheet would include human, material, and social capital, but it would omit money or other financial instruments! Money is just a tool, a means to truly good things. Necessity makes the household manager pursue natural wealth, but life puts a limit on this pursuit. One needs only so much food, drink, shelter, and friends, after all, in order to live well.

The unnatural type of wealth, money, arises from exchange. Aristotle calls the art of acquiring it commerce. (He regards usury, or charging interest on loans of money, as a subdiscipline: commerce in money itself.) Commerce, Aristotle complains, has caused most people to mistake money for true wealth and to deprecate natural wealth, the very things that money was invented to buy.

A deeper problem is that commerce—unlike household management—puts no limit upon pursuing its end, money. How can this be, when money neither feeds, nor quenches thirst, nor provides shelter, nor ensures true companionship—all the things that natural wealth does? Aristotle responds, "The reason for this mistake is that people are serious about living, but not about living well. And since this desire to live has no end, there's no end to their desire for the means of living." Likewise, he adds, "Even those who aim at living well seek it in bodily enjoyments," and since possessions appear to deliver that enjoyment, people spend all their time making money. Though we all know that there is more to a good life than "stuff," people have a hard time getting beyond amassing money and means.

The Good Life

Aristotle's teaching about wealth leads to basic insights that can aid us as we reflect upon our own situation. Whether we speak of "natural wealth," assets that can be monetized, or money itself, wealth is no more than a means. Wealth is *for* something else, namely, the pursuit of the good life. Not life in general, lacking a definite shape or quality, but the good life, a life lived well.

The concept of the good life adds definition to the ultimate end virtuous activity pursues. It defines wealth and wealth acquisition in a way that commerce alone cannot. To put the same point another way, there is no financial answer to the question, "How much is enough?" Only reflection upon the good life, its activities and its shape, can do that, and such reflection depends on our ability—through intellect—to see human being-in-action. Once again intellect and being-at-work not only define the goal but illuminate the means to get there.

In short, we do not even know what we have—our "wealth" is really nothing—until we connect our capacity to a definite end or aspiration, the good life, which is defined by happiness and virtue. Our purposes and aspirations give character to our resources and generate living well. Without purposes, our possessions—large homes, fancy cars, even huge bank accounts and high-placed "contacts"—may become liabilities, bringing down upon us distractions, envies, worries, and complications.

Using Resources Liberally

To recall, our central question is how we can thoughtfully connect wealth or other material resources to our ultimate aspiration, which Aristotle defines as happiness. Aristotle found two virtues to be specifically related to the virtuous use of wealth: liberality and magnificence. We have mentioned liberality as an expression and embodiment of the grand virtue of friendship. Now let us return to liberality, and also explore magnificence, in the context of using our "equipment" well.

Long before Andrew Carnegie and John D. Rockefeller, Aristotle was famous for saying in his *Ethics* that it is more difficult to give money away well than to make it (2002: IV.1). This giving well, which depends upon thought and deliberation, is liberality. Aristotle is also famous for saying that every virtue is a mean between two vices. In other words, in every sphere of thought and action, there is one way to go right and many ways to go wrong. The trick is to find the mean.

One might expect Aristotle, then, to define liberality as simply seeking a mean between excessive giving (wastefulness) and insufficient giving (stinginess). Actually, Aristotle's notion of liberality reveals itself more dialectically than that, coming to light by twists and turns (see IV.1). At first Aristotle says the liberal person should give in proportion to his particular degree of wealth: people with little give little, people with much give much.

This "means test" is practical and makes sense. But it is not Aristotle's last word. Truly liberal people often tend to "go to the excess in giving," "leave less for themselves," and do not "look out for themselves," he writes. In other words, people may give beyond their means yet remain true to the virtue. Indeed, giving beyond your means looks like a mark of liberality! Here we might recall Luke 21:1–4: Jesus praises the widow who gave her two pennies because she gave "all that she had to live on." She wasn't giving "within" her means but beyond them.

But isn't there something wrong with giving (hence living) beyond your means? In Aristotle's account, liberality at times sounds as though it has begun to edge toward wastefulness. But he stops short by distinguishing between that vice and liberality. Wasteful people may have to take money from ugly sources (such as stealing or gambling) in order to support their habits. The liberal person gives from a morally safe source, such as his or her own possessions.

But the larger distinction between liberality and wastefulness has more to do with *disbursing* than *acquiring*, with the destiny, rather than the source, of giving. Wasteful people give for many reasons: out of sympathy, or guilt, or fear, or to show off. They may lavish gifts on flatterers or toadies. Liberal people, on the other hand, give away money "for the sake of the beautiful." This doesn't mean they spend money only on that which is physically beautiful. "The beautiful" refers to what is fitting, upstanding, right, excellent, and fine. The judgment required is less aesthetic than moral. Liberal people desire to do a beautiful thing with their resources.

LIBERALITY'S BEAUTY

The giving of liberal people is motivated by a vision of beauty. For Aristotle, all the ethical virtues, which include courage, temperance, greatness of soul, gentleness, wit, and justice, aim at the beautiful. But the beauty of courage differs from that of temperance or gentleness. So what is the special beauty of the liberal deed? How do liberal people know they are "doing a beautiful thing"?

First they ask themselves: Is this the right amount? For the right person? At the right time? And in the right manner? In other words, Aristotle's liberal soul thinks about many of the same things that contemporary givers and their advisors puzzle over: size, capacity, effectiveness, timing, manner, and so forth. These are the concern of practical judgment, the virtue we consider in the third part of this chapter. Practical judgment connects reflection with action.

But the beauty of the liberal deed shines not only from its thoughtfulness and reflection but from its very doing. Recall the apparent likeness between liberal and wasteful people. What defines wasters is that they destroy their own means, on which living depends; hence they seem to destroy themselves. To someone interested only in the "bottom line," the liberal person does the same thing: his or her property ends up diminished.

But the "bottom line" approach misses the point. For the truly liberal person, acquiring and maintaining property does not equal being. Such people find their work, their flourishing and happiness, in giving away what looks to be most their "own." This is a twist on the familiar human propensity to lay claim to property, to equate it with our very being. How many people feel a personal attachment to their homes, or cars, or businesses! But liberal people take a step beyond this, and realize a higher aspect of human nature, when they turn property into a gift. Indeed they add a new facet to the concept of what one "owns." They develop a self, as Ignatius put it later, that is internally free and thus can focus on deeper ends.

Aristotle confirms this in his *Politics,* in which he argues that the good legislator should make sure that people hold and care for property privately, but use it as much as possible for public purposes (1998: II.5). One reason he gives for preserving private property is that one cannot perform a liberal action without something to give away. Abolishing property will not change the human desire for more goods, which, as he notes, finds no limit in itself. Instead, legislators should make sure that "naturally decent people are disposed not to want to be acquisitive, and that the base ones cannot be" (1998: II.7).

FRIENDSHIP IN ACTION

But how is it that givers find a new facet of "their own" in giving? This question brings us back to friendship, or *philia*. As with other virtues, friendship involves thinking and doing. At its most thoughtful, in the friendship of the wise, friends share thoughts and speeches. But all friendship depends upon a mutual perception and practice of some good. Friendship in action strives to achieve that mutual benefit. In regard to our question about wealth, liberality is a key way friends benefit each other. Given our topic, we should spend a moment getting to know better the dimensions of this form of friendship in action.

"The giver," Aristotle writes, "is the most beloved of all the virtuous, because he benefits others" (2002: IV.1). But he also notes that givers tend to love those they benefit more than those benefited love their benefactors (IX.7). This observation might surprise us. After all, givers have given something up, while those they benefit have received something. Why shouldn't they love their benefactor more than the benefactor loves them? The answer is that benefactors, practicing liberality, don't only give things away: they find great good in their benefaction.

Aristotle likens benefactors (and friends in general) to people who make things. Poets, he says, always love their poems inordinately. If statues could come to life (as in the story of Pygmalion), one suspects their makers would love them more than the statues would love their makers. Givers are the same way. A poet, a sculptor, and a giver all produce something: poems, statues, gifts. More importantly, they all put something of themselves into their products. They are "in action" in what they make. Since people love their own "being-in-action," they love the product of this special activity, whether it is a poem, a statue, or a gift. A shared "being-in-action" is not something that givers simply see externally; they perceive it with *nous,* intellect. Givers and recipients, and friends in general, can share in this intellectual and moral perception.

In other words, as people love their friend for the friend's own sake, so too, benefactors find their own flourishing in the flourishing of those they benefit. Though in different ways, the beneficiaries' flourishing is their benefactors' flourishing; benefactors nourish themselves when they nourish others.

Liberality is fundamentally an expression of friendship, and friendship, as a moral virtue, embodies care. In modern terms, we might say that care is liberality implemented. It involves sacrifice, yes, but this does not necessarily mean loss. The caring person finds his "being-in-action" in the happiness of others. Liberality offers a worthy end toward which one might direct one's wealth or other gifts. It connects wealth with happiness by transforming personal property into personal being-in-action, under the auspices of friendship and care. It is not a loss, but a gain, for everyone.

Human beings' wondrous ability to be at work "in" one another, through giving or friendship, helps explain why many donors identify with those they benefit—whether children, the sick, the elderly, people close at hand, or others far away—and why this is such an incentive to giving. It also helps explain why wealthy donors, as hyperagents, also seek to change the conditions under which others live. Building organizations or major parts of them amounts to "being-in-action" on a large scale, which for Aristotle is the virtue of magnificence.

Using Resources Magnificently

Magnificence is the second virtue Aristotle specifically links to the use of wealth. It involves making big gifts or expenditures. At first glance, it looks a lot like liberality. Indeed, Aristotle says that magnificence is liberality writ large: while the liberal person gives small or moderate amounts, the magnificent person distributes huge sums of money (2002: IV.2).

But on closer inspection we find that magnificence, unlike liberality, does not depend upon sacrifice. And while liberality embodies and fosters friendship, magnificence requires and fosters contemplation, a major element of wisdom. Magnificence does not directly seek to benefit others as much as to inspire wonder. It aims at "greatness." The magnificent person may build huge buildings, deck out enormous ships, and throw big parties.

Sheer magnitude, however, is only part of magnificence's greatness—and it may not be the greatest part. Aristotle contends that to be truly magnificent, a work must also suit the person doing it. These doers should be recognizable as great. It also helps if their family is great. A great family, a great personal reputation, and great amounts of money all contribute to the greatness of the magnificent expense.

The "great" in greatness is relative. A magnificent gift must suit the spender and the occasion. Thus Aristotle says that a very beautiful bottle or ball, given to a child, may be a magnificent gift even though such items do not cost much and hence require little or no liberality. A magnificent person and a liberal person might even spend the same amount on the same object and produce different results. The magnificent person, Aristotle says, will make the result "more suitably grand." The magnificent person knows how to spend even small or moderate amounts with grand results. Magnificence has much more to do with grandeur and consequential effect than liberality does.

WONDERFUL SPENDING

These points of contrast with liberality reveal another facet of magnificence: Aristotle never says that practicing magnificence requires persons to spend their own money! As we have seen, spending one's own money is an important element of liberality. One can't really be liberal with other people's money. That is why Aristotle says that tyrants should not properly be said to be liberal, since they share nothing by simply taking and then giving away others' property.

Magnificence, in contrast to liberality, resides less in the expense or its source and more in the display. The magnificent act also possesses greatness and beauty. It inspires wonder. Whatever magnificent people spend on, they evoke the response, "Wonderful!" And they do so whether they are spending their own money or others'.

But why should spending money in an awe-inspiring way be a virtue? Imelda Marcos spent an awesome amount on shoes. Few people would call this a worthy expression of any virtue. Indeed, people increasingly recognize that the "conspicuous consumption" of our affluent age reflects and deepens a sort of spiritual emptiness.

The key is that magnificence, while indeed conspicuous, is far from consumption. We can understand this point by comparing magnificence with a nearby vice, which Aristotle calls "vulgarity." Vulgar people miss because they spend "not for the sake of the beautiful, but to make a show of their wealth and so to make *themselves* wondrous" (2002: IV.2). Vulgar people aim at "wonder" through spending, but they miss the mark by trying to make the object of that wonder . . . themselves.

The magnificent person may lavish funds on civic feasts and weddings, or the building of temples and warships. But such magnificent acts direct people's attention toward "things shared in common," not toward the giver. For this reason, Aristotle likens the expenditures of the magnificent person to offerings devoted to the gods. Such offerings direct the eyes of onlookers toward things much greater than ourselves.

COSMIC SPENDING

This focus on directing attention to communal things reveals a moral quality of magnificence and why it offers a worthy path in the good life amid prosperity. "Magnificence" is *megaloprepes* in Greek, literally "greatly conspicuous" or "greatly fitting." The ambiguity between conspicuous and fitting in this translation reflects the complexity of the virtue. Magnificence is about the wonder evoked by a great display. But what does that display display? What does it cause us to wonder at? The expense must not only be "conspicuous." It must also be "fitting." A truly virtuous expense evokes our wonder at how fitting it is.

In the largest sense, then, the magnificent gift "fits." It fits its givers, their renown, and their family. It fits its purpose. But most importantly, Aristotle holds, it fits "the common things." This refers to our common human nature, our common social structure, or both. Spending a huge amount on yourself, on your own personal needs—such as buying one thousand shoes—just doesn't fit, even if you tried them all on before you bought them. Only a millipede could use that many shoes, except that it doesn't wear any. Certainly no person can. By its disproportion, the vulgar expense makes the world seem off-kilter.

The magnificent act also reveals how "fitting" our world is. It helps us see that the things we hold in common fit together. Aristotle says that magnificent gifts resemble offerings to the gods: they knit together the universe, the high and the low. Whatever the magnificent person spends on, writes Aristotle, is a *cosmos*—in Greek, an "ordered whole." The magnificent gift fits together the way that the cosmos fits together; it dazzles with reflected cosmic light.

Just as liberality finds its full meaning in friendship, magnificence ultimately points to living out the virtue of wisdom. Aristotle suggests the connection this way: "The magnificent person resembles the knower, for he can contemplate what's fitting and spend great amounts harmoniously" (2002: IV.2). That which is most harmonious and most of all constitutes "the common things" is, of course, the universe itself. This cosmos is the object of the eternal contemplations of God and the more limited contemplations of wise people. The magnificent person is a reflection of God and the wise person. Magnificence thus emerges as a sort of conspicuous philosophy. To use present-day terms, we could call the philanthropist a public philosopher. Magnificent persons or philanthropists do not create a private world (neither does God, in Aristotle's view!), but, when fully "being-in-action," they reflect the ordered nature of the world and its ordered beauty in their grand expenditures. Whether by building a school or a church or a hospital, philanthropists knit together the public and the personal, the natural and the conventional, the high and the low—indeed, at their best, the whole of things.

Just as liberality relies upon friendship, magnificence relies upon wisdom. Similar to hyperagents, magnificent persons need to direct their energetic being-in-action with care. They need to recognize the limits on property and on what good it can do. Magnificent people use property not to satisfy their own or others' personal needs but to excite their own and others' highest psychic capacities. By exciting the capacity to wonder, they activate wisdom—their own and others'. A truly magnificent expenditure, therefore, gives all its onlookers a taste of the best that human life has to offer, and sets them on the path to happiness. By tying magnificence to wisdom, Aristotle shows that a virtue we may have thought was only "about money" actually taps into the ultimate reality of our common life. Contemporary great philanthropy can be well instructed by Aristotle's philosophy of magnificence in practice.

Practical Judgment

Thus far we have come to understand better, from Aristotle's point of view, two of the three elements in our question about how to live well in an age of affluence: purposes and resources. For Aristotle, these are complementary. We cannot know our resources without knowing our ultimate ends. And we cannot attain our ends without the necessary resources.

We now turn to the third term: discernment. Discernment seeks to clarify and unite purposes and resources, which, though complementary, often seem to stand far apart. How do we make wealth serve virtue? How can we apply our principles to our possessions? These are the questions that, in decision after decision, discernment tries to answer.

Several terms in Aristotle's Greek capture facets of discernment. The one that stands out from the others as being the most comprehensive and powerful is *phronesis,* or "practical judgment." Practical judgment is a virtue, and hence a good activity, a form of being-in-action. Like wisdom, it is rooted in careful thought. Like friendship, it gives rise to deeds and also seeks the good, for oneself and others. Practical judgment unites wisdom and friendship, thought and deed by enacting wise choices for putting resources into action in accord with fitting purposes. It makes the virtuous life possible.

As a virtue, practical judgment has four characteristics. (1) Its primary aspect is deliberation. Simply put, this means deliberating well (2002: VI.5). (2) Because it involves thinking, it relies upon *nous* or intellect to guide it toward its goal. (3) It also involves reflection—on ourselves, our predispositions and desires. (4) And practical judgment results in our making a choice. Let us examine each of these four characteristics of practical judgment.

Deliberation

Before one can choose a course of action, one must deliberate on the possibilities and consequences. Deliberation is the mental activity of "connecting the dots" between the present and a wished-for end. Deliberating well connects us to good ends in a good way.

We all have some sense of what deliberation is. Examining many different automobile models and interrogating dealers before buying a car is an example of deliberation. So is thinking about all the consequences of, say, taking a new job. But Aristotle deepens our understanding of deliberation. He calls it a type of "inquiry" (2002: III.3). A scientific experiment is an obvious sort of inquiry. So is trying to prove something in mathematics, trying to remember someone's name, or simply trying to get from A to B in any context. Not all inquiries are deliberation, since they don't all aim at choice and action. Figuring out a mathematical proof is not a form of deliberation. You don't end a proof by "choosing" whether x = y. Deliberation is practical inquiry. It connects the means that lie at hand with the action we want to accomplish. It clarifies the wise choices we will implement.

Because of the power of imagination, deliberation can proceed in two ways: from the means to the end, or the other way around. Aristotle uses mathematical terms to describe these ways. He likens the first way to "demonstration." In a demonstration or proof, mathematicians begin with what they know, the already proved, and proceed to what is not yet known—the answer.

People undergo the same process on a larger scale when they project mentally from current circumstances to a wished-for end. One way to perform such a "proof" easily enough is to ask yourself a series of "Why?" questions concerning your activities. Why am I reading this book? *I want to learn about giving well.* Why do I want to learn to give well? *I serve as a trustee of a foundation and need to decide this quarter's grants.* Why do I bother making grants? *I want to make the best expenditure for the best purposes.* That final step—the best grant—is the wished-for end.

But mathematicians also find it practical, when they haven't figured out a proof yet, to proceed from the desired end back to what they know. This Aristotle calls "analysis." In analysis, one endeavors to "see" the end as clearly as possible, even if the way to get there is unknown. (In the example above, this would be "the best grant.") Analysis seeks the causes of an outcome. One moves from the desired result to something that could lead to it. One keeps up this backward movement until one arrives at something that one *does* know or a choice that one *can* make. Now there exists a path from the end to oneself.

We do the same thing all the time in travel, when we work our way "back" from a destination to where we are now. We imagine being at the place where we want to be, and then we figure out a path from there to our present location. This is indeed how Aristotle envisions deliberation operating. But from the start it requires "seeing" the wished-for end with great clarity. For example, one might say, I really want to do something good for the kids in my hometown. But first I need to clearly picture what that "good" is, and for whom. Who are those kids? What do they really need? What would be good for them? Once I perceive that end with utmost clarity, I can imagine my way "back" to my situation and means.

This need for "seeing" the end clearly illuminates the role of intellect in deliberation. Left to itself, deliberation, like any other inquiry, might go on forever. There are dozens of ways, for example, to prove the Pythagorean theorem. Intellect, in the service of practical judgment, puts a stop to deliberation and results in action. Aristotle likens this to our knowing that a triangle forms the simplest rectilinear figure. Try to imagine a straight-lined figure (not just a line or a point!) with fewer than three sides. No matter how you manipulate the lines in your mind, you can't form one. Something similar happens for people with practical judgment: no matter how they imagine the situation being otherwise, nothing "looks right" except the action they choose.

As wisdom equals intellect plus deductive knowledge, so, too, practical judgment amounts to intellect plus deliberation. And just as intellect provides the starting point and the logical tools for knowledge, so too it allows us to better see the means we have, including our spiritual capacities, material resources, talents, and even our weaknesses, to get from "here" to "there." It's time then that we look more closely at intellect, and try to understand its marvelous ability to inspire wisdom and practical judgment.

Intellect

Aristotle calls *nous,* or intellect, the "eye of the soul" (2002: VI.12). Human beings, at our best, are not so much givers as receivers. We receive the world into our souls. In his book *On the Soul,* Aristotle goes so far as to claim that the world—the things we apprehend through intellect—"shapes" our souls when we perceive and understand it. In other words, our intellect becomes the very things we know.

What do we "see" through intellect? Aristotle begins with the perception of two sorts of what he calls "ultimate particulars." There are changeless principles that can be demonstrated, such as that the whole is greater than the sum of the parts or that human beings differ from dogs. Wisdom can know nothing unless its knowledge is grounded in enduring first principles, which come to us through intellect.

But the ultimate particulars include more than enduring first principles. Actions are also "ultimate particulars." Even though actions are not enduring, for they could always change, halt, or go awry, they are nevertheless the special province of practical judgment. Why? Practical judgment does not deliberate about whether the world is round. It is, or it is not; that is a matter of reality or wisdom. Practical judgment *does* deliberate whether or not one should travel around the globe. Choosing to travel is within my power. Deliberation over whether to engage in it, like the ultimate particular of the world's roundness, comes to me through intellect (2002: VI.11).

By making wisdom and practical judgment as well as the subordinate virtues possible, intellect unifies a human being. Here is where Aristotle, in his *Ethics,* comes to the threshold of the central teaching in his *Metaphysics.* What is truly first is not practical judgment, or wisdom, or even intellect, but the ultimate particular or its being. Some particulars or beings (e.g., nature, the cosmos, and numbers) exist forever. When the intellect perceives them and knowledge gives order to this perception, one has wisdom. But ultimate particulars can also change, as in actions, and intellect informs our deliberation about them as well. When judgment leads us to stop deliberating and act, it is not on a whim. We stop where intellect tells us we will find the good for ourselves and others. Intellectual perception thus determines when good actions begin and when they end.

The best way to perceive the end of deliberation is by seeing it in ourselves, in our own experience of living well; intellect permits this. People know what living well is like and keep doing it. On the other hand, because no single perception of our being-in-action is always better than any other, Aristotle allows that we can also learn first principles from others, through our experience of *their* lives.

To become good choosers, then, we should not only reflect upon our own experience but also try to get to know other people, what they think and the particulars of their situations. If we observe them faithfully and reflect on our observations, we will enhance our ability to know the direction for our own being-in-action. Such perception can even come from books, such as Aristotle's *Ethics,* as long as these books reproduce human living and human choosing in its particulars. Aristotle's understanding of human being-in-action and of choice underlies even this book's attempt to expand our moral imagination by surveying how great thinkers have approached wealth and the will of God.

Reflection

To review, we are examining discernment, the third main topic in our question about wealth and happiness. We have seen that it involves deliberation, which helps us imaginatively connect ends with means, and intellect, which allows us to better see both our ends and the means to bring them about. Now we turn to the third aspect of practical judgment: reflecting on our own personal predispositions and desires, which affect the character and outcome of our deliberation.

All human beings have desires. These desires reach out for (or flee from) all sorts of things in the world but generally *for* pleasure and *from* pain. Desire, for Aristotle, is firmly rooted in the body. It is not reflective by itself, but desire can become the object of reflection.

Desires move us—this is why we call them e-*motions*—and if one moves us repeatedly, we begin to develop a habit or predisposition. Most people think of habits, "good" or "bad," as unthinking and mechanical. But Aristotle respects them as the essential patterns of our lives. Seen in this light, habit is essential to choice. For a choice to be true, it must not be flighty, arbitrary, or unpredictable. It must spring from a settled disposition involving thought. On the other hand, thought alone does not produce a choice. Our habits or predispositions play a large role. In effect, we choose in certain ways because we have become accustomed to acting and choosing in those ways. Habits provide the backbone of choice.

Predispositions may be seen as desires solidified. Some of us are habitually greedy. Some of us are habitually self-denying. In Aristotle's notion of moral self-reflection, the key thing is to recognize whether our habitual desires harmonize with wished-for ends. Assume, for example, that intellect presents climbing a mountain as a good end to pursue, making it a goal for deliberation. Deliberation identifies the means—the boots, ropes, packs, maps, and so forth—that we should marshal to reach that goal. A thorough process of deliberation issues in a choice, such as organizing our trip and starting forth. If our habits are well formed, they incite a desire to pursue that wished-for goal. If, instead, we are lazy, or timid, or habitually indecisive, our choice will be stymied.

Our desires, alas, are frequently at odds with our wished-for goals. An overpowering habitual desire out of harmony with one's desired ends may be called a "bad" habit. Most people "know" that habitual stinginess is bad. When we hold back a gift—even though we "want" to give—we reveal an absence of choice. The familiar desire and its repeated motions crowd out any deliberation. But there are steps that we can take to redress this absence of choice.

The first step is to perceive our habits and predisposed desires for what they are. Aristotle would remind us that, most commonly, these desires concern themselves with pleasure and pain. In Aristotle's view, pleasure is never simply a stimulus; it is more active than that. When we feel pleasure, we reveal that we are "in action" in a certain way. Pleasure or pain can serve as a diagnostic tool. We discern our own activities when we feel pleasure. For example, if we give to others only grudgingly and with pain, Aristotle would say that we are not truly "in action" as liberal people. We may go through the motions, but the moral character is not there. An even more telling sign would be if we pay lip service to liberality but take pleasure in hoarding or even stealing from others. Here the pleasures and pains reveal that we are predisposed to greediness or even injustice. Observing what makes us feel pleasure and pain goes a long way in revealing to us what our habitual predispositions are.

The next step in correcting bad habits, Aristotle suggests, is to conceive of the virtues or good activities in human life as a middle road between two extremes. We can identify courage as the mean between cowardice and foolhardiness, liberality between stinginess and wastefulness, magnificence between chintziness and vulgarity, and so on. To be sure, things are not always so simple. As we saw with liberality, the virtue may not sit exactly between its two vices. But the general point holds. After all, if human beings have characteristic activities, it is likely that we'll go awry in one way or another, too much or too little.

If this is so, one way to improve oneself is to reflect upon one's predispositions and to observe to which extreme one is drawn—then to aim in another direction. This is a rough-and-ready way to habituate oneself to want right things. It does not represent the fullness of moral life, nor does it constitute a "rule" for living and choosing well in all circumstances. For example, simply aiming at the middle between wastefulness and stinginess would not make one liberal, for liberality, in important respects, more closely resembles wastefulness.

Aristotle illustrates this point by recalling Odysseus's navigation between the twin dangers of Scylla and Charybdis in the *Odyssey*. Odysseus was sailing home from Troy, but he was driven off course by a storm. To get back, he had to make it through a narrow channel, on one side of which lurked the vicious dragon Scylla. On the other side was the all-devouring whirlpool Charybdis. Odysseus knew that if his ship went anywhere near Charybdis, all would be lost. If it got too close to Scylla, a few crewmembers would be lost. Neither course was good, but aiming slightly toward Scylla avoided the greatest harm, which simply shooting down the middle would not have achieved.

It is up to intellect to perceive the Scylla and Charybdis—the known features of our predispositions—clearly and honestly. If people do not take the time to do so or have corrupted their intellects so thoroughly that they cannot see these predispositions as problematic, there will not be much successful "navigating" to do. They will keep sailing along with the bad habits. By the same token, if we successfully aim at the middle and avoid our predisposed actions, we may begin to see another way of acting. Through reflecting on our predispositions and advancing our good habits, we open up the "eye of his soul" more widely and see more clearly.

Choice

Choice is the product of practical judgment: it is the end of deliberation and the beginning of action. It involves a great deal of thought, making use of intellect at every step to inform agile deliberation. But we also saw that choice is produced not only by thought but by desires and predispositions. "Thought alone moves nothing," Aristotle reminds us. Desire serves as the engine of action, through choice. Aristotle defines choice this way: it is "intellect desiring or desire intellecting." As if this definition were not marvelous enough, he adds: "And such a source is human being" (2002: VI.2). In other words, Aristotle defines what it is to be human by this amazing combination of intellect and desire, generating choice.

Choice is always active, in Aristotle's view. Bad habits such as biting your fingernails or overeating are usually not a choice; these reveal the absence of choice. True choice springs from a free and conscious being. Our choices, in other words, reflect who we are, our settled dispositions or character. It is because we are a certain way that we choose a certain thing, and character defines and limits future choices. We are always free to choose this or that. But we are not always free to choose to be this or that way. We may have once been free to choose to be, say, liberal or stingy. But after many such choices, it becomes harder and harder for us to change who we are. Still, because each and every choice remains in our power, we have some ability over time, although perhaps with great difficulty, to change our character.

The choices we make in turn contribute to the formation of habits, which, when fully settled, become character. Choices are like bricks in a wall: each holds up those that come later while giving form to the complete structure, the desired shape of which guided the bricklaying from the start. In essence, our being-in-action and our choosing are often one and the same. We are "in action" in our choices. Someone who chooses to watch TV alone differs in certain ways from someone who chooses to go to the theatre or to play cards with friends.

Choice even affects our intellect. This "eye of the soul" is not always wide open. One may open it wider through active seeing, listening, reading, and other experiences. But by the same token we can begin to close the intellect through bad habits. For example, if some people allow themselves to become thoroughly stingy, their intellect will become blind to liberal actions. They will call them "stupid," "irrational," or "inexplicable." They won't consider them as possible choices. This is why it is so important, in Aristotle's view, to develop the best habits and predispositions we can in youth: they prepare us to see the beautiful end in beautiful actions or at least do less to obscure that vision.

Making good choices, developing good habits, and improving our characters open the intellect wider and make it more receptive. The liberal person sees what it is to be stingy or wasteful and is repelled, but he also sees liberal action as an object of choice. That is why Aristotle makes the seemingly odd statement that no one can possess practical judgment without possessing subordinate virtues (2002: VI.12). Practical judgment allows us to deliberate well and to choose virtuous actions. But the virtues themselves define the good ends that the intellect proposes to practical judgment. There is no morally disengaged way to become good, no "trick" or shortcut. You do the best you can to choose the good, and, little by little perhaps, come to see the good more clearly. The clearer perception incites better choices, and so on. That is what it is to be a human being.

Conclusion: Reflection and Reverence

We began by asking Aristotle, how can we most thoughtfully connect our material resources with ultimate purposes? His answer, as it were, is that practical judgment allows us to deploy equipment (of whatever sort) with virtue for the sake of happiness.

Virtue, we saw, falls under two main banners: friendship and wisdom. And when it comes to that equipment known as wealth, two foremost virtues may direct its deployment: liberality and magnificence. Wealth itself is nothing, or next to nothing, until it is directed toward a purpose, whether that purpose is the maintenance of life itself (through "natural wealth") or the pursuit of the good life (through both natural wealth and money). Wealth and virtue are coexistent: wealth needs virtue to direct it, and virtue often relies on wealth (or "equipment" more generally) to support its strivings.

Finally, Aristotle has opened our eyes to that reflective but decisive virtue he calls practical judgment, a term that aptly corresponds to our special focus, discernment. At the heart of practical judgment lies good deliberation, which depends on an agile imagination, incisive intellect, and reflection on and, when necessary, amendment of one's own predispositions or existing desires. Practical judgment issues in choice, an activity peculiar to human beings. Aristotle even defines us as a marvelous combination of "intellect desiring and desire intellecting." This observation, like everything else Aristotle writes in his *Nicomachean Ethics*, attempts to unveil the complex yet inspiring being-in-action that is human life.

One final reflection: Given our concern with the will of God, Aristotle's human-centered approach in the *Ethics* may appear to be in contrast to the deeply theological perspective of the other writers in this volume. Unlike many classical Greek thinkers, Aristotle does not look to the Muses, God, or the gods for direct guidance. He relies on unaided human reflection (rather than prophecy or providence)—that is, on our natural human capacities and agency. To make matters more striking, in the *Ethics* he does not praise piety or reverence, which was held by his culture to be a virtue that any decent person possessed. Aristotle argues that while reverence is well and good for children or bad people, it has no place in the soul of the confident, truly virtuous adult (2002: IV.9). Aristotle instead praises a virtue he calls "greatness of soul," an element of which involves looking upon nothing else as great (IV.3).

This approach might not inspire people to kneel down and pray. But Aristotle's criticism of reverence and praise of individual greatness of soul do not reflect the whole of his thought. To see this whole, we must evaluate human being-in-action in all its many facets as it quests for happiness. At the height of being-in-action are wisdom, friendship, and practical judgment, all of which rely on the ability to perceive the highest principles for all they are worth. Cultivating this quality, intellect, means opening ourselves to the ultimate—whether the ultimate end, the ultimate being, or the ultimate particular. It may even mean, as we suggested earlier, imitating and uniting with the divine. Doing so entails seeing everything around and within us with the imagination of new eyes, as strange and wonderful. Aristotle's approach is characterized more by wonder than by pride, and in this respect provides a natural introduction to the more God-centered reflections of the great minds that follow.

2 ⁓

Aquinas

"Distinguish Ends and Means"

When reading Saint Thomas Aquinas (c. 1225–1274), it is easy to forget the writer behind the deftly poised arguments of the *Summa Theologica*. Aquinas seems to disappear amid the delicately balanced objections and responses. Even when he proclaims, "I answer that . . . ," his individuality pales beside the authorities he cites and proceeds to defend. The very immensity of his work also makes it seem impossible that a single human being could produce it.

Yet it is all the more important to remember Aquinas the writer, the human being, when we study his thoughts on such topics as wealth and giving. Both Aquinas's parents belonged to noble families. As a young man, he enjoyed honor, power, and many possessions. And yet he chose to abandon all these goods for a mendicant order and a life of learning, teaching, advising, and writing. He gave up in order to give. As he himself explains, "even as it is better to enlighten than merely to shine, so it is better to give to others the fruits of one's contemplation than merely to contemplate" (1947: II–II.188.6).

Aquinas's example reminds us from the start that there are many ways to give of oneself. It also reminds us, forcefully, of how much the giver may give up. And it presses home the question of the end: that for which the giver gives. Aquinas abandoned wealth in order to pursue what he understood as his own natural and divinely ordered end. In what follows, we will review his thoughts on the general ends or purposes of human life, especially in the virtues of liberality, magnificence, and charity. We will then turn to his comments on wealth and money and the challenges he thinks wealth poses to its possessor. In the chapter's final section, we will look more closely at the deliberative process that Aquinas recommends for ordering our possessions to our ultimate ends, a process that he explains most fully in the context of almsgiving.

Happiness and Charity

Supernatural Happiness

Like Aristotle, Aquinas envisions perfect happiness as the ultimate goal of human life. But he sees this state as comprised of two parts. The first, natural happiness, results from work done in accord with our particular nature as human beings, a work defined by various excellences or virtues.

Unlike Aristotle, Aquinas finds that natural happiness does not exhaust human happiness; to be a truly worthy end of life, it must culminate in the second part, supernatural happiness. "Final perfect happiness (*beatitudo*) can only come from the vision of the divine essence" (1947: I–II.3.8).[1] Aquinas offers two reasons for this claim. First, people cannot be perfectly happy as long as they still need or desire anything. But every natural being eventually succumbs to needs and desires. Only God stands above necessity or want. Human happiness thus finds perfection in union with God.

Second, "the perfection of any power is related to the characteristics of its object" (1947. I–II.3.8). The greatest power that human beings possess is the intellect (*intellectus*, Aquinas's Latin version of Aristotle's *nous*). It seeks the very being of things. But, in Aquinas's view, all beings are creations. They find their ultimate source in the one uncreated being, God; and they find their fulfillment of perfect happiness in God.

For Aquinas, natural inclinations, such as compassion or the desire to know, direct us toward natural ends. Similarly, we are directed toward our supernatural ends by "certain supernatural principles," especially faith, hope, and the desire for spiritual union that is realized in charity (see 1947: I–II.62.3). These three theological virtues do not replace the natural virtues but rather perfect them. Let us begin by considering what Aquinas calls the "mother of all virtues," charity. In the second part of this chapter, we will return to the more subordinate virtues, liberality and magnificence, that have to do with wealth.

The Excellence that Shows the True End of Life

The present age almost completely misunderstands charity. When we think of charity, we tend to think of its *objects*—the poor, the hungry, the ignorant. The term has come to mean something as broad as any organization devoted to the good of others, a "charity." We equate charity with its handouts and recipients: a "charitable gift," a "charity case," or a "charitable organization."

For Aquinas, charity is not an object; it is a virtue. Today the virtue has almost entirely disappeared behind its object or means of expression. Neither those persons who benefit from charity nor those organizations that engage in

---

1. References to the *Summa Theologica* (Aquinas 1947) cite the book and part (e.g., book 1, part 2), then the chapter, then the paragraph.

it *are* themselves "charity." The virtue does not even primarily concern poverty, need, or self-denial.

As a virtue, charity reigns supreme in Aquinas's view. Thus, he says, citing the Psalms, "The ultimate and principal good of man is the enjoyment of God, according to Ps. 73.28: 'It is good for me to adhere to God,' and to this good man is ordered by charity" (1947: II–II.23.7). Likewise, "Charity tends towards the last end considered as last end: and this does not apply to any other virtue" (1947: II–II.26.1). Indeed, charity not only stands above all the other virtues; it also can be understood as their source: "Since a mother is one who conceives within herself and by another, charity is called the mother of the other virtues, because by commanding them, she conceives, by the desire of the last end, the acts of the other virtues" (1947: II–II.23.8 *ad* 2). Far from being an object, charity is the excellence that inclines us toward the true end of human life.

LOVE AND FRIENDSHIP AS UNION

Most importantly, charity is a form of love, specifically, a grace-infused friendship. It is that which animates the loving person. "Now charity is a kind of friendship," Aquinas tells us. "Therefore it consists in loving rather than in being loved" (1947: II–II.27.1). As Psalm 73 reveals, charity is a particular type of friendship: "the friendship of man for God" (1947: II–II.23.1).[2] From ancient times to the present, most people have taken the possession of wealth as a sign of God's friendship: if someone is well-off, it must be because "God loves him." But charity's friendship is not so self-serving. The goal of charity is drawing near to and resting in God: "charity attains God Himself that it may rest in Him, but not that something may accrue to us from Him" (1947: II–II.23.6).

This does not mean that charity amounts to self-denial or self-annihilation. Every virtue contributes to our happiness, whether natural or supernatural. Charity does so most of all. Aquinas approvingly quotes Paul's famous declaration that "If I should distribute all my goods to the poor, and if I should deliver my body to be burned, and have not charity, it profiteth me nothing" (1 Cor. 13:3). Aquinas concludes, "Accordingly no strictly true virtue is possible without charity" (1947: II–II.23.7). Charity brings us the greatest fruits.

Furthermore, charity rests upon the "fellowship of happiness," which "consists essentially in God, as the First Principle, whence it flows to all who are

---

2. In this definition of charity, Aquinas closely follows St. Augustine. So, for example: "By charity I mean the movement of the soul towards the enjoyment of God for His own sake" (*De Doctr. Christ.* iii.10, quoted in Aquinas 1947: II–II.23.2). "Charity is a virtue which, when our affections are perfectly ordered, unites us to God, for by it we love Him" (*De Moribus Eccl.* xi, quoted in Aquinas 1947: II–II.23.3). "There are four things to be loved; one which is above us, namely God, another, which is ourselves, a third which is nigh to us, namely our neighbor, and a fourth which is beneath us, namely our own body" (*De Doctr. Christ.* i.23, quoted in Aquinas 1947: II–II.25.12).

capable of happiness." Aquinas recognizes that true lovers do not seek to annihilate themselves in their love. He takes a similar stance toward love of God: people seek rest in God not to destroy themselves but rather to find a truth and fullness that makes them completely happy. "Therefore," Aquinas continues, "God ought to be loved chiefly and before all out of charity: for He is loved as the cause of happiness, whereas our neighbor is loved as receiving together with us a share of happiness from Him" (1947: II–II.26.2).

THE SURPRISES OF CHARITY

This vision of charity as friendship with God can lead to surprising conclusions. For example, we tend to think about charity in times of need, hardship, or disaster. But since charity amounts to fellowship in God's happiness, it truly comes into its own, into its fullest state, only in heaven, where there are no needs, hardships, or disasters. Aquinas explains, "Nature is not done away, but perfected, by glory. . . . then [in heaven] one man will no longer succor another, as he needs to in the present life . . ." (1947: II–II.26.13).

Likewise we tend to think of charity as for certain other goods: comfort, health, shelter, etc. Aquinas, in contrast, summarizes its general outcome this way: "charity is the good which we desire for all those whom we love out of charity" (1947: II–II.25.2). In other words, whatever good we do for others out of charity, what we should truly wish for them, the greatest good we can hope that they attain, is charity itself.

These observations reveal how perfect charity is. It is the supreme end for human beings. It accompanies the highest happiness. Aquinas's charity is as perfect as anything human can be, but it attains its completeness or perfection by pointing beyond itself and toward God and friendship with God. Its perfection is a reflection of God's own.

Loving God does not exclude our loving other people. Far from it: loving God gives us a reason to love other people, since they are made in God's image and promised a place in His friendship. But Aquinas never hides the truth that charity requires loving other people secondarily: "God is the principal object of charity, while our neighbor is loved out of charity for God's sake" (1947: II–II.23.5). Likewise, "The love of one's neighbor is not meritorious, except by reason of his being loved for God's sake" (II–II.27.8).

One might complain that Aquinas denigrates loving other people as inferior. Could not this opinion promote proud proclamations of piety, while beyond the church doors actual human beings starve and die? It could. But one can also say that Aquinas elevates and saves love for other human beings, by assimilating that love into the love we have for God. Charity is the love of other human beings *in* God. Without that elevation, loving other people, caring about them more than about all other creations in this world, begins to look parochial, as if it were a particular narrow tribalism that claimed to embrace the whole human race.

This end—the love of God above all else—also leads to surprising results concerning friends and enemies. Aquinas argues, "it is better to love one's friend, since it is better to love a better man, and the friend who loves you is better than the enemy who hates you" (1947: II–II.27.7). But such meritoriousness is only part of the story. He continues:

> In [another] way, however, it is better to love one's enemy than one's friend, and this for two reasons. First, because it is possible to love one's friend for another reason than God, whereas God is the only reason for loving one's enemies. Secondly, because if we suppose that both are loved for God, our love for God is proved to be all the stronger through carrying our affections to things which are furthest from us, namely, to the love of our enemies, even as the power of a furnace is proved to be the stronger, according as it throws its heat to more distant objects. Hence our love for God is proved to be so much the stronger, as the more difficult are the things we accomplish for its sake, just as the power of fire is so much the stronger, as it is able to set fire to a less inflammable matter. (1947: II–II.27.7)

At first glance, loving other people "for the sake of God" has a frigid air of distraction about it, rather like the people who greet others at a party while continually scanning over their shoulders for someone else they would rather talk to. What a cold embrace such a "friend" offers! But Aquinas makes clear that the charitable soul does not simply stare at God and, with whatever attention and strength it has left, attend to other people. Charitable love is not only love *for* God but also *from* God. God does not act as a chimney, sucking up the passion of charitable souls into a gusty flue, leaving everybody chilly; God rather acts as a generous furnace, pumping warmth into us and *through us* into others.

True, there are only so many BTUs of divine love that the human heart can handle. And Aquinas does not demand us to do what is beyond human nature: "[charity] does not require that we should have a special movement of love to every individual man, since this would be impossible" (1947: II–II.25.8). But the furnace of divine love is inexhaustible. And so Aquinas explains that truly charitable persons should be ready to feel a special movement of love for every individual they meet, whether friend, enemy, or sinner. What already exists in God—universal love for every person—remains potential in us, ready to be thawed into life at any moment.

THE FRUITS OF CHARITY

To round out our understanding of charity, we need to see not only its roots in love and friendship but also its fruits. Given our focus on wealth, we shall take a glance at two of these: mercy and gratitude.

Mercy

Mercy today also goes under the names of compassion or sympathy. It gets mixed reviews in the modern world. No one really argues against compassion; indeed, many people define their philanthropy as grounded in compassion rather than in "charity." But mercy also raises feelings of discomfort. We speak of people "begging for mercy" or "showing others mercy," implying that the one showing the mercy is superior to the one who begs. Such an elitist posture does not fit well in a democratic world.

Aquinas recognizes this ambiguity in mercy. It may be "a movement of the sensitive appetite, in which case mercy is not a virtue but a passion." This is the mercy people liken to compassion. Such emotion may not be wrong, but there's little of moral worth in it. Mercy may also "denote a movement of the intellective appetite, in as much as one person's evil is displeasing to another. This movement may be ruled in accordance with reason, and in accordance with this movement the lower appetite may be regulated." In short, mercy can take the form of compassion compounded with rational choice. When mercy acts this way, Aquinas agrees that it can be a virtue (1947: II–II.30.3).

Since this mercy is a virtuous response to the distress, misery, and evil that afflict human life, is it then a supreme virtue? No, says Aquinas. Mercy does stand before other virtues in the sense that the merciful person gives bountifully to others and takes care of them in their need, he concedes. In this way, the merciful person resembles God. But is a merciful person the greatest and most surpassing being? Not at all. Such a giver is kind and thoughtful, but there is something greater. The needy desire the goods of the giver or the happiness the giver enjoys. So, too, we should do as the needy person does and desire union with the greatest and most perfect giver. Such union comes about not through mercy, but through charity.

Thus, Aquinas concludes, "as regards man, who has God above him, charity which unites him to God is greater than mercy, whereby he supplies the defects of his neighbors. But of all the virtues which relate to our neighbor, mercy is the greatest, even as its act surpasses all others, since it belongs to one who is higher and better to supply the defect of another, in so far as the latter is deficient." And so one can divide the whole of religion between mercy and charity: "The sum total of the Christian religion consists in mercy, as regards external works: but the inward love of charity, whereby we are united to God preponderates over both love and mercy for our neighbor."

Long before Luther and other Reformers would elevate faith (and hence love) above works, Aquinas effects an elevation of this sort in his distinction between mercy and charity. There can be love without the work of caring for distress and loss; such love exists in heaven. But there cannot be work without love. Love moves all things. Only at such moments when love cools and when we lose sight of anything higher than ourselves, does mercy (understood as compassion) eclipse charity, and at the same time assume the temptation to take on the dark trappings of power.

Gratitude

People have always praised gratitude, but in an era of affluence, when fortunes spring up seemingly overnight, it has emerged as a preferred response to success. It is not exactly seen as a virtue, since it sometimes appears to require little deliberation, thought, or discrimination. It more resembles a passion, a sort of spontaneous thankfulness that arises in reply to having or achieving good things. At the same time, however, gratitude is expected. Those who do not express gratitude for their good fortune are seen as unworthy of it. Gratitude thus softens the edges of great achievements, which might otherwise foster envy or hatred, by reminding us that the achiever owes much toward many benefactors. It is the public piety of an Oscar-mad world.

Aquinas takes a different view. For him, gratitude is a virtue and as such a fruit of charity's tree. But it is not anywhere close to charity itself. Gratitude amounts to "giving thanks to our benefactors" (1947: II–II.106.1). Aquinas distinguishes this thankfulness from other forms of thanksgiving or respect. For example, the thanks we owe to our ultimate benefactor, God, he locates within the virtue of "religion," which brings with it a whole host of special actions, honors, observances, and obedience (see 1947: II–II.79–100). Likewise, the thanks we owe to our parents and country, Aquinas finds in "piety" (see 1947: II–II.101). Gratitude extends to those who do not offer us the ultimate goods of life, nurture, and education. It inspires thanks to those who give gifts but not life itself (see Joubert, cited in Aquinas 1947: 3323).

Aquinas also distinguishes gratitude (and these other virtues) from justice, that is, from paying off debts and maintaining order. If exercised carelessly, gratitude may come to resemble justice (see 1947: II–II.106.4), but in such cases gratitude almost ceases to be what it is. For gratitude truly embodies a return of love rather than a return of principal. This difference distinguishes ingratitude from injustice as well. Unjust persons who, say, default on a loan, injure someone else, the creditor. The ingrates, who forget to offer thanks for a gift, injure themselves (see Joubert, 3323; Aquinas 1947: II–II.107).

For this reason, gratitude always yields a return that exceeds the benefit that prompts it: "We should repay those who are gracious to us, by being gracious to them in return, and this is done by repaying more than we have received" (1947: II–II.106.6). As a consequence, gratitude's generous giving and returning does not end (Joubert, 3324). This result could seem to lead to an endless escalation of gift and re-gift (see 1947: II–II.106.6.2). But that escalation would occur only if gratitude were the same as justice, which requires an equal return. Instead, it flows from charity, "which the more it is paid the more is due" (1947: II–II.106.6. *ad* 2). Truly grateful givers and re-givers gradually lose count, cease keeping score and upping the ante, and unite in love and friendship. But this is another way of saying that gratitude, in its fullest form, does not stand on its own, but transforms itself back into its source, into charity.

Wealth's Perils and Promise

Unlike Aristotle, Aquinas locates his thoughts on wealth within a worldview ruled by a creator God. God's creation and grant to people of worldly dominion settles, for some minds, the issue of ownership and possession. The view that reason may help us fulfill God's plan for the earth's resources is further justification in this view. Even if we concede a common human right of possession and domination of nature, however, it is still a big step to ownership of private property (see MacLaren 1948).

Many early Christian thinkers drew this line firmly. While recognizing that property helped people survive, they also saw it as a sign of humanity's Fall. It was legitimate in our condition but not part of God's perfect world (see O'Brien 1920: 59). Some Patristic writers criticized private wealth harshly. "Giving alms to the poor is not a gift to them of what is yours but rather a restitution of what is their own," Ambrose of Milan, one of the most eminent fourth-century bishops, declared. "You usurp for yourselves alone what was given for the common use of all." What God meant as a common gift, he writes in *On the Duties of Ministers,* "usurpation . . . has made a private right." Ambrose's fellow Christian bishop in Syria and Constantinople, John Chrysostom, also a saint, held that "common and not private property" accords best with God's plan. Most bracing is the comment of Jerome, the master translator of the Bible and patron saint of theological learning, who lived from about 347 to 420: "All riches are descended from iniquity . . . Hence the common saying seems to me to be most true, 'A rich man is either a thief or the son of a thief!'" (see O'Brien 1920: 59).

Aquinas agreed with the Patristics—up to a point. The philosopher-monk from a rich Naples family was no idealist or absolutist. Aquinas uses the criticism of these Fathers and Doctors of the Church, as they are known in Catholicism, to weave a coherent and sophisticated defense of private property, one that includes a survey of wealth's perils and promises. Within that defense, he, just as his pagan predecessor, also weaves in his own account of the virtues to do with wealth, liberality, and magnificence.

The Perils of Possession

Aquinas begins by citing Aristotle, declaring: "Everything whatsoever that men own on earth and all things which they possess are called money" (Aquinas 1947: II–II.117.2.2). He quotes Aristotle's laconic (if not tautological) definition: "We call all those goods money whose worth is measured in money" (Aristotle 2002: IV.1). Aquinas then pulls a neat rhetorical trick. He strips wealth of its moralistic or aristocratic trappings (e.g., the *landed* estate) by equating it with its most liquid and transferable form, money. Yet at the same time, Aquinas also widens the meaning of "wealth," or *divitiae*. At certain points, he argues that it includes all external goods (Aquinas 1947: II–II.2, 66, 84, and 118; Aquinas 1945: III.134; see Richey 1940: 1). Its compass can also escape material bounds altogether to include "spiritual riches."

Without denying the goodness of bodily goods, and appealing to Aristotle again, Aquinas goes on to show that they cannot satisfy our desire for happiness. He gives three reasons. First, the body needs the soul to live, so the soul and its goods must be superior. Second, animals as well as people enjoy bodily goods such as health or strength, whereas human happiness should be proper to humans alone. Third, animals surpass humans in certain goods of the body (such as speed or agility), from which it would follow that human happiness must fall short of theirs—a conclusion he calls "obviously false" (see 1945: III.32).

After describing the insufficiency of external goods, Aquinas adds a potential harm: they may directly threaten our happiness. Some external things, such as love or the desire for money or honor, he says, incite powerful passions that resist reason, making it necessary for virtues to counter that passion. Why does money, in particular, cause such resistance? Each coin might be trivial, but money is desirable as a class of goods because it provides life's necessities. Our deep-seated desire for life expresses itself in an almost unquenchable longing for the very means to sustain and advance life (see 1947: II–II.129.2). Money itself does not make the greedy person hoard it or trick others in order to get more of it. It is the soul's penchant to cling tenaciously to the means and hope of life that must be moderated by the virtues of liberality and magnificence. Aquinas's argument here resembles Aristotle's: that people overvalue money because they value merely living over living well.

Aquinas adds another level of moral peril: money's status as a means. As we have noted, the point of money is to spend or give it, to use it for some purpose. Therefore merely acquiring or preserving it is as pointless (and thus as bad) as squandering it. This is the ultimate danger: that money's status as a means will overshadow its importance as an end. It may cause us to ignore the need for a "final cause." Such ignorance amounts to "evil by reason of its incompleteness" (Richey 1940: 50).

MONEY AS VIRTUAL HAPPINESS

One time-honored strain of religious asceticism, which claims to find sanction in the teachings of Jesus, sees wealth or money as too "bodily," too "corporeal," and not "spiritual" enough. A truly spiritual life, this view holds, involves denying interaction with sordid matters such as the body and money. Aquinas does not subscribe to this point of view. True, he elevates the goods of the soul over those of the body; but he never asserts that the latter are not also good. He does not even see money as entirely physical! Aquinas recognizes that money takes material form as a coin of precious metal (or, today, paper). But he sees that money, unlike bread, feeds no body. Nor can it alone excite physical pleasure. As he says, in his discussion of the virtue of liberality, "Delight in money is not referable to the body but rather to the soul" (1947: II–II.117.5). It does not pose a bodily threat, like hunger, but rather a spiritual one.

The problem is that money is good for attaining almost everything. The greater that power, the more money begins to resemble the ultimate good, happiness. And the more it resembles happiness, the more money takes on the hue of an ultimate end. Money, however, lacks a critical condition of happiness: that of being self-sufficing, capable both alone and endlessly to "set man's appetite at rest." In reality, he continues, money offers only a type of virtual happiness. "It is true that money is directed to something else as its end: yet in so far as it is useful for obtaining all sensible things, it contains, in a way, all things virtually. Hence it has a certain likeness to happiness" (1947: II–II.118.7).

Money's outsized hold on our imagination hangs on the universal desire for happiness. The slippery downward slope from riches as means to riches as end is predicated on the erroneous belief that if we get all that money promises, we will be truly self-sufficient and thus happy. This slide also blurs the distinction between the theoretical possibility of attaining something and the actual possession and use of it.

Aquinas makes this clear with his contrast of finite and infinite desires (see 1947: I–II.30). Desires for an end are "always infinite: since the end is desired for its own sake." Aquinas gives the example of health; no one desires only a moderate amount of health or a reasonable amount of health and no more. The reasonable amount has no end: one wants health, health, and more health. Health is not for the sake of anything else; other things, such as medicine, diet, or exercise, are for it. Thus, among bodily goods, health is a properly infinite desire and medicine a properly finite one. It is right to want medicine when you are sick. But if you want more and more medicine, and if you do so in the absence of the disease the medicine treats, then your desire has grown inordinate; the desire for a cure has become a sickness.

From this Aquinas draws a conclusion for wealth: "Those who place their end in riches have an infinite," and unquenchable, "concupiscence," or desire, for riches, "whereas those who desire riches on account of the necessities of life, desire a finite measure of riches, sufficient for the necessities of life . . ." (1947: I–II.30.4; see also Richey 1940: 4). Once more, the problem is a confusion of ends and means. It is right to desire ends to an infinite degree. But people sometimes confuse wealth with happiness and so improperly pursue wealth as an end. The fault lies in their confusion, which is the result of people's "incomplete" use of our God-given critical faculties, not in their desire.

Aquinas sees other perils in wealth. One may pursue money because that person is "presumptuous in his solicitude, considering his own powers sufficient without the aid of Providence to provide for the satisfaction of his needs." Or on the other hand, he may fall prey to fear and become "diffident and over anxious, distrustful of Providence, fearful of lacking necessaries if he does as he ought." Similarly, the money-seeker may have real needs—but worry about them at the wrong time. Perhaps most commonly, we may desire money "out of all proportion to any known or anticipated needs" (Richey 1940: 14, citing Aquinas 1945: III.141, Aquinas 1947: II–II.55.6 and 55.7, and Aquinas 1947: I–II.108.4.5). Those who do so may even keep wealth in its place, but their failings of pride, diffidence, or imprudence lead them to ascribe greater powers to wealth than it actually has.

COVETOUSNESS

This manifests itself in the sin of covetousness. Observing the maxim that every good has its measure, Aquinas argues, "Hence it needs be that the man's good [in respect to riches] consists in a certain measure, in other words, that a man seeks, according to a certain measure, to have external riches, in so far as they are necessary for him to live in keeping with his condition in life." The fault lies in ignoring this limit: "It will be a sin to exceed this measure, by wishing to acquire or keep them immoderately. This is what is meant by covetousness, which is defined as *immoderate love of possessing*" (1947: II–II.118.1). This direct opponent of liberality may manifest itself not only in acquiring and keeping riches, but also in an immoderate "interior affection" for money (II–II.118.3).

Many preachers and commentators, from ancient times to the present, have identified covetousness as the source of all evil. Although Aquinas does not consider covetousness to be the gravest sin, he still sees it as a serious matter because it broaches on idolatry. The insatiable desire for possessions devours a person's capability to care for others and activates anxiety in the soul. For Aquinas, such covetousness or greed is not only about external goods. An excessive love of money is a spiritual failing because it envelops the spirit:

> Sins are seated chiefly in the affections: and all the affections or passions of the soul have their term in pleasure and sorrow . . . Now some pleasures are carnal and some spiritual. Carnal pleasures are those which are consummated in the carnal senses—for instance, the pleasures of the table and sexual pleasures: while spiritual pleasures are those which are consummated in the mere apprehension of the soul. Accordingly, sins of the flesh are those which are consummated in carnal pleasures, while spiritual sins are consummated in pleasures of the spirit without pleasure of the flesh. Such is covetousness: for the covetous man takes pleasure in the consideration of himself as a possessor of riches. Therefore covetousness is a spiritual sin. (1947 II–II.118.6)

One cannot eat, drink, or make love to one's riches. Covetousness does not merely pervert a bodily appetite. It upsets the proper ordering of love itself, a disorder which strikes against the love of God, the ultimate guarantor of human happiness and peace. Covetousness sometimes takes the shape of excessive getting, which can cause an "insensibility to mercy." The covetous person sees the needy not as fellow human beings in God's friendship, but as potential drains on one's earthly treasures. This person sees not people but rather expenses and liabilities. This is a mortal sin.

Covetousness also causes people to be "restless" and creates "excessive anxiety and care," says Aquinas, quoting the poet of Ecclesiastes that "a covetous person shall not be satisfied with money." One might call this a fitting revenge that covetousness exacts upon the sinner. In the extreme, covetousness may give rise to force, violence, deceit, perjury, fraud, and treachery in the pursuit of others' goods (1947: II–II.118.8).

Finally this insensibility to mercy, restlessness, and a host of other ills can all combine into a larger social sickness caused by covetousness. It is this social ill that makes Aquinas, at times, concerned about the effect of trade. Trade seems to stoke its fires, opening the way to many vices, Aquinas warns. His argument harkens back to Aristotle, who also found fault with trade, as well as to the Patristic sources mentioned earlier. As Aquinas explains, "since the object of tradesmen leads especially to making money, covetousness is awakened in the hearts of the citizens through the pursuit of trade. The result is that everything in the city will be offered for sale: confidence will be destroyed and the way opened to all kinds of trickery: each one will work only for his own profit, despising the public good; the cultivation of virtue will fail, since honor, virtue's reward, will be bestowed upon anybody" (1988b: II.3; also see Richey 1940: 37–38). What begins in the individual mistaken judgment blossoms into a civic ill. Here Aquinas anticipates, and offers a basis to rebut, the Enlightenment dictum centuries later that commerce derives public good from private vice.

USURY

These thoughts on the perils of wealth come together in Aquinas's treatment of usury, that is, the practice of charging interest or some other expense for the use of money. The modern world tends to view the medieval prohibition on usury as imprudent, outlandish, and altogether unworkable. But Aquinas's criticism of usury is not simple or dogmatic.

In criticizing usury, Aquinas once more moderates and tempers Aristotle's and the Bible's criticisms. Aristotle had attacked usury as commerce in money itself. It inspires a narrow lust for money as an end rather than as a means, he held, threatening the health of any community that allows it to thrive. Aristotle also argued that it perverts the very nature of money, since money cannot produce gains on its own. Aquinas does allow that money by itself produces nothing, but he also recognizes that human labor can produce new goods from money as it can from other sources. Aquinas takes a more balanced position, acknowledging that while commerce can distort our understanding of money's proper place in the hierarchy of goods it can also provide the means and opportunity for virtuous actions. This stance causes Aquinas to look for ways to allow a lender to gain from a loan while not charging for the use of the money itself (see Flynn 1942: 63).

Aquinas does call usury, by itself, a sin. Nor does he restrict its meaning to charging exorbitant rates of interest. In his view, any charge simply for the use of money is usury: "To receive usury for lending money is unjust in itself." He reasons that, in usury, "something is sold that does not exist," which creates an inequality contrary to justice.

In order to explain this claim, Aquinas distinguishes between things that are consumed when they are used and those that are not. When we "use" wine or wheat, for example, we consume it; we cannot separate the use from the thing itself. Giving someone use of such things is the same as giving the things themselves. If I "loan" wine to someone, I give him the bottle.[3] I cannot sell wine to one person and its use to another person, nor can I sell both to the same person for separate prices. In contrast, some goods may be used without being consumed. Houses can outlive many users, whether owners or renters. The same obtains for anything that can be rented or leased again and again; Aquinas would not see income from such rental as usury.

Aquinas puts money in the former category. I cannot both use a dollar bill and "own" that dollar—that is, keep it the way that I can both use and own a house or car. Thus I cannot keep a dollar and let someone else use it. If I do, I take payment for something that does not exist. Charging for the use of money apart from compensation for its transfer is as unjust as charging for the use of wine or wheat while not selling the ownership rights in these comestibles. In sum, Aquinas does not prohibit usury because of some wicked taint in money itself, but because money's nature does not allow us to separate its ownership from its use (see 1947: II–II.78.1).

Nevertheless, having established this point Aquinas does not prohibit virtuous citizens from making use of loans. He approves of certain loans, for example, that benefit both borrower *and* lender. A lender may rightly charge for late payment or defaults (which might suggest that owners of video rental stores

---

3. Terms from Roman law might help make Aquinas's moral distinctions even clearer: "A loan made on such terms was called a *mutuum* because what was mine (*meum*) became thine (*tuum*); that is, the ownership was transferred. If the ownership was not transferred, the loan was called a *commodatum* and the owner expected the return of the original article" (Dempsey 1947a: 3373).

have acquaintance with Aquinas) or apply a surcharge to cover the credit risk involved in making a loan (see Dempsey 1947a: 3374).

Two conditions Aquinas places on usury are especially significant. One is that lenders cannot require the borrower to pay over and above the loan but they can rightly receive whatever the borrower chooses to pay as a matter of custom and courtesy as a sign of gratitude (1947: II–II 78.2.2; see O'Brien 1920: 193–194). The other is that the borrower, not the lender, produces the gain and thus owns it (see O'Brien 1920: 200). This condition protects against confusing what in philosophy are known as principal and instrumental causes. Labor is the principal cause of capital growth; money (today mischaracterized as "principal") is but its instrument. To reverse these roles is to exalt the instrument over the person in violation of human dignity (see Flynn 1942: 65–66).

Aquinas thus breaks with modern economists who say "Caveat emptor!" to all marketplace transactions. Aquinas wants loans or sales to do justice to both parties, thus preserving any actual or possible amity between lender and borrower. This economic ideal is worth preserving, even in the absence of its practice. At its best, the market should prove to be a means to increase the friendship of mutual benefit within the community. Usury not only violates justice but also impedes or destroys friendship.

Aquinas's successors recognized that his teaching could open avenues to use wealth to benefit those in need. Thus the Franciscan order created revolving credit facilities for the poor. The first was founded at Orvieto in 1462, and they soon spread throughout Italy. They called these funds *montes pietatis*, literally a "mountain" or "heap" of credit for good or pious use, and they, in essence, offered philanthropic loans. They charged a small fee to defray working expenses. The monks also reasoned that if poor people must borrow, it is better for them to borrow at low cost from friends than at extortionate rates from usurers (see O'Brien 1920: 196–197). In time, these funds broke away from their orders and transformed themselves into some of the largest cooperative banks in Italy and Switzerland, whose successors still exist today.

ECONOMICS: FIELD OF VIRTUE

Aquinas's views of wealth and money challenge what the nineteenth-century French moralist and economist Joseph Joubert called the goal of the modern economic life: "entertaining" after paying all of one's bills "that smug feeling enjoyed by money-minded men at having 'money in the bank.'" Anyone who yearns for that self-complacent, "I-am-indebted-to-no-one" feeling, Joubert warns, "will decide that St. Thomas is entirely insufferable" (Joubert, 3306). The reason is that Aquinas proceeds from a different starting point than that of classical economics, which subordinates human beings to wealth and consumption to production. O'Brien compares Aquinas and other medieval economists favorably on this point: "They insisted that all production and gain which did not lead to the good of man was not alone wasteful but positively evil," O'Brien writes, "and that man was infinitely more important than wealth" (1920: 8–9). When Aquinas's contemporary, Antoninus of Florence, "exclaims, 'Production is on account of man, not man of production,' [he] sums up in a few words the whole view-point of his age" (O'Brien 1920: 9).

That is not to say that Aquinas is at odds with all modern economic approaches. For example, he allows that cost (of production) affects the value of something. But he approaches economics, as a whole, not simply as an art or science but as a human excellence, a virtue, which has as its end "the common good of the family" (see 1947: II–II.47.11).

Therefore, Aquinas argues that "[Economics] has more to do with people than with the possession of inanimate things such as wheat, wines, and other things of the sort; and it should deal more with the virtue by which people live well, than with the virtue by which we procure and multiply those possessions which are called wealth" (1988a: I.10). In the same treatise Aquinas compares economics with sailing in order to make crystal clear the difference between economics and acquisition: "It is clear that . . . the art which uses is different from the art which acquires or makes, just as the art of sailing a ship is other than the art of shipbuilding; therefore, economics is different from the art of acquisition" (1988a: I.6).

Economics, as Aquinas understands it, provides the end that guides the acquisition of money: a comprehensive vision of the human good that acknowledges both material and spiritual needs. By reducing economics to something like a science of acquisition, the modern age destroys it as the practical judgment Aquinas envisioned and eviscerates the moral depth he gives it. It also contributes to the basic problem that Aquinas identifies: mistaking wealth's role as means versus as an end.

Liberality

Aquinas envisions a twofold response to these perils of wealth: personal and communal. We will take up the personal responses first, in the form of the virtues of liberality and magnificence. We will then turn to more communal responses.

As the foregoing discussion of economics reveals, one must begin to answer the challenge of wealth in one's own soul, in virtue. Like Aristotle, Aquinas identifies two virtues as especially concerned with money: liberality and magnificence. However, Aquinas expands upon Aristotle's presentation in the scope of each virtue; he also differs with his teacher in important ways over their value and limitations.

Liberality for Aquinas "tends to set in order one's affection toward the possession and use of money" (1947: II–II.117.6). It perfects a passion, namely, a passionate attachment to money. In this case, the virtue appears to quiet the passion so that other desires can emerge. As Aquinas explains, by becoming liberal and thus "not being lovers of money," people more readily make use of it, "whether for themselves, or for the good of others, or for God's glory" (1947: II–II.117.6; see also Richey 1940: 66). Two observations must be made here: First, Aquinas treats liberality as subordinate to other virtues. Liberality, he says, "derives a certain excellence from being useful in many ways" (1947: II–II.117.6)— that is, from making it possible for liberal people to use their money for various purposes. Second, Aquinas does not attempt here to rank or categorize those other ends. Liberal people may use the money "for themselves, or for the good of others, or for God's glory." From the first, Aquinas allows judgment, rather than rule, wide sway when it comes to distributing our goods.

Aquinas argues that, as its verbal root suggests, liberality "liberates" or frees. It frees (in Latin, *liberat*) wealth from those who possess it and it frees them from their attachment to it (see Aquinas 1947: II–II.117.2). This act of freeing is not the same as losing or forgetting something. It takes the moral form of unencumbered choice.

Liberality allows money to work. It allows it to move, which is what money is for. Aquinas connects liberality to movement. We should aim, he says, not only to generate, acquire, or preserve money, actions which have a role but are, at this point, the storage of energy, like a person at rest. Rather we should aim to *use* money, which "consists in parting with it." He also compares liberality to throwing something. "The farther we put it away, the greater the force (*virtus*) employed. Hence parting with money by giving it to others proceeds from a greater virtue than when we spend it on ourselves" (1947: II–II.117.2). This parting can be difficult. But liberal persons surmount that difficulty and allow money to work. In a way, they *throw* money—not away, but into a wise activity.

Liberality is ultimately about desire, not dollars; it has more to do with moral worth than net worth. A person can cease to spend and to give, and yet remain liberal if this is a wise choice. So may a liberal person under circumstances want money, even lots of money. One need not make a vow of poverty to prove one's liberality. What is essential is that the liberal person frees earthly goods for their best and highest use (see Richey 1940: 56–57).

"Best use" involves considerations beyond simply letting go. A virtuous person's task is "not simply to use well the goods which form the matter of his actions, but also to prepare the means and the occasions to use them well," writes Aquinas. A soldier, he notes, must sharpen and keep a blade in his scabbard in order to use it against the enemy. "In like manner, the liberal person should prepare and reserve his riches for a suitable use" (1947: II–II.117.2). Aquinas includes within liberality activities such as saving money or even buying insurance (if it is purchased to preserve resources against possible disasters).

Aquinas's argument allows a similar conclusion about investment as a form of "natural generosity." If liberality requires using property well, this implies acquiring or preserving it, which can be said to extend to investment, particularly that which benefits the whole community by creating needed goods and jobs. Thus Pope Pius XI, in "Reconstruction of Social Order" (paragraph 51), teaches that persons possessed of superfluous income who employ the excess to create employment opportunity through investment practice the virtue of liberality, a teaching the pope derives from Aquinas (also see O'Brien 1920: 72–74; Dempsey 1947b: 3364n40; and Richey 1940: 112).

If pursued to generate and preserve wealth only, investment undermines liberality. As Aquinas puts it, natural or untutored generosity can degenerate into "grandiose undertakings," "impulsive giving," prodigality, and squandering. At the same time, he acknowledges that people undertake virtuous works before becoming virtuous themselves; developing the habit of liberality is part of the process of attaining virtue (see Aquinas 1947: II–II.117.1.3; and Richey 1940: 54–55). To transform natural generosity into true liberality requires, as Richey explains, "that reasonable habit of mind, that spirit of detachment from external goods, which is according to Saint Thomas, the very essence of true liberality . . ." (1940: 115).

PRUDENCE, DETACHMENT, AND FREEDOM

Aquinas recognizes three traits of the liberal person. The first, perhaps paradoxically, is moderation in exercising liberality. One troubling aspect of Aristotle's account is the suggestion that liberal people may think so little of their own good that they eventually ruin themselves, putting an untimely end to their giving. Aquinas acknowledges this potential problem, and he takes a more moderate position, arguing that true liberality need not lead to bankruptcy. Truly liberal people, he says, do not give to everyone. They exercise foresight. After all, some people do not deserve gifts, for they would not use the money well. Liberal people also recognize that their liberality "would be hindered were they to give to everyone: for they would not have the means of giving to those to whom it were fitting for them to give" (1947: II–II.117.4.3).

Even in material things, liberal people never completely lose sight of themselves and those who depend upon them. Aquinas quotes Ambrose that "it is a commendable liberality not to neglect your relatives if you know them to be in want" (1947: II–II.117.1; see also II–II.117.4.2). Pursuing the spiritual good of providing for others does not obliterate the spiritual good of providing yourself and your dependents as well (see Richey 1940: 54 and 92). Prudent thrift cooperates rather than competes with liberality.

Indifference is a second key quality of the liberal person. Anticipating Ignatius, Aquinas says, "it belongs to liberality that one be not hindered by an immoderate love of money, either from spending it becomingly, or from making suitable gifts" (1947: II–II.117.3). In the bestowal of gifts, he writes, two things must be observed. "One is the thing given outwardly, while the other is the inward passion that a man has in the delight of riches. It belongs to liberality to moderate this inward passion, so as to avoid excessive desire and love for riches; for this makes a man more ready to part with his wealth. Hence, if a man makes some great gift, while yet desiring to keep it for himself, his is not a liberal giving" (1947: II–II.31.1).

Liberal people thus develop an attitude of "indifference" toward material goods, an attitude that finds its roots in Aristotle and reaches perfection in Ignatius. As we have seen, it does not equal contempt. Liberal people know that material goods are good both for exercising liberality itself and for sustaining our families. They know wealth to be an instrumental good—a means to something else. Thinking this way frees them from pursuing wealth as an end in itself.

The third quality of liberal people is that they freely choose to be liberal. Aquinas would no doubt agree with philanthropists and social activists today who see thoughtful giving as central to both social cohesion and freedom. Great wealth or income inequalities foster covetousness, envy, hatred, and social strife, tearing apart the community upon which much of our happiness depends. Aquinas argues that liberality should help tie together the community. Following Aristotle, he cites the case of the Greek colony at Tarentum, in which wealthy citizens during times of need gave freely of their surplus to the poor (Aquinas 1988a: VI.5).

For these reasons, Aquinas believes that liberality loses its moral force when it becomes forced, by official action or private threat. As a student of Aristotle, Aquinas believes that government should encourage beneficence and guide citizens toward good deeds. Likewise, he recognizes that to ensure that no citizens are left in dire want, a state may have to take some of the surplus of the rich to fulfill the needs of the poorest (see Richey 1940: 88–89). But it is equally important that the communities preserve the moral freedom required for the existence of generous gifts.

LIMITATIONS OF LIBERALITY

Liberality is not without its limits. Liberality and almsgiving, for example, both concern giving money. But liberality simply removes an obstacle (such as an excessive love of money) to the more important act of giving expressed in almsgiving, as we shall see (see Richey 1940: 64, and Aquinas 1947: II–II 32.1.4). Indifference is a step on the way to something better, but only a step. Aquinas's notion of liberality says little about what one does with material things after attaining "letting go." Other supernatural virtues, above all charity and almsgiving, take on that role. As a natural virtue, liberality simply clears the way.

Aquinas indicates this virtue's limits by rejecting the claim that God, who created the entire world as a free gift, is the most liberal being of all. Aquinas answers that "God's giving proceeds from His love for those to whom He gives, not from His affections towards the things He gives, wherefore it seems to pertain to charity, the greatest of virtues, rather than to liberality" (1947: II–II.117.6). God never feels any attachment to material things; He does not have to possess or exercise a virtue of detachment or indifference. God is not the most liberal being but is the most loving one. This does not negate the importance of liberality for human beings. Quite the contrary: because we are not God, we need such virtues as liberality. But it does reinforce the impression that there are virtues that surpass liberality.

A final indication in that direction comes from Aquinas's comments on the popularity of liberal people. In his day, as in Aristotle's (and as in our own), generous people attracted a great deal of attention, confirming Aristotle's view that liberality is the most loved of the virtues. But why is that? Aquinas answers, "The friendship whereby a liberal person is beloved is not that which is based on virtue, as though he or she were better than others, but that which is based on utility, because he or she is more useful in external goods, which as a rule men desire above all others. For the same reason the liberal person becomes famous" (1947: II–II.117.6). Some people may appreciate liberal persons for their virtue. After all, liberality is an excellence. But, Aquinas suggests, such fans will be few. Most people love liberality because they love material goods, and, to all appearances, the liberal person is a means to material goods. Warren Buffett and Bill Gates, take note! As is true with many popular judgments, liberality's popularity largely rests upon a misunderstanding.

Magnificence

Aquinas devotes less attention to the virtue of magnificence, which concerns spending large amounts of money, than he does to liberality. But he keeps the two virtues closely linked. As he says about liberality, "every liberal man has the habit of magnificence, either actually or in respect of a proximate disposition thereto" (see I–II.129.3.2, I–II.65.1, and II–II.134.1). But whether every magnificent person remains thoroughly liberal is another question.

"The matter of magnificence," he says, "may be said to be both the expenditure itself, which the magnificent person uses to produce a great work, and also the very money which he employs in going to great expense, as well as the love of money, which love the magnificent person moderates, lest he be hindered from spending much" (1947: II–II.134.3). Although Aquinas is ever attendant to the soul, here he focuses not as much on the magnificent person's soul as on the greatness of the expenditure, the money spent, and the work. In fact, it even seems that the magnificent person's love of great amounts of money (which undermines liberality) provides the fuel to the fire of magnificence. Not that the magnificent person seeks to amass and hoard great funds. But loving great sums could foster magnificence if it leads to huge, well-considered expenditures. "Indifference" seems to hold little weight in the face of greatness's charm.

LIMITS OF MAGNIFICENCE

Aquinas reviews the strengths of magnificence, as well as its natural and supernatural limits. The highest end of magnificence reveals itself directly: "The intention of magnificence is the production of a great work. Now works done by men are directed to an end: and no end of human works is so great as the honor of God: wherefore magnificence does a great work especially in reference to the Divine honor." To support this claim, Aquinas cites the pagan philosopher Aristotle's comment about magnificence (2002: IV.2), that "the most commendable expenditure is that which is directed to Divine sacrifices: and this is the chief object of magnificence" (see Aquinas 1947: II–II.134.2).

Aquinas does not limit magnificence only to spending for the honor of God. Like Aristotle, he mentions many other possible objects of magnificence: buildings, theater productions, communal feasts, and private weddings. Nor does he say that the magnificent person always tries first to honor God directly and only after that turns to more terrestrial projects. Such choices depend upon the circumstances, upon what is needed and what opportunities are available.

Concerning the natural limits to magnificence, Aquinas develops a line of thought that is more surprising still. As we have seen, Aristotle does not subordinate magnificence to any other practical virtue though he hints that, in his view, there are deep connections between magnificence and the highest intellectual virtue, wisdom.

Instead of connecting magnificence with wisdom, however, Aquinas annexes it to courage, the most visceral of the virtues. He explains his choice this way: "magnificence agrees with courage on the point that, as courage tends to something arduous and difficult, so also does magnificence" (1947: II–II.134.4). For this reason, Aquinas regards courage and magnificence as virtues that perfect the "irascible" part of the soul, the part that tends to strive, to fight, and not to yield. It is the part that can fly with hope, sink in disappointment, and burn with anger.

But magnificence, he continues, "falls short of courage," since the arduous thing or danger that courage overcomes actually threatens the person, while the challenge to magnificence is simply "the dispossession of one's property, which is of much less account than danger to one's person" (1947: II–II.134.4). Magnificence then takes courage, but the difficulties involved in spending large amounts of money pale in comparison with risking your life.

Aquinas also contrasts the psychic roots of liberality and magnificence. As we've seen, liberality concerns a spiritual disposition of indifference or letting go. Magnificence concerns personal aspiration, for which liberality clears the way. In more contemporary terms, liberality involves work on self, while magnificence involves work on the world.

In Aquinas's terms, liberality and magnificence both concern spending; however, they face different passions. "Liberality regards expenditure in reference to the love and desire of money" (Aquinas 1947: II–II.134.4). This love and desire are passions of "the concupiscible" part of the soul, the part that loves and desires things. "On the other hand, magnificence regards expenditure in reference to hope, by attaining to the difficulty [through] expenditure" (ibid.). Magnificence aims to attain a certain hope in the face of certain difficulties. The hope it pursues is to spend large amounts of money well and to produce a grand result. Because it operates with a view to hope, it belongs to the "irascible" part of the soul, the hoping, striving, sometimes angry part (see ibid.). Though different, then, the two virtues are very much related. Liberality is comparable to the *via negativa*—the path of negation—and magnificence to the *via positiva,* or constructive approach.

KNOWING FOR DOING

It may appear that Aquinas simply ignores Aristotle's attempt to link magnificence to contemplation. However, Aquinas preserves this connection in altered form, enriching his presentation of this grand virtue. Aristotle says that the magnificent person "is like a knower" and makes a "cosmos" with his wise expenditures. Aquinas does not deny this intellectual side to magnificence. He comments, "it belongs to the magnificent person to use his reason by observing the proportion of expenditure to the work at hand. This is especially necessary on account of the greatness of both those things, since if the magnificent person did not take careful thought, he would incur the risk of a great loss" (Aquinas 1947: II–II.134.4). The fear of hugely overspending your resources helps concentrate the mind.

Furthermore, Aquinas argues, magnificence must be preceded and accompanied by much thought: "it belongs to magnificence not only to do something great, *doing* (*facere*) being taken in the strict sense, but also to tend with the mind to the doing of great things." For support, he cites the pagan Roman philosopher Cicero, himself a planner and doer of great exploits, to the effect that "'magnificence is the discussing and administering of great and lofty undertakings, with a certain broad and noble purpose of mind,' discussion referring to the inward intention, and administration to the outward accomplishment" (see 1947: II–II.134.2).

With regard to magnificence, Aquinas remains much more down-to-earth than his teacher. In his view, it perfects a kind of thinking for the sake of doing. It is therefore not thinking for the sake of knowing and knowing alone, as is contemplation. Instead, it partakes more of courage's struggle against obstacles. At a certain level, and in the best way, it seeks to succeed, not to get.

Communal Responses to the Challenges of Wealth

VIRTUOUS TRADING

Liberality and magnificence need not restrict themselves to giving. They may also operate in the realm of production. This consideration brings us back to the communal responses to the challenges of wealth.

As we have seen, Aquinas criticizes trade generally because "it satisfies the greed for gain, which knows no limit, and tends to infinity. Hence trading, considered in itself, has a certain debasement attaching thereto, in so far as, by its very nature, it does not imply a virtuous or necessary end" (1947: II–II.74.4). Economic gain alone, which is the end of trading, does not connote anything virtuous or contrary to virtue. So, Aquinas continues, nothing prevents gain from being directed to some necessary or even virtuous end.

This admission opens possibilities for virtuous trading: "Thus, for instance, a man may intend the moderate gain which he seeks to acquire by trading for the upkeep of his household, or for the assistance of the needy; or again, a man may take to trade for some public advantage—for instance, lest his country lack the necessaries of life—and seek gain, not as an end, but as payment for his labor" (1947: II–II.74.4). Social investment deserves a worthy return.

In developing his view that wealth can be an instrument of virtue—for, as Aquinas himself notes, "We can easily accomplish things by means of riches, power, and friends" (1947: II–II.129.8)—he utilizes and develops early Christian thought about the nature of wealth. For example, earlier we noted Ambrose's condemnation of private property as usurpation of a common gift from God. However, Ambrose gave moderation its due by also noting that "riches themselves are not wrongful. Indeed, 'a man's riches are his soul's redemption,' because he who gives to the poor saves his soul," he wrote in one letter (63.92, quoted in Aquinas 1947: II–II.129.8). "There is therefore a place of goodness in these material riches." Addressing the wealthy, Ambrose said, "You are as steersmen in a great sea. He who steers his ship well, quickly crosses the waves, and comes to port; but he who does not know how to control his ship is sunk by his own weight. Wherefore it is written, 'Possessing riches is the strongest city.'" A Church council in 415 also condemned the Pelagian claim that "the rich cannot be saved unless they renounce their goods" (see O'Brien 1920: 61).

PRIVATE PROPERTY, PUBLIC BENEFIT

This understanding of liberality, magnificence, and virtuous economics allows Aquinas fruitfully to recast the Church's traditional criticisms of wealth and property. Although to some modern ears Aquinas's stance may sound like communism or socialist forms of distributing wealth, in fact it differs greatly from them. Aquinas attends carefully to the need for the just distribution of goods, as he does to the need for production or consumption (see O'Brien 1920: 227). But he never abstracts individual producers and consumers from the larger society. He also addresses his teachings to individual wealth holders, which in his day included leaders of the Church, and urges them to see wealth in a different way. Moreover, even when drawing attention to community needs, Aquinas never loses his focus on the individual soul.

Aquinas's recasting of ownership and community proceeds in several steps. He begins by making the case that one must look at the goods of the earth from the point of view of their use. In doing so, one sees that "people have a natural authority over external things since people have a reason and a will that can make use of external things for human benefit." For this reason, human beings are more perfect than the external things, and "imperfect things are for the sake of the more perfect." From the standpoint of human nature (as opposed to the nature of the things), human beings are right to exercise authority over external goods (see Aquinas 1947: II–II.66.1).

Aquinas elaborates his understanding of the "use" of things by distinguishing it from the "care" of them. Private property is necessary and legitimate, as far as care is concerned, Aquinas says, for three reasons. "First," he says, "everyone is more concerned to take care of something that belongs only to him than of something that belongs to everyone or to many people, since in the case of common property people avoid effort by leaving care to others, as occurs when one has a large number of servants." He then continues with a more organizational point: "Secondly, human affairs are more efficiently organized if the proper care of each thing is an individual responsibility. There would only be confusion if everyone took care of everything in a disorganized fashion." Finally, he raises the defense of private property to the political level by saying it preserves peace: "Peace is better preserved among people if each person is content with his property. So we see that quarrels frequently arise among those who hold a thing in common and undivided" (1947: II–II.66.2).

Aquinas does not defend private property absolutely. Instead, he shows that under most conditions, given our fallen nature, private property offers the best way to ensure a fair and peaceable distribution of external goods (MacLaren 1948: 21). And he couches his defense in "relative" terms. He says people are "more concerned" with their own things, that human affairs are "more efficiently organized" when all persons have their own responsibilities, and that peace is "better preserved" this way (see ibid.: 20). But his point is that private property allows for the production of more and better goods, as well as a greater and better community (see Dempsey 1947b: 3361).

Concerning use, Aquinas makes this radical suggestion: "In regard to this a person should not possess external things as his alone but for the community, so that he is ready to share them with others in case of necessity." This "readiness" is a relative matter. As we will see in the last part of this chapter, many considerations precede any thoughtful act of sharing. But in cases of great necessity, forethought has no room to operate. In such a case, "everything is common property and thus it is not a sin for someone to take the property of another that has become common property through necessity" (1947: II–II.66.7). No claims of private property are absolute; all bow before need and use.

Aquinas's thoughts thus describe a natural trajectory of wealth: care, give, use. This template parallels the modern economic classification of production, allocation, and consumption. But the moral distance between these two classifications is immense. To mention only one point, Aquinas would never restrict use to consumption.

Nor would he reduce care to production. At first glance, Aquinas's defense of private property may seem to indicate that private property simply allows for increased production, and hence the care that Aquinas mentions in this context disappears into producing. But *cura* implies much more than watchfulness; it implies acquisition, development, and complete management (Dempsey 1947b: 3360). Aquinas's template solves the difficulties posed by material wealth, by recognizing the ends of wealth and putting them in their proper place of dignity.

TITHING

Before turning to the process of deliberation that Aquinas recommends to match resources with ultimate ends, we should note that he does enjoin one way of doing this that requires little deliberation: the practice of tithing. Aquinas canvasses the topic of tithing carefully, examining the apparent dissonance between the Old Law and the New. He catalogues the tithing commanded in the Old Testament: tithes to the Levite priests, tithes accompanying sacrifices, and tithes for the poor. He acknowledges that some Christians believe that is unnecessary, for the Levites are no longer, ceremonial offerings are forbidden, and every Christian has a duty to relieve the suffering of the poor.

Following the authority of Augustine, Aquinas argues that Christians still must tithe (1947: II–II.87.1). However, he moderates the practice as presented in the Hebrew Bible. He explains that the demand for exactly one-tenth of one's earthly goods was a matter of judicial precept; it was a law that God designed specifically for ancient Israel and its conditions, and is therefore no longer binding. Aquinas leaves it to the Church and its representatives to decide, on the basis of existing circumstances, what percentage the tithe should amount to. He does not leave this decision to individual believers, for tithing responds to deeply communal concerns.

Aquinas also clarifies the purposes of the tithe. The tithe primarily supports the ministers of the Church, the present-day successors of the Levites. The tithe should also go to the ministers for the use of the poor; ministers will distribute to the poor whatever they do not need for their own support (1947: II–II.87.1 *ad* 4, and 1947: II–II.87.3 *ad* 1). Insofar as the tithe benefits the poor, it represents an office of charity, which relieves others' distress. But supporting the clergy is not charity. Such tithing reflects "the debt whereby carnal things are due to those who sow spiritual things" (1947: II–II.87.2). It is part of the infinite debt human beings owe to God in an era when Church authority and God's authority were less critically separated than they are for many today.

This same principle causes property, not just income, to become subject to tithing. "Whatever man possesses comes under the designation of carnal things," Aquinas holds. "Therefore tithes must be paid on whatever one possesses" (1947: II–II.87.2). Nor should one tithe after subtracting wages, taxes, or other expenses paid; tithing comes "off the top" of whatever "carnal" goods God has blessed you with.

Ministers may use their own judgment in distributing that part of the tithe set aside for the poor. They may distribute it themselves. Or they may arrange that it goes directly to the needy (1947: II–II.87.3 *ad* 3). Also, the poor owe the same duties (to support the ministers and contribute to the support of the other poor) as do other citizens. Thus while the clergy are exempt from paying tithes, the poor are not (1947: II–II.87.4 *ad* 4).

In conclusion, we may say that Aquinas's thoughts on wealth's ambiguities, its danger and its promise, remind us that it is human agency—not the resources at our disposal—that determines which way our engagement with riches moves: toward virtue or toward vice. This reflection is encapsulated beautifully in his treatment of the question of whether one should pray for wealth: "When our mind is intent on temporal things in order that it may rest in them, it remains immersed therein; but when it is intent on them in relation to the acquisition of beatitude, it is not lowered by them, but rather raised to a higher level" (1947: II–II.83.6 *ad* 3; see also Richey 1940: 13).

Discernment: Reflecting Well to Give Well

It is plain from our brief description of tithing that it does not solve the larger need for deliberation and judgment in matching material resources to spiritual ends. Tithing itself contains no guidance as to its proper distribution. It meets the Church's needs and cements bonds among citizens, the Church, and the poor. But as a mechanism it tells us little about the substantial meaning of these operations.

What we need is a process to choose deliberately the most excellent of many possible ways of directing our means toward particular ends—while keeping in mind the ultimate ends and virtues discussed earlier. This commonly results in charity, which Aquinas, as we have seen, regards as "the mother of all virtues." Charity, to review, is not something shown only to the poor or the distressed, nor is it a grudging concession to social cohesion. Still less does Aquinas limit the meaning of charity as being about those who receive beneficence or the organizations devoted to its practice. Aquinas holds charity to be the preeminent form of human agency; it guides all the other virtues, ties together human communities, and provides a goal for every human life.

The principal form of charitable love is almsgiving, which has many different objects. The reality is that we cannot act beneficently to all those for whom we have this love. Aquinas therefore places these objects in a hierarchy, the "order of charity," according to their goodness or contribution to our happiness. While it may superficially appear to be a rigid hierarchy, the order of charity truly sets forth a range of options that require perception, deliberation, and judgment. It is however also true that Aquinas created his ranking of almsgiving's possible objects in a historical, and maybe religious, context that differs from our own. We must use our own reason and judgment to adapt it. It nevertheless provides a useful framework for discernment and choice on the use of resources.

The Order of Charity

Aquinas does not produce this rank in abstraction. He keeps his focus on the end of human striving: "the fellowship of happiness" on which charity rests. Charity does not establish a "cold" relationship with others; it reaches out for a friendship that wraps itself in the mantle of joy. The more an object of charitable love actualizes this joy and happiness, the higher its place in the order of charity.

For these reasons, God stands as the preeminent object of charitable love. God, after all, is the "First Principle," the cause of being, and hence the ultimate cause of all happiness. Charity loves God above all else, not because it "has to," but because from God springs the happiness it seeks (see Aquinas 1947: II–II.26.2).

As a consequence, "man ought, out of charity, to love God, Who is the common good of all, more than himself." This claim may seem paradoxical: if I want happiness, for myself, how can I love someone else more than myself? Aquinas responds that we should do so, "since happiness is in God as in the universal and fountain principle of all who are able to have a share of that happiness" (1947: II–II.26.3). Without God I can have no happiness "for myself." Or put otherwise, human beings find "our own" happiness in God; we cannot generate it by ourselves.

After loving God, one should love oneself over one's neighbor. The reason lies in the distinction between unity and union: "Wherefore just as unity surpasses union, the fact that man himself has a share of the Divine good, is a more potent reason for loving than that another should be a partner with him in that share." But the primacy of self-love does not lead to selfishness or less care for others. It strengthens our commitment to the virtues. A sign of the primacy of self-love is that "a man ought not to give way to any evil of sin, which counteracts his share of happiness, not even that he may free his neighbor from sin" (1947: II–II.26.4). Self-love demands bettering ourselves (and not just financially), for the sake of happiness, rather than merely satisfying ourselves at others' expense.

Our neighbor holds a surprising and complicated place in the order of charity. After explaining that one should love oneself more than one's neighbor, Aquinas adds the qualification that one should love one's neighbor more than one's own body. For "fellowship in the full participation of happiness which is the reason for loving one's neighbor, is a greater reason for loving, than the participation of happiness by way of overflow, which is the reason for loving one's own body" (1947: II–II.26.5). Our bodies can experience true happiness only indirectly, in a shadowy way. In contrast, our souls experience happiness directly, through sharing that fellowship with God and with other people. In this surprising way, the order of charity does unite love of God, love of self, and love of neighbor.

Aquinas does not demand that we love all other people with the same intensity. We must be ready to love all others as God's children, but that love often remains potential; after all, we do not know all these others as individuals. In actuality, we will love some people more than others. To clarify this distinction, Aquinas again returns to his starting point: the source of happiness in fellowship with God. Our love should increase as one or another other person comes closer to that fellowship. Most generally, then, we wish all people well, out of charity, and are ready to love any one of them in an active way. But because we cannot love everyone with equal intensity, nor can we do good for everyone all the time, we should love actively and do good for those who are more closely united to us with a view toward our shared, ultimate end (see 1947: II–II.26.6 and 7).

Aquinas's order of charity is not a rigid hierarchy. We may love certain other people even more than we love our own bodies. Aquinas left his own family and their comforts for a life of serving other, more distant friends. The essential message, however, holds true despite such allowable personal and situational variables: "it can be argued that, if any man loves not his neighbor, neither does he love God, not because his neighbor is more lovable, but because he is the first thing to demand our love" (1947: II–II.26.2). Certainly God rightly demands our highest love, as the best object of that love. But if we cannot experience that love indirectly (in other people), then we can hardly expect to experience it in its direct and full form.

Almsgiving

Almsgiving is the practical outcome of reflection on the order of charity. It has a poor reputation at best in the modern world. The root word, "alms," seems almost an insult. Anyone claiming to give "alms" to another today would be looked upon as joking, arrogant, or even spiteful. The connection between almsgiving and charity has been stood on its head.

Aquinas in contrast sees almsgiving as a specific form of beneficence. Beneficence means doing good to another; it is charity expressing itself in work. It may not be the highest expression of charitable love. Nonetheless, there can be no beneficence (and hence no almsgiving) without charity.

Though almsgiving properly belongs to charity, it also finds support in liberality. Both liberality and almsgiving concern themselves, at least in part, with giving material goods. More specifically: "Almsgiving belongs to liberality, in so far as liberality removes an obstacle to that act, which might arise from excessive love of riches, the result of which is that one clings to them more than one ought" (1947: II–II.32.1). This comment reinforces our earlier impression that liberality serves more as a defensive virtue, a remover of obstacles, than as a true guide to behavior. This observation also elevates the standing of almsgiving: just as charity does, it too provides an end for the actions that liberality makes possible.

DEFINITION AND SCOPE

It is important to recognize both what almsgiving is and what it is not. It involves voluntarily giving one's own goods to those in need as a sort of act of beneficence and a form of charity. Thus, giving what one does *not* need to someone whose need is extreme is, properly speaking, an act of justice (Richey 1940: 74–75). People who mistake almsgiving for obligatory sharing see only the demands of justice and miss the critical role of charity, and hence love, in true almsgiving.

It may be helpful here to summarize Aquinas's understanding of almsgiving. We will begin with four general principles that encapsulate it, after which we will consider his more detailed definition and organization of almsgiving. According to Richey (ibid.), the principles are as follows:

- Giving what is superfluous is a precept of charity and a demand of justice when urgent human need is manifest.
- Giving what is relatively necessary is a counsel of charity and assumes more force of obligation as the recognized need is greater and the inconvenience to oneself and one's dependents is less.
- Giving what one absolutely needs lacks charity toward oneself and both charity and justice to one's dependents, except under extraordinary circumstances as an act of devotion to the common good.
- To give all for Christ's sake belongs to the perfection of charity and to a special state of life.

Aquinas then identifies two classes of "alms deeds": corporal and spiritual. Each class is divided into seven types.

The corporal alms deeds are to (1) feed the hungry, (2) give drink to the thirsty, (3) clothe the naked, (4) harbor the harborless, (5) visit the sick, (6) ransom the captive, and (7) bury the dead. The spiritual alms deeds are to (1) instruct the ignorant, (2) counsel the doubtful, (3) comfort the sorrowful, (4) reprove the sinner, (5) forgive injuries, (6) bear with those who trouble and annoy us, and (7) pray for all.

Aquinas's readers, of course, could not store such lists on their computers or PDAs. Hence traditional verses were conceived to help people remember them. For corporal alms, it is: "To visit, to quench, to feed, to ransom, clothe, harbor, or bury." For the spiritual ones, the verse goes: "To counsel, reprove, console, to pardon, forbear, and to pray," including in "counsel" both advice and instruction (see Aquinas 1947: II–II.32.2).

These lists underscore the powerful point that almsgiving does not require or necessarily involve money. Giving money appears nowhere in these enumerations.

SPIRITUALITY AND ALMS

Perhaps one of the most surprising characteristics of Aquinas's list of alms deeds is the inclusion and elaboration of spiritual alms. This prompts two questions: Does Aquinas show a preference between corporal and spiritual alms? Although many people see almsgiving as a material response to human need, Aquinas does not hide his judgment that, in general, "spiritual alms deeds are preferable to corporal alms deeds." In line with the implications of Proverbs 4:2, "I will give you a good gift, forsake not My Law," Aquinas concludes that a spiritual gift surpasses a corporal gift. Also, he argues that just as each of us ought to care more about our souls than about our bodies, so should we do in respect to our neighbors in need. Finally, the nature of the relation between the body and the soul reveals that the body serves the soul, and hence corporal gifts ultimately serve the spirit.

However, Aquinas reasons that, in some cases, corporal alms may excel spiritual alms. For example, a starving person needs food rather than instruction. Or, as Aristotle admits (*Topics* III.2), for a needy person "money is better than philosophy," although philosophy is better simply (Aquinas 1947: II–II.32.3).

In their substance, corporal alms deeds have a merely corporal effect: clothing someone who is naked does exactly that. But substance is not the only cause of things: one must also reckon the action's source and its object. The ultimate source of corporal alms deeds (and alms in general) is charity, the love of God, which extends to love of neighbors. In this respect, even corporal alms have a "spiritual fruit." And the object of alms is the good of our neighbor. One of their effects, then, an effect of corporal alms as well, is to succor one's neighbor and move them to pray for their benefactor. Aquinas quotes Proverbs 4:15: "Shut up alms in the heart of the poor, and it shall obtain help for thee from all evil." In short, "He who gives alms does not intend to buy a spiritual thing with a corporal thing, for he knows that spiritual things infinitely surpass corporal things, but he intends to merit a spiritual fruit through the love of charity" (1947: II–II.32.4).

Another reason many people look askance at almsgiving is that they perceive it as something commanded rather than something voluntary, and many prescribed actions look less worthy than those we freely choose. For example, most parents praise children who clean their room on their own volition more than those who need nagging to get it done. This judgment confuses several considerations. The acts of virtue are always matters of precept. For example, we are not to be courageous only if we feel like it or if we want to; we should be as courageous as we can be. The same reasoning applies to charitable actions, including almsgiving. The most meritorious actions, the virtuous deeds, are commanded.

But a particular command ("Clean your room now!") differs from a general prescription ("Always be courageous"). Virtue depends upon practical judgment, which must survey the time, place, and other circumstances; its dictates address particular situations, and so do not speak with the inflexibility of particular orders. Even more importantly, virtue's voice speaks from within, through our own reason. The major difference between children and adults is that the former cannot be expected to hear that voice clearly; they require amplification from without. Adults give and obey their own commands. Free will and precept unite.

Thus when Aquinas argues that almsgiving is a matter of precept he is alluding not to its operation but to the deeper truth that Christian virtue commands that we love our neighbors as ourselves. It commands us to do whatever is necessary as part of that love. Since love requires not only well-wishing but also doing good, we must, as a matter of precept, attend to our neighbors' needs, in the form of almsgiving.

Aquinas does identify one area where a specific type of giving is required under all circumstances: when the giver has received something unjustly from someone else who gave it unjustly. An example would be a priest who engages in simony, receiving material goods in exchange for performing a sacrament. In this case, it does no good for the sinful recipient to return the goods to the giver, for the giver gave them unjustly. Nor, clearly, can the recipient keep what was given. The recipient should become a giver, and hand over the property as alms (1947: II–II.32.7). This is the only situation in which Aquinas appears to identify almsgiving as a way of "cleaning" "dirty money." But needless to say, the almsgiving does not expunge the sins of the original two parties.

Before leaving this topic, it is worth reiterating the narrow-mindedness of the view that acts done out of obedience lack moral merit. Obedient people do not negate or annihilate their own will. Instead, they order their will so that it cleaves to and follows the love of God: obedience opens the heart to that divine furnace. Just as liberality prepares the way for charity vis-à-vis material things, so an obedience aligned to God paves its way in the soul.

Deliberating about Alms

FACTORING ONE'S OWN NEEDS

Giving alms well relies upon reasoned judgments about one's own needs, one's surplus (the excess of property and income over one's needs), and the needs of others. Aquinas includes within the consideration of one's own needs consideration for one's dependents, first and foremost one's family members.

Aquinas treats care and saving as worthy habits to inculcate as part of the ownership of wealth. For use relies upon acquisition of resources and care of them. Personal and familial savings can prepare not only for future needs but also for future exercise of liberality or magnanimity. Like all the other moral virtues, these virtues cannot operate in their active forms at all times. Saving does not detract from their operation but rather makes their excellent expression possible (see Richey 1940: 92).

Aquinas also offers some priorities for this savings plan, beginning with two main types of needs of wealth holders and their family: the need to sustain life and the need to support one's station. These considerations shape the surplus one might give as alms.

People are right to save in order to secure their need for food, clothing, and shelter. These needs come first, as far as material sustenance is concerned. Second, people can save in order to educate or train themselves to take up a profession that will itself invest them with regular income satisfactory to meet their basic needs. Third, personal and familial thrift can operate to meet the necessary obligations of the church and state, that is, necessary expenditures for the common good. Fourth, savings may be established in order to purchase and keep a suitable home for oneself. Fifth, one may save to meet the needs of rearing and educating one's children, if one has children. Sixth, since relaxation is a necessary part of the active life, one may put aside money in order to enjoy "wholesome and appropriate recreation." Seventh, one may certainly save so as to perform in the future acts of kindness, friendliness, mercy, and friendship. Eighth, one may put aside funds in order to provide suitable insurance for oneself and one's family members against old age, disability, and sickness. Ninth, since the body has needs after death, one may save for a decent burial. Last, after having considered all these other needs and opportunities, savings may be kept in order to leave a suitable inheritance for one's children or other dependents (see Richey 1940: 93–95).

Aquinas does not offer this list as a strict and unyielding hierarchy. Prudent deliberation about circumstances must decide among these priorities in the given moment as well as with a view to one's whole life. Also, Aquinas does not order this list by the intensity of motives or from most worthy to least. For example, since we use things in order to preserve our lives, and since parents naturally seek to preserve their children's lives, it is "naturally befitting" that parents should leave to children material support in order to continue that care after the parents have died (see Richey 1940: 10–11).

Given human self-concern, and the concern people have for their own families, it is easy to imagine that readers of this list might easily allocate all their wealth or income to savings, eliminating any possible funds for almsgiving. But Aquinas puts limits upon these (often well-meaning) expressions of self-concern. First, it is just as easy to observe that the worthy objects of savings include several altruistic ends: for example, having money to contribute to the common good, or making funds available for acts of mercy.

Aquinas also gives readers some instruction on limiting their natural concern for their own needs and security. In deciding which goods are superfluous, one need not "consider every case that may possibly occur in the future, for this would be to think about the morrow, which Our Lord forbade us to do (Matthew 6:34), but he should judge what is superfluous and what necessary, according as things probably and generally occur" (1947: II–II.32.5). Attention to the natural order of things, and not to improbable disasters, should guide our discernment about the level of savings for our own security.

Again, Aquinas never requires that givers ruin themselves or their families in order to give. He does offer counsel—a matter of choice—that raises this possibility. This counsel also raises one's own "station" as an important standard for giving. For example, Aquinas does allow that "it would be praiseworthy" even to endanger your own life or your dependents' lives, in order to help "a great personage" or to support the church or state, "since the common good is to be preferred to one's own." Such great crises do not come along all the time, nor is it often clear whether one's own personal sacrifice would make the difference. But in such cases as it might, Aquinas's counsel is clear.

Aquinas also considers a different sort of "necessary," one's own station in life, and the things that support that station. Station may sound like an archaic term, but it applies today as well as in the middle ages. The fluidity of modern classes is not an argument against the existence of a "station" appropriate to a particular person. One's station reflects one's stance toward life, one's goals and aspirations. Social striving implies a particular stance, but not one that everyone need share. A self-imposed modest station offers a limit to the infinite striving (and consequent anti-charitable tendencies) fostered by modern economic theories.

Aquinas offers as a matter of counsel, not precept, that one should give alms from this kind of "necessary," the things necessary to one's station. He does not counsel that one should completely undermine one's station in order to give alms. But station should not be an impenetrable bulwark against others' needs: "It would seem praiseworthy" to drop the "needs" of one's station if in presence of "extreme poverty" in an individual or "great need" in the commonwealth. Once more, the common good surpasses the individual good, but Aquinas does not require that individuals sacrifice their own "necessary" in order to serve that good (1947: II–II.32.6). And so, once again, prudent deliberation is necessary for practical action.

The "necessary" of station differs from the more basic "necessary" of life and security, since the latter springs straight from nature in a uniform manner for all people, while the former takes on different shapes for different individuals. This difference does not mean that station is "merely" conventional. It reflects a communal order, which derives from the differences in individual needs and abilities, which themselves spring from natural differences.

Many readers may worry that Aquinas, in treating station as somehow natural, may think that human beings can never change their station in life. Not at all. People should be content with the things that accord with their social position—if that social position suits them (see Richey 1940: 98). But all people must undergo a process of discernment to discover their "suitable" station. The overall justification for station makes sense: that "the thing in which man excels is given to him by God, that he may profit others thereby: wherefore a man ought so far to be pleased that others bear witness to his excellence, as this enables him to profit others" (1947: II–II.131.1). But sometimes it takes time and self-reflection in order to discover this excellence and to bring it to bear for others' good.

So, as long as people attend to justice and charity, and avoid covetousness, we may acquire and save wealth with no limit but the good that we can do with it (Richey 1940: 100). The two kinds of necessary, life and station, combine to provide a guideline for determining our own needs, and hence the surplus we make available for others.

RECIPIENTS

Thus far we have focused on Aquinas's thoughts about the donor of alms. But he applies some of the same considerations that the giver must face, such as about life and station, to the recipient as well. For the recipient, Aquinas begins not with surplus but with defect: "On the part of the recipient it is requisite that he should be in need, else there would be no reason for giving alms." Aquinas then turns to the most basic "necessary," the need to sustain life: "Yet since it is not possible for one individual to relieve the needs of all, we are not bound to relieve all who are in need, but only those who could not be succored if we did not succor them. For such cases the words of Ambrose apply, 'Feed him that dies of hunger: if thou hast not fed him, thou has slain him'" (1947: II–II.32.10).

Aquinas also applies some of the conditions or questions that almsgivers face to recipients. Donors must give from their surplus (what they have, minus what they need to sustain life and station) and must give whatever they can to those in extreme need. Anything beyond their surplus or to people not in extreme need is a matter of choice. "On the part of the recipient, alms may be abundant in two ways; first, by relieving his need sufficiently, and in this sense it is praiseworthy to give alms: secondly, by relieving his need more than sufficiently; this is not praiseworthy, and it would be better to give to several that are in need . . ." To determine what is "sufficient" requires thinking about both the life and the station of the recipient. As Aquinas explains, we should give alms "not so that he may have an easy life, but that he may have relief." We should secure life. But, "we must bring discretion to bear on the matter, on account of the various conditions of people, some of whom are more daintily nurtured, and need finer food and clothing. Hence Ambrose says (*On Duties* I.30): 'When you give an alms to a man, you should take into consideration his age and his weakness; and sometimes the shame which proclaims his good birth; and again that perhaps he has fallen from riches to indigence through no fault of his own'" (1947: II–II.32.10; see also Richey 1940: 81). The station of the recipient should guide giving no less than the station of the giver—and perhaps even more so.

Aquinas's commentary on Aristotle's *Politics* makes a similar point. There (Aquinas 1988a: VI.5) Aquinas follows Aristotle in praising the ancient Carthaginians, who pooled some of the money of the rich in order to give each poor family enough to buy a small piece of land for production, or to pay for the education needed to learn a trade. The community thereby does not support (or keep) the poor in a state of poverty, but provides the opportunities for them to support their own lives and to rise to their own proper station. Riches and philanthropy thus become a natural support to the natural and divine order.

Almsgiving for Aquinas, in sum, is partly a matter of precept, partly a matter of individual initiative. In any case it requires reflection, thought, and choice. We have a duty to share with others our surplus, the wealth or income that exceeds our needs of life and of station. We also have a duty to give alms to those whose need is "evident and urgent," and who are not likely to get any help from elsewhere. In all such cases donors may still consider their needs too, though they should not engage in too-fine judgments about future needs, when someone else's present necessity presses (see Aquinas 1947: II–II.32.5 *ad* 3).

In choosing to whom to give alms, Aquinas navigates between the poles of benefiting those closest to us or those we know and love and providing succor to the apparent stranger. On the one hand, he does not allow arbitrariness. The order of charity, that hierarchy of loves, provides guidance in this respect. On the other hand, Aquinas does not impose a rigid scheme. The hierarchy is not a mechanical template; human wit, prudence, and judgment must guide our decisions. The very need for such discernment in a sense reflects the sinful state of our fallen world and our own individual material and physical limitations. But it also honors our ability to reason and judge, and reflects also the great variety of ways charitable love puts itself to work.

Ultimately, almsgiving provides the centerpiece for giving. It does not detract from liberality, for liberality clears the way to make almsgiving possible. It is fueled by charity, by a desire for fellowship with God that energizes fellowship with humanity. It looks to do good for those in need, but such need encompasses the entire human condition, corporal and spiritual. Thus almsgiving is not a rote disbursement. It encompasses comprehensive reflection on one's own needs, one's surplus, and the needs of others. Such reflections depend upon practical judgment and put into work Aquinas's conception of a community of needs.

Wealth Raised to Another Level

Aquinas's thoughts on wealth, giving, and the ends of human life owe much to Aristotle, but his deep Christian faith decisively modifies his predecessor's lessons. To natural happiness in this life Aquinas adds the possibility of a divine happiness in the life to come. Accordingly, he treats the natural virtues of liberality and magnificence as excellent correctives to our human tendency toward desire and anger—the "concupiscible" and irascible parts of our psyches, as he puts it. The twin virtues correct our natural disorder with regard to property with a view to a supernatural end: the love of and fellowship with God, which is embodied in the virtue of charity. Charity orients human life, and giving in particular, to its complete and perfect end: the unity of love of God, love of self, and love of neighbor.

This vision transforms Aquinas's understanding of property and deliberation about giving. He defends private ownership for the sake of care, efficiency, and peace. Concerning its proper uses, he extends property to anyone in the community in need. At the same time, he does not subject decisions about property to clumsy rules. True, one should tithe, as an act of religion—*religio* arising from the older Latin verb *ligo*, meaning "to bind." But the exact amount must be set according to personal and community needs and conditions. Also one should abstain from usury, owing to the very nature of money and for reasons of justice, but not from proper charges for loans.

Although almsgiving is considered a benighted concept in twenty-first-century America, Aquinas depicts it as a practice of charity arising from the furnace of divine love, which warms our affections for other people. Nothing about it implies a giver's superiority over the recipient. As it presupposes careful judgment about one's needs, situation, and station, it does not demand super-human actions or lead to personal ruin. Indeed, his conception of almsgiving passes beyond the transfer of money to paying "watchful" attention to the whole continuum of needs, corporal and spiritual, in the human condition.

3

Ignatius

All Things Ordered to Service of God

The American postmodern philosopher Richard Rorty once said that we modern, Enlightened people must find Ignatius Loyola "mad." Ignatius's life (1491–1564) was unusual. Born and bred a nobleman like Aquinas, he took a vow of poverty. He had visions of angels and divine beings. He begged his way across Spain, Italy, and the Holy Land. Even as he faced the intimidation of the Inquisition, he managed to give spiritual direction and nourishment to hundreds of souls. And Ignatius founded a major and still influential Roman Catholic religious order, the Society of Jesus, known commonly as the Jesuits.

Although atypical, Ignatius hardly qualifies as insane. One of his enduring legacies, the set of meditations, prayers, and mental exercises known as *The Spiritual Exercises of Ignatius of Loyola,* are known the world over. Though written around 1523, they remain an excellent path to discernment and can serve as an anchor of sanity in our confused age. To make use of them, in particular as we seek to discern God's will in relation to wealth and material resources, we do not have to see heavenly beings or adopt a particular worldview. It is particularly amid the conflicting voices calling out from diverse faith traditions that the principles of Ignatian discernment can help us find our way (see Buckley 1973, 20; Spohn 1996, 244–245).

We begin with Ignatius's exercises themselves and the purposes or ends toward which they direct us, from (initially) a martial-like service under the "standard" of Jesus Christ, to collaboration with Christ in God's work, and finally to friendly love and obedience to God's will above all else. As in the previous chapters, we then turn to the question of life's resources and means, as well as the kind of reasoning they require in the Ignatian perspective. Finally, we consider Ignatian discernment in its main forms: discernment of spiritual influences and of God's will. The practical elements of the exercises are emphasized, for they are the easiest to translate into a secular framework. Through them

Ignatius helps us find a lively spiritual purpose in our everyday lives beyond passive submission to abstract religious or moral laws.

Principal Purposes: To Praise and to Serve

Good Knights

Following Scripture, Ignatius reaffirms that the primary end of human life is to serve God and glorify Him (*Exercises*, § 23, tr. Ganss; references to the *Spiritual Exercises* will generally cite the numbered paragraph of the text). Yet Ignatius does not immediately prescribe rules and regulations to attain that end. Instead, he offers his spiritual exercises as means to find God's will in our actual decisions and daily work. That Ignatius chose to describe these practices as "exercises" reveals one way in which we are to understand our relation to God. *Exercises* derives ultimately from the Latin *exercitus*, or "army." The word originally meant those things an army does as it prepares for victory in war.

Ignatius served as a sort of gentleman soldier as a young man, and he greatly enjoyed chivalric romances about knights and battles. He knew of the military overtones of *exercises* and employs them to the fullest. He recommends that the person undergoing the exercises consider how "good subjects" in a realm should respond to the demands of a generous and kind sovereign; he also asks the participant to imagine how a person who shirked that duty would be "scorned and upbraided by everyone and accounted as an unworthy knight" (*Exercises*, § 94, tr. Ganss). The king, of course, is God; we are his soldiers and his knights; earthly life is a battle. Our goal in this battle is Christ's goal, says Ignatius: "to conquer the whole world and all my enemies, and thus enter into the glory of my Father" (§ 95). Likewise, Ignatius asks sinners to imagine themselves as knights "shamed and humiliated" before a king and his court (§ 74). Ignatius pictures the personal struggle against sin in overtly military terms: we are on a field of battle between "two standards," that of Christ and that of Lucifer, and how we live determines the outcome (§ 138). Performing the exercises means taking part in a life-and-death struggle, in which the greatest forces in the universe are arrayed.

Grand language—but perhaps questionable to those of us who have come to suspect that neither side in a fight is all right or all wrong. This military talk is but the beginning of Ignatius's invitation to spiritual deepening. Ignatius's understanding of our relation to God transcends the military metaphor. The "standard of Christ" does not simply wave over our heads. Nor does God command us from afar. God has a plan for each of us, and God wants us to discover that plan and, through our choices, act upon it. God is a direct and immediate source of purpose and meaning for us, not a distant and abstract justification for certain values (see Buckley 1973, 20–21).

Thus we are not simply God's troops, much less His pawns or puppets, but more like His loving coworkers, His interlocutors in a searching conversation.

God does not simply boss us around. The will of God awaits our discovery. In Ignatian spirituality, God evokes mystery and transcendence while at the same time choosing to submit His will to human discovery and judgment. Through the spiritual exercise of discernment, we are able to figure out what we are to do with God.

Principle and Foundation

Ignatius's fullest and simplest expression of the purpose of human life appears in the "Principle and Foundation" section of the *Exercises:* "Human beings are created to praise, reverence, and serve God our Lord, and by means of doing this to save their souls" (§ 23). Outwardly, the goal is twofold: first, to praise and serve God, and second, to save our souls. But these twin goals embrace each other. For Ignatius, salvation includes readying ourselves for eternal life through continual spiritual progress (Ganss 1992, 150, and *Exercises,* § 20). Salvation means praising and glorifying God in a beatific state (see Ganss 1992, 149, and *Exercises,* § 167, 179, 180, 189, and 240). There is no salvation apart from God and His glory.

"Principle and Foundation" makes clear that we shall reach this goal primarily through work rather than contemplation alone: "The other things on the face of the earth are created for the human beings, to help them in the pursuit of the end for which they are created," Ignatius writes. "From this it follows that we ought to use these things to the extent that they help us toward our end, and free ourselves from them to the extent that they hinder us from it" (§ 23, tr. Ganss).

Ignatius lays out here not so much a static claim of ownership as a reason for use. God is kind and benevolent. He does not set us up for failure. He lets us use all other things in order to pursue our goal: serving God's glory and saving our souls. Our care for things stems from the importance of our work, for God. But the exact path that we take toward that goal, Ignatius continues, cannot be prescribed in detail; each of us must discern it in conversation with God's will. We must converse with God, within a state of submission to God's will that Ignatius calls indifference: "We ought to desire and choose only that which is more conducive to the end for which we are created" (§ 23, tr. Ganss).

Ignatius reminds us at the beginning of every exercise that our goal is God's glory, service, and salvation. He does so with a "Preparatory Prayer" that asks God for the grace "that all my intentions, actions, and operations may be ordered purely to the service and praise of the Divine Majesty" (see § 46). Just as this goal permeates the *Exercises,* so, too, it should permeate our lives, from our first earthly moment to our last.

To be clear, we do not praise and serve God *in order* to be saved; rather we are saved in order to serve, praise, and revere. Service takes the form of work, which, in turn, takes shape in the concrete situations of our lives, under the guidance of the will of God. Whatever our situation, the means with which to do this work are everywhere evident: the rest of creation. Human beings are coworkers with God in creation. We orient to God's service things that otherwise may be aimless or disordered, including our fellow human beings. One expression of the goal laid out in the "Principle and Foundation" is to work for "the salvation and perfection" of our neighbors (Ganss 1992, 150; see *Exercises* § 3). Our work opens a critical avenue through which the will of God permeates the world.

Companionship

So, despite his use of the military metaphor, Ignatius does not ultimately envision life as a constant battle. Nor does he propose that we should see ourselves as mere drudges in God's workhouse. Ignatius teaches us to take on the service of God as a calling—as our highest work. It is work sweetened with friendly feelings and uplifted by a sense of loyalty. These feelings arise through developing sympathy with Christ. Many of the *Exercises* ask us to imagine ourselves in Christ's place: undergoing His struggles, His successes, even His Passion. Again and again, Ignatius prods us to imitate Christ, at least in our imaginations. For example, at the end of the first week, he recommends Thomas à Kempis's *The Imitation of Christ* as occasional reading for the remaining three weeks (§ 100). Beyond any particular event or scene in the book, we are asked to imitate Christ in this spiritual attitude: the love of God. That settled attitude should dominate our work, providing guidance and passion to our pursuit of the goals of human life.

This stance permeates the numerous colloquies or conversations Ignatius prescribes in the *Exercises*. He repeatedly asks the reader to imagine him- or herself in a searching conversation with Mary, Christ, or God the Father. For example, in the first exercise of the first week, Ignatius says,

> Imagine Christ our Lord suspended on the cross before you, and converse with him in a colloquy: How is it that he, although he is the Creator, has come to make himself a human being? How is it that he has passed from eternal life to death here in time, and to die in this way for my sins? (§ 53)

What an incredible though simple exercise: to converse with Christ on the cross—and what questions Ignatius poses!

Sometimes the colloquies are not interrogative but express thanks, as when the sinner thanks God for his life (§ 61) or gives thanks that Christ did not let him die in sin (§ 71). Other colloquies ask for particular favors, as when Ignatius begs Mary for the grace to know his own sins, to amend them, and to detest worldliness (§ 63); or when he asks Mary (then Christ, then God the Father) for "the most perfect spiritual poverty" (§ 147). But most of the colloquies are open-ended, such as the one at § 109, where Ignatius says, "I will beg favors [of God] according to what I perceive in my heart, that I may better follow and imitate Our Lord . . ."

The first colloquy (§ 53) is typical in these respects. After the imagined conversation focused on the purpose and meaning of Christ's actions, mentioned earlier, Ignatius turns the questions back to the human interlocutor: "In a similar way, reflect on yourself and ask: What have I done for Christ? What am I doing for Christ? What ought I to do for Christ?" These questions finally give way to the free expression of the human heart: "In this way, too, gazing on him in so pitiful a state as he hangs on the cross, speak out whatever comes to your mind."

These "conversations," then, are practice in companionship with God. This is not just WWJD: "What Would Jesus Do?" It is doing with Jesus. These colloquies seek to help us understand God's work in the world as a lived experience; they help us put ourselves in Christ's place, as though we are Christ's companion or literally the sharer of His bread. They prompt us to discover and express what we think about God's work in this world, implying that we think God cares, as a friendly companion would, about what we have to say. They show that our decisions are not only from God but also for God. These conversations are about discovering God and also about discovering ourselves vis-à-vis God.

Love and Gratitude

This sense of companionship is preparation for highest goal of the *Exercises,* which Ignatius calls "contemplation to attain love"—not only God's love for us, but also our love for God. Ignatius describes this deepening of love as "contemplation" because of his belief that when one loves something, one comes to know it more deeply and personally. He takes pains to make sure that we do not take this as merely intellectual: from the start he reminds us, "Love ought to manifest itself more by deeds than by words" (§ 230). He then explains what he means by love, emphasizing its mutuality:

> Love consists in a mutual communication between the two persons. That is, the one who loves gives and communicates to the beloved what he or she has, or a part of what one has or can have; and the beloved in return does the same to the lover. Thus, if the one has knowledge, one gives it to the other who does not; and similarly in regard to honors or riches. Each shares with the other. (§ 231)

Ignatius's vision of human life is permeated by the mutual enjoyment of goods more than by the sacrifice of such goods. That is not to deny that we may sacrifice and suffer, as Christ did. But sacrifice is not the end of the story. Ignatius's world is dominated by love, not loss. We give and we get, in friendship and in love.

Accordingly, contemplation focuses on four ways that we receive goods from God. First, one reflects that God has given us creation, redemption, and particular gifts (§ 234). Second, God dwells in all things, in all the creatures and elements, giving them existence, and giving intelligence as well to me and other human beings (§ 235). Third, "God labors and works for me in all the creatures on the face of the earth; that is, he acts in the manner of one who is laboring" (§ 236). And fourth, "all good things and gifts descend from above" (§ 237).

This approach is summed up in Ignatius's prelude to the exercise of contemplation, in which he asks that we imagine ourselves before God and that we also then ask, as he did, "for interior knowledge of all the great good I have received, in order that, stirred to profound gratitude, I may become able to love and serve the Divine Majesty in all things."

The spiritual exercises continue to evoke this sense of gratitude. The first point—in which we contemplate God's bounty—inspires a famous, grateful response in the prayer *Suscipe*: "Take, Lord, and receive all my liberty, my memory, my understanding, and all my will—all that I have and possess" (§ 234). Grateful giving is a *return*. It depends upon the primacy of the original gift: God's love for us and our love for God. Ignatius has us pray: "Give me love of yourself along with your grace, for that is enough for me" (ibid.). Gratitude follows love. The preexistence of love and friendship makes it possible. Attaining such gratitude is critical to spiritual growth.

But gratitude is not the goal of human life. At the end of the *Exercises* proper, we return to the beginning: praise, reverence, and service. Ignatius seeks knowledge so that he may love and serve. True love is never without works. Conversely, works presuppose love. God does not want us simply to do good works but rather to love and worship Him. To focus on our companionship with Christ, we should not merely do what Christ tells us to do; we should strive to incarnate His deeds and teachings in our own lives, in our giving and all we do.

Indifference

One of the pillars for the spiritual life Ignatius establishes in the "Principle and Foundation" is an attitude of indifference. Indifference may sound like apathy or not caring, but it is anything but. Today we might use "detachment" or "submission to a higher purpose" to describe what Ignatius meant. As we will see, it can also be a form of liberation. Understanding life's purpose requires understanding what this special type of indifference means. It is crucial to Ignatian discernment concerning wealth and giving.

THE SPIRITUAL DIRECTOR

To begin to consider indifference, let us anticipate, for a moment, what Ignatius said about "the one who gives the *Exercises*," known today as the "spiritual director." The director is a sort of spiritual adviser who guides the discernment process of someone seeking to understand himself and God's plan for him. He or she eschews telling others what to do or not to do. The director does not say, "Become a priest," or "Live a life of poverty," or "Marry her." Instead, the director attempts to balance the discerner's own spiritual affections, to help the pupil make sense of the thoughts and passions moving him or her.

The wise director recognizes that no prescriptive advice, no matter how sound or well-meaning, can completely address the particularity of our situations and our persons. God may want something very different for me or for you than what even a wise observer might think is best. A good choice for the spiritually maturing person might be a very bad choice for a spiritually degenerate one. Lest the spiritual director wrongly impose an end at odds with God's will, or recommend means unsuitable to the individual, he or she must remain indifferent to these particulars.

In normal relationships, not immediately reacting emotionally to a choice someone makes might signify a disorder rather than healthy indifference (see Toner 1995b: 92–93). And indeed, spiritual directors may possess clear and definite ideas about which choices are better or worse. But the director steps back—out of the way, one might say—and helps the discerner find God's will for him- or herself. Although good spiritual directors strive to maintain this sort of "indifference," they do care for the people under their direction. And on one matter they cannot be indifferent: they assume that one should follow God's will. In sum, Ignatian indifference is not a lack of care but rather a trusting openness to God's will and wisdom.

LIBERATION FOR SERVICE

From the beginning of the *Exercises,* we learn the importance of this quality of detachment from particulars and outcomes, not just in a spiritual director but in anyone undergoing discernment. As noted, in the "Principle and Foundation" (§ 23) Ignatius first explains the overall purpose of humanity: "Human beings are created to praise, reverence, and serve God our Lord, and by means of doing this to save their souls." All the other things on earth, he says, have this purpose: "The other things on the face of the earth are created for the human beings, to help them in the pursuit of the end for which they are created." From the combination of these two principles, there follows this critical conclusion:

> we ought to use these things to the extent that they help us toward our end, and free ourselves from them to the extent that they hinder us from it. To attain this it is necessary to make ourselves indifferent to all created things, in regard to everything which is left to our free will and is not forbidden.

So, Ignatius claims, "we ought not to seek health rather than sickness, wealth rather than poverty, honor rather than dishonor, a long life rather than a short one, and so on in all other matters." Instead, "we ought to desire and choose only that which is more conducive to the end for which we are created" (*Exercises,* § 23). This is Ignatian indifference even more fully expressed: maintaining a balance before competing goods, a balance of affections as well as of judgments, so that appetites and biases and fears and ambition do not dictate our choices.

This idea follows as a corollary to Ignatius's first principles. Because we should serve the will of God first, we ought to put all other goals or things second (at best). Ignatian indifference does not require that we empty ourselves of any interest in these things, much less that we despise them. He describes all the things on earth as created specially for our use, in achieving our true end. All play a vital role in our serving and praising God. Thus we are encouraged to appropriate them if this serves our primary goal (and doing so meets certain moral conditions). This way, Ignatius recommends, we will truly own our possessions rather than being owned by them. To liberate our use of things, we must approach them with indifference—not contempt or lack of care—in the service of God's will. Indifference, then, is a type of liberation. As the Jesuit theologian Karl Rahner explains,

> It is probably correct to say that indifference is the same as what Paul calls the freedom conferred by the Spirit of God himself—freedom with regard to all the individual powers and forces in our human existence, both in our inner life and in our external situation.

Or, as Rahner adds in the same passage, "Indifference and freedom, seen as one and the same thing, signify the infinite and open space in which God becomes the event we encounter in our existence" (Rahner 1980, 4). Indifference frees us from the tyranny of the trivial and liberates our concrete existence with God's presence.

Ignatius makes the character of this indifference even clearer later in the *Exercises,* when he introduces a "Meditation on the Three Classes of Persons" (see § 155). This meditation has a grand purpose: "to aid one toward embracing what is better" (§ 149). He asks us to imagine three people, each with 10,000 ducats. The first person feels very uncomfortable about the money; he feels that it impedes his finding God and being saved, and so he does not touch it even to the hour of his death. The second person also feels uneasy about his attachment to the money. But in contrast to the first, this person still wants to keep the money for himself; as Ignatius puts it, such a person hopes that "God will come to where this person desires." Each of these people somehow fails, in Ignatius's view, to achieve a proper stance toward the things around them.

The third person does much better. He too would like to get rid of his attachment to the money. But he neither donates it nor keeps it for himself. Instead, he "desires to get rid of the attachment, but in such a way that there remains no inclination either to keep the acquired money or to dispose of it." This person has achieved indifference toward the money. And he does so with a view to his overall purpose: "such a one desires to keep it or reject it solely according to what God our Lord will move one's will to choose, and also according to what the person himself will judge to be better for the service and praise of the Divine Majesty."

The third person does not love the money, nor does he hate it. He does not worship wealth, nor does he despise it. He is indifferent. As Ignatius says, "this person endeavors to take an attitude by which, as far as the affections are concerned, he is giving up everything." But an appearance of apathy is merely that, apparent only, for this third person "strives earnestly not to desire that money or anything else, except when one is motivated solely by the service of God our Lord; in such a way that the desire to be able to serve God our Lord better is what moves one to take or reject any object whatsoever" (§ 155). What from a materialistic perspective looks like contempt or apathy reveals itself, spiritually, as wholehearted commitment to use, or not to use, whatever you have for this transcendent end. Ignatian indifference is not a timid "balance" between contending desires, but a wholehearted choice-before-choice to serve the will of God, whatever it may be (Toner 1995b: 8–9). Indifference is not the positive goal of human life; the service of God's will is. But because the service of God's will is the end, it is critical to attain indifference with regard to all the possible means. Discernment, which indifference prepares, takes place within an environment of freedom—and love.

Spiritual indifference is the beginning and the end of Ignatian discernment. Discernment helps us perceive and choose God's will without being drawn or distracted by lesser ends. It results in indifference to anything but God's service and praise. While it is true that, if we are to serve God, we cannot serve things, it is also true that serving God may require closer attention to things we can use in that effort. So indifference to all but God's will is a prescription for deeper care for the things of this world. It is many people's experience that, without this transcendent goal, subjection to the things of the world ultimately leads to anger with, and rebellion against, the world and its things.

Material Wealth, Spiritual Poverty

As we have seen, the overall goal with Ignatius is clear: to praise and serve God, and to do so with love and friendship. As part of this goal we should cultivate benign indifference toward anything besides God's will. This goal raises the question of how, in particular situations, we may discern that will. Before exploring the Ignatian method of discernment, however, let us look at the question of the means and resources at our disposal to fulfill the overall goal. Ignatius does not formulate specific rules for dealing with material wealth, but from his own actions, and from his larger teaching, we may infer how Ignatian spirituality applies to choices about wealth.

Ignatius's Money Management

Ignatius's teaching on discernment grew out of his own experience, and, to a large degree, his teachings about wealth were tempered on the same anvil. As noted, Ignatius grew up in a noble family, with luxuries and responsibilities. After being wounded as a soldier and deciding to join the priesthood, he abandoned his family wealth and took up a life of poverty. Ignatius began his spiritual growth with a sort of asceticism about wealth and material things. He kept this resolution even when it made it difficult for him to achieve other spiritual goals, such as traveling to the Holy Land. But over time, Ignatius became less purely ascetic. He saw the importance of not simply denying ourselves goods but of navigating the choices among goods. Ignatius's *Autobiography* provides a moving account of his own spiritual development during the early and middle portions of his life. In it we find suggestions of this shift from the rejection of wealth toward openness to a more positive use of resources.

For example, before he left Spain for Italy (the first stop on his way to Jerusalem), Ignatius had to beg for the money to supply himself with provisions, for the ship captain would give him none from the common store. When he was done begging and buying, he found that he still had a few pennies left. Instead of keeping them as a reserve for the future, he decided to leave them on a bench near the shore, a bonus for whoever discovered them next (Ignatius 1996: 30). Ignatius reveals here the good uses of money: it sustains him in his apostolic mission, his need for it brings him into contact with the needy, and it can be left for others to use in the fulfillment of their needs. A radical ascetic approach might require one, after eating enough to keep life and limb together, to cast the remaining lucre into the sea.

In a slightly different manner, when he was traveling from Rome to Venice, Ignatius found that he had a couple of surplus coins that his friends had given to him for the journey. In the words of his autobiography, "He thought about whether it would be good to leave them somewhere. But in the end he decided to spend them generously on whoever crossed his path, who were normally poor people, and did so, with the result that when he later arrived in Venice he didn't have more than a few coppers on him, which that night he needed" (1996: 31–32). When he arrived at Venice, he again supported himself by begging and slept in St. Mark's Square: "He had a great conviction in his soul that God was to give him the means of going to Jerusalem . . ." (1996: 32). In this case, not just begging but spending brings Ignatius into contact with others' needs. Money can separate spiritual advisors from those in need, but it can also bring them together.

Ignatius's desire to live simply and give to others had consequences beyond the physical difficulties it imposed upon him. Ignatius was interviewed several times by the Inquisition. On one occasion he and a friend arrived at the interview wearing poor and outlandish clothes, for they had given whatever good clothes they had to the poor. The examining friar asked why they were dressed so oddly, and, after hearing their story, muttered, "Charity begins at home." Clearly, their response did not please him (Ignatius 1996: 45). Ignatius was perhaps motivated by the avarice of church officials that insulated them from the needs of their flocks and sought to correct that problem in his own way. But while rejecting finery may inspire some, it may anger others.

Ignatius was also sometimes not careful with his money. In Paris, some friendly Spaniards gave him a tidy sum for his support. He gave the money in turn to a student companion for safekeeping, but his confidant quickly spent it all, leaving Ignatius with nothing (Ignatius 1996: 49). Ignatius was not angry, but neither was he pleased that his friend lost the money. The story warns the reader about despising wealth too much, and thus impeding God's work.

Even though he chose a life of poverty, Ignatius, being a good spiritual director, did not seek to impose that life upon all other people. Nor would he have us simply copy him and give everything we have to others. The Ignatian spirit calls us to do all that we can to discover God's will for our money and to use our resources accordingly.

Spiritual versus Actual Poverty

Ignatius was nonetheless worldly enough to recognize that the power of these resources makes them a constant source of temptation. Among the "snares and chains" that the evil spirits use, they "tempt people to covet riches" so that such people seek honor from others and finally burst with pride and fall into many other vices (*Exercises*, § 142). Christ makes the opposite appeal:

> He recommends that they endeavor to aid all persons, by attracting them, first, to the most perfect spiritual poverty and also, if the Divine Majesty should be served and should wish to choose them for it, even to no less a degree of actual poverty; and second, by attracting them to a desire of reproaches and contempt, since from these results humility. In this way there will be three steps: the first, poverty in opposition to riches; the second, reproaches or contempt in opposition to honor from the world; and the third, humility in opposition to pride. Then from these three steps they should induce people to all the other virtues. (§ 146)

It is important to recognize that in both these spiritual motions—from love of riches to vice, from poverty to virtue—the riches themselves are not the motive source. Wealth opens a door for evil, and for good. What matters is that we see wealth as an opportunity, not simply as a predetermined limitation.

This point bears on Ignatius's reflections concerning "spiritual poverty" versus "actual poverty." Spiritual poverty has to do with attitudes of indifference and humility rather than material goods. It is the stance of one who, seeking total dependence on God, "has emptied his or her self of the love of earthly things" and "filled that self with God and his gifts" (see Ganss 1992: 168–169n72). Spiritual poverty does not necessarily dictate what we should do with our resources; it prepares us to discover what God's will is for them. Consider the rich young man in the Gospel of Mark. He wished to follow Jesus, but turned away when Jesus told him to sell all that he had and give it to the poor. It is because he lacked spiritual poverty that he balked at the thought of actual poverty, not the other way around. (We consider this story further in our discussion of discernment.)

Ignatius's words about spiritual poverty reveal his radical understanding of means and resources. In a sense, for Ignatius there are no means or resources. The end—the will of God—is so complete, so potent, that it renders meaningless any talk of "other" resources. The person who has attained spiritual poverty attaches himself to nothing beyond God's will. All "else" appears as agent to accomplish this. There are no resources apart from it; God's will is the means and the end in one.

In the condition of spiritual poverty, all of one's wealth in the broad sense (including conveniences, independence, and social prestige as well as possessions) becomes subject to discernment and deliberation. Wealth is a prime locus for such attention, for it offers a great opportunity for self-improvement and spiritual joy. But in authentic deliberation about wealth, we put aside the commonplace urge to possess. We must keep in mind the example of Christ's love of people rather than things and we desire to live simply in order to come closer to Christ and those he loves.

These themes emerge in a case of discernment Ignatius offers: choices we make about our households and families. For, as he explains, people not called to a formal religious vocation "should examine their resources, how much they ought to assign for the house and household, and how much for the poor and other good works." Let us put ourselves in the role of Ignatius's "elector." How large a house should I have? How many persons should I support? How ought I and my partner to govern its members? How can I teach those in my household by word and example? We might today call this deliberation about sustainability. Will my material resources sustain this household? Can my emotional resources? After taking care of these others, will I have spiritual resources to serve God? Sustainability is not primarily about the environment but about ourselves.

"In all this and by it," Ignatius concludes, "each one should desire and seek nothing except the greater praise and glory of God our Lord" (*Exercises*, § 189). This kind of discernment may appear simplistic. But it is precisely in our habitual routines and possessions that we fall most easily into conventional "rules" and social habits—overlooking or ignoring the potential freedom we have to discover God's will in our everyday lives.

Getting and Giving Alms

Because he was a priest and the leader of a religious order, Ignatius spent a great deal of his latter years considering the duties and responsibilities incumbent upon the officers of the Church. One matter he considered closely was the Church's acquisition, possession, and distribution of wealth. Though his thoughts along this line were directed to priestly practice, they give another example of how we can think about our wealth and giving.

As a supplement to the *Spiritual Exercises,* Ignatius developed "Rules Concerning the Ministry of Distributing Alms." These were meant to guide priests who must distribute the alms of their churches, institutions, or parishes, but they speak as well to anyone considering giving to others. They begin with the recommendation that you make sure the love you feel for those you wish to benefit flows from love of God. We should be moved not merely by sympathy or a sort of tribalism, but by love for that being in whose image we were all made. This advice resembles Aquinas's teaching that we should love our neighbor "for God's sake."

He then proposes three imaginative experiments: First, imagine an ideal or "perfect" person, whom you've never actually seen or known, and ask how you would wish him or her to act. Second, put yourself on your death bed and ask how you wish you had acted. Third, imagine yourself on the day your life is judged by God and ask how you wish you had acted. These exercises achieve several goals. The first separates your giving from your individual person and thus your prejudices or predispositions. The second and third return the focus to yourself, the first from the perspective of your whole life, the second from the perspective of eternity. They liberate our personal act of giving from any confusing particularities and place it within a universal context.

Ignatius also advises that in giving alms you should always try to reform yourself, to make yourself a better person. He also turns to the "revenue" side of the transaction, for giving presupposes some means from which to give. In order to increase what we can give, he recommends that we reduce what we spend:

> In regard to our own persons and household arrangements, it is always better and safer to curtail and reduce our expenses. The more we do this, the more do we draw near to our high priest, model, and rule, who is Christ our Lord. . . . The same consideration should be applied to all the styles of living, in accordance with the condition and state of the persons under consideration.

Finally, he offers a model to guide our spending and giving:

> In the state of marriage we have Sts. Joachim and Anne. They divided their possessions into three parts, gave the first to the poor, the second to the ministry and service of the temple, and kept the third for their own support and that of their family. (*Exercises*, §§ 338–344)

Again, this "rule" stands more as inspiration than as command, and the resources it governs are not just material but also spiritual. Ignatius did not follow this rule in his own life, nor would he have everyone else follow it in an exacting way. It introduces areas of expense for our mental and spiritual deliberation (the poor, the ministry), rather than demands upon our purse. The exact direction of our giving we must discern by seeking God's will in a communicative and responsive manner.

The same lesson emerges if we consider Ignatius's writings about the Society of Jesus and poverty. Early on, Ignatius concluded that his order should avoid owning property and that its members should devote themselves to lives of poverty. But he did not come to this by applying some unbending rule. Instead he underwent a long and involved discernment process. Ignatius produced a long list of "pros and cons" concerning the order's poverty. The "pros" of owning property were quite obvious. But the "cons" of property held their ground as well. Poverty would strengthen the order, because the life of poverty imitates the life of Christ, and it would instill onlookers with confidence in God's power. It would force Jesuits to attend more closely and sympathetically to the poor, cementing a union between the Church and the poor. And it would serve as a healthy example to lay people, who are tempted to live all-too-worldly lives (Ignatius 1996: 70–72, 190–193, and 247). The conclusion Ignatius reaches follows from the particulars of the situation. It does not leap from a dogmatic and preconceived position. It arises from observing and reflecting upon the needs of the Jesuit order and those it serves. It reflects the recognition that the will of God does not draw us in predictable ways but attends to the particulars with greater wisdom than any human being could muster.

Ignatius does not view wealth as something either to be fled or to be pursued. It is an amazing resource. As such, it opens the door to great virtue and to great vice. This is why so many people pursue wealth—and why so many hate it. To use wealth well, as to use anything well, one must attain indifference—indifference to anything except for our true purposes and ends, properly considered. In particular, one must put aside an ambition to possess things (even while it is permissible to continue possessing them). A desire for such indifference or "spiritual poverty" must proceed any honest attempt at discerning God's will. True discernment will strengthen that "spiritual poverty" and it makes it possible to marshal our wealth for the best and most comprehensive ends: the glory of God and the benefit of those whom God loves.

Finding God's Will through Discernment

In his comments on the art of discernment and the role of the spiritual adviser, Ignatius expands on a long Christian tradition about ascertaining God's will for one's life. A basic premise of this tradition is that God makes God's will known to us through our thoughts and our passions. Discernment clarifies our attention so that we can receive these promptings and choose accordingly. This is crucial to our role as thoughtful and loving collaborators in serving God, a work that uses the rest of creation. While the choice to follow God's will is our own, we need not make it alone: spiritual advisors can help us achieve the balance and liberty needed to perceive and choose God's will.

Discernment in Ignatian spirituality is not so much a process as a way of living. It prepares one for the "battle," as it were, between the twin poles of good and evil, between Christ and Lucifer. Indeed it is the field on which that battle is fought. Love and indifference are the spiritual dispositions that characterize our stance toward the goal of life: praising, revering, and serving God. Discernment is the spiritual practice and disposition that illuminates the details of how to pursue that goal in the particular situations in which we find ourselves.

For Ignatius, "spiritual exercise" includes "any means of preparing and disposing our soul to rid itself of all its disordered affections and then, after their removal, of seeking and finding God's will in the ordering of our life for the salvation of our soul" (*Exercises*, § 1). There are many types of exercises (such as examinations, meditation, and prayer), but discernment stands at the center. It diagnoses which passions move your soul. It prompts self-improvement—advancing spiritual maturation or combating degeneration—and provides a way to judge the improvement wrought by other exercises. Discernment is a way to answer the question, "How do I want to work with Christ?"

This is not to say that one begins the spiritual exercises with discernment. Discernment presupposes that the person seeking to make a choice is coming closer to the ultimate source of direction: God. The first half of Ignatius's discernment exercises focuses on God's love, the consequences of separation from it, and Christ as the mediator between God and humanity—all oriented to create a collaboration with Christ on the journey to becoming more whole.

Ignatius identifies two types of discernment, discernment of the will of God and what is known in classical theology as the "discernment of spirits." The second, so-called because we have within us both the worldly spirit of error and the spirit of Christianity, addresses the spiritual influences or predispositions capable of impelling us toward good or evil. It is a means to achieve the first type of discernment.

Discernment requires that I desire to find and to embrace what God leads me toward and that I be able to see the directions my affections, thoughts, inspirations, and so forth take. In the *Spiritual Exercises,* Ignatius describes discerning God's will in his directives on making an election or choice (§ 135, §§ 169–189) and covers the discernment of spirits in a separate section (§§ 313–336; see Ganss 1992: 195).

These two types of discernment contribute to each other's operation. One must use discernment of spirits to "rid" the soul of disordered passions, so that, through the discernment of God's will, it can find that will and choose it. The operation can proceed the other way, too. One must find the will of God here, amid certain particular choices, in the midst of various strongly felt spiritual affections. To discern the will of God, people must ask, "By which option am I, with my personality and in my circumstances, likely to bring greater glory to God? Or to serve God better?" These questions will excite thoughts and feelings, some from the good spirit and some from the evil. Seekers must appeal to the discernment of spirits, and perhaps a counselor (see Ganss 1992: 195n156), to interpret them.

With these distinctions in mind, we can examine Ignatian discernment in four stages: matters general to discernment, preparatory practices, discernment of spirits, and discernment of God's will. Because the process has a communal dimension, a fifth section covers Ignatius's thoughts on the role of the spiritual advisor. Ignatius approaches each stage of discernment as a way to answer the question, "How do I want to work with Christ?" The sections describing each include ways that people outside the realm of Ignatian spirituality can adapt them.

On that note, we must acknowledge that much in what follows may sound strange to ears unused to Ignatian or Catholic teaching. What's all this about "spirits," "good and evil," and God's will? While acknowledging its foreign quality, it is important also to give Ignatian spirituality a chance. Part of the attraction of Ignatius is that he teaches that we live in a world that respects the kinds of beings that we are. This world cares about our choices. We are not an anomalous, choosing part of an otherwise uncaring, necessary universe. But these two types of discernment have another lesson for us as well. If we imagine that there are no such "spirits" that move us from without, no evil spirit, no Holy Spirit, no God even, what follows? We would still have to admit that we often become confused, that we often choose things we somehow don't "want," that we deceive ourselves or even try to deceive ourselves without success. How can we do these things? How is it possible, for example, both to want something and not to want the same thing, as the rich young man in the Gospel story does? Without talking about spirits and discernment, the human soul quickly starts to look like a pitch-black well, whose bottom one can never probe. Someone might think that speaking about "spirits" intrudes unnecessary obscurities into psychology. But we should ask ourselves whether avoiding such language only makes the world, and ourselves, all the more obscure.

Matters General to Discernment

Ignatian discernment operates with three areas: human emotions and thoughts, and supernatural influences. These shape the first part of the discernment process. For example, rules five and six show how to confront the emotion of "desolation"; rules seven to eleven focus on thoughts that arise from desolation; and rules twelve to fourteen advise on the confrontation with "the evil spirit" (see Buckley 1973: 29). Spirits, good or bad, do not simply determine human life. We must work with and learn from our own thoughts and feelings. But our own thoughts and feelings are not a prison, from outside of which nothing else can touch us. True, we have human agency and must choose for ourselves—but we live in a world in which God cares what we do.

Discernment involves four stages. It aims at a choice, called by Ignatius an "election." An election may concern something as profound as choosing to follow a vocation in the priesthood. But it may concern our work, our schooling, our home life, or any other subject whose importance leads us to seek for God's will and guidance.

Ignatius calls the stages in the discernment process "weeks," though each stage may take much longer than a calendar week to complete. The first week focuses on perceiving and identifying your sins—those things that have kept you separated from God. The second week uses Gospel stories to help the discerner open his heart to God's will, and to remove any preconceptions or prejudgments that might impede his perceiving that will. This stage culminates in election. The latter weeks use contemplation of Christ's passion and resurrection to seek confirmation of the election and to draw the discerner closer to God's love.

As noted, one source of "data" in discernment are your own passions or feelings. The most important ones are "spiritual consolation" and "spiritual desolation" (see *Exercises*, §§ 315–316). It is important not to confuse these passions with feelings of pleasure and pain. Consolation may feel painful and desolation pleasant. These feelings take their bearings not from us or our bodies but from God. Consolation is the spiritual state of growing closer to God: stronger in faith, firmer in resolve, deeper in love. Depending on one's relation to God, it can take the form of beatific visions or tearful grief. Desolation involves falling away from God: faith weakens, confusion grows, hate may kindle. In a spiritually mature person, desolation can feel terrible and terrifying; in the spiritually shallow, it can feel very pleasant, at least for a time.

Preparing to Discern

Several practices prepare the Ignatian discerner. First, Ignatius recommends that people undergoing the spiritual exercises subject themselves to a "particular examination" twice each day (see §§ 25–26). These examinations allow some latitude, depending upon the person or the day. But in general he advises that one examination should take place at midday and one in the evening. The purpose of each examination is to catalogue any sins committed in the morning or afternoon. To aid the memory, Ignatius also recommends that one keep a spiritual log, and make a mark for each sin recollected. This type of examination has been reproduced in many ways through the ages, from people's personal diaries to the discipline of "moral perfection" that the American polymath Benjamin Franklin practiced.

In addition to a particular introspection, Ignatius also recommends that one undertake a "general examination of conscience." This involves several steps. As with most of Ignatius's exercises, first one gives thanks to God for all the benefits one has received. Next, one asks God's help to know one's sins and to get rid of them. The third step comprises the general examination proper. In it, one "asks" for an account of one's soul from the moment of waking up to the present moment, "hour by hour or period by period." This examination focuses on one's thoughts, words, and deeds. After this examination, the discerner should ask God's pardon and resolve, with God's grace, to improve. The examination closes with an "Our Father" (§ 43). Such an examination not only prepares one for confession; it almost comprises a confession in itself.

Ignatius then recommends extending this reflection to the whole of one's life. In this meditation, Ignatius asks the person undergoing the exercises to produce "the court-record" of his or her sins. Speaking as though he were undergoing the exercise, he says, "I will call to memory all the sins of my life, looking at them year by year or period by period." Such a task might seem impossible. But Ignatius offers some shrewd advice: "For this [recollection] three things will be helpful: first, the locality or house where I lived; second, the associations which I had with others; third, the occupation I was pursuing" (§ 56). What he wants us to catalogue are not possible sins or categories of sin but sinful acts. Localizing the memory helps in such a task.

Ignatius's goal in these remembrances of sin is not to make the sinner feel bad or to tip him or her into desolation. Discernment is a path of self-knowledge, and that self-knowledge begins with recognizing one's own predilections and temptations. Battling effectively with evil desires requires knowing where they will strike: Where are your weak points? There is no better way to recognize those weaknesses than to see where evil has struck in the past.

The use of the imagination is also critical. A great many of the spiritual exercises consist largely of meditations upon the Gospel. In these meditations, the exercitant is asked to think closely about a particular scene or event, the meaning of which is related to the person's spiritual development. Ignatius would have us imagine these scenes in great detail and perspicuity. For example, in a meditation on the Nativity, he advises, "Here it will be to see in imagination the road from Nazareth to Bethlehem. Consider its length and breadth, whether it is level or winds through valleys and hills. Similarly, look at the place or cave of the Nativity: How big is it, or small? How low or high? And how is it furnished?" (§ 112). He advises a similar method throughout the contemplation of Christ's life and passion.

The purpose of this detail is not to simply exercise the discerner's imaginative capacities. Ignatius means for us to draw all the more closely to the life of Christ. As we have seen, the spiritually mature person is a loving coworker with Christ, someone who reconceives his own life in the image of Jesus's. Imagination fosters that imitation.

Discernment of Spirits

Ignatius's rules for the discernment of spirits grow from the preparation. The first "rules" frame our expectations: Spiritually degenerating or sinful people will face assault from apparent pleasures (say, of food, drink, or sex). Spiritually maturing people, on the other hand, will suffer at times under anxiety and sadness. Knowing what to expect helps a great deal in understanding oneself and preparing for future struggles.

Next, Ignatius describes the consolation that the spiritually maturing person will feel—"hope, faith, and charity, and every interior joy which calls and attracts one toward heavenly things and to the salvation of one's soul"—and the opposite, the desolation that instills feelings that "move one toward lack of faith and leave one without hope and without love" (*Exercises,* §§ 316–317). Recognizing these affections is crucial, and determines how one should act. As Ignatius recommends, when in desolation, the discerner should not make any changes to his or her habits or choices. Changing your mind when desolate may lead you to give up good resolutions. In contrast, when you are feeling consoled, you should make vigorous changes for improvement.

The distinction between consolation and desolation shapes the rest of the discernment of spirits. We might ask, "Why does God allow desolation to befall us, even very spiritually mature people?" Ignatius answers that, most of the time, it is God's way to test us, to exercise us, and to make us stronger. If we understand desolation this way, then we should endure it with patience, and we should reflect that it reveals our need for grace. In contrast, when we enjoy consolation we should use our strength to prepare for a future desolation. We should also exercise humility, trust in God, and watch out for the wiles of "the enemy" (§§ 318–327).

Let's consider an example of discernment of spirits appropriate to our subject of wealth and giving: the Gospel parable of the "rich young man" (Mark 10:17–22) who asks Jesus how one might attain life eternal. Jesus responds that he should keep the law, in particular loving God and his neighbors. The man responds that he does so. Jesus adds that the young man should sell all he has, give it to the poor, and follow Him. The young man looks sad and turns away, "for he was very rich."

This young man lives in the conflict between the Holy Spirit and "the evil spirit." The Holy Spirit moves the young man to ask Jesus for help, and to inquire about eternal life. The evil spirit moves him to cling to his gold and all the trappings of the wealthy life. The young man's predisposition, in the end, is toward acquiring and keeping his wealth. The evil spirit draws the young man in the direction of that disposition. But this evil spirit does not explain why the young man becomes sad. If the evil spirit had its way, the young man would run to his treasury and count his shekels joyfully. It is the Holy Spirit that pains him as he turns from Jesus. The Holy Spirit affects the young man in two ways: it draws him to seek Jesus's advice in the first place (in seeking salvation), and it pains him when he returns to his predisposed attachment to wealth (see Toner 1995a: 71–72).

A good spiritual director would counsel this young man not to give up his resolve to seek Jesus and to pursue salvation in the face of his desolation. Discernment of spirits reveals this young man not as the plaything of mysterious "drives" or "impulses" within himself, but as a choosing agent, confronted by the world and its momentous choices. These "spirits" and forces may be formidable, but he still has a choice. Better discernment would help him make it more ably.

Discernment of God's Will

Let us turn to the discernment of God's will. As noted, discernment of spirits can serve as a precursor to discerning God's will; but the practices can work in reverse as well. Discerning God's will aims most closely at an election, a choice. For that reason, Ignatius particularly emphasizes that discerning God's will requires distinguishing clearly ends and means in one's choices. As he explains,

> I ought not to order or drag the end into subjection to the means, but to order the means to the end. In this way it happens, for example, that many choose firstly to marry, which is the means, and secondly to serve God our Lord in marriage, although the service of God is the end. Similarly, there are others who first seek to possess benefices, and afterwards to serve God in them. Thus these persons do not go directly to God, but desire God to come directly to their disordered attachments. As a result they transform the end into a means and the means into the end; and consequently what they should fasten on in the first place they take up in the last. For I ought to aim first at desiring to serve God, which is the end, and secondarily at accepting the benefice or marrying if that is more suitable for me, which is the means to the end. (*Exercises*, § 169)

Here Ignatius reinforces his teachings, discussed earlier, about the priority of ends over means. And they imply that no true election chooses between a spiritual and a non-spiritual choice, or between two non-spiritual options, but between two possibilities both of which would advance man's true end and God's glory. That's where the real difficulties and opportunities lie.

There are different situations in which we make choices. In rare cases, supernatural factors are involved. God may immediately and directly reveal a course of action: it remains for us to choose to follow or not to follow. Or God may strongly move the soul of the chooser, making him or her feel strong consolation when confronted by one option and desolation when confronted by others. In such cases, Ignatius recommends that one still meditate methodically upon the choice, though these spiritual urgings carry great weight. No matter how strong the superhuman urgings or evidence, the choice still lies with the human being.

But in most cases, Ignatius recommends a "method" for "making a sound and good election." Indifference plays a critical role. First, you should put before yourself the matter about which you're making an election. Next, you should keep in sight the end of praising God, and you should maintain indifference toward all else. You should then ask God to move your will to do what is right, and you should take notice of any such urgings. Most importantly, however, you should weigh up the pros and cons of the proposed action, and you should examine which way your own human reason inclines. Finally, you should pray to God after making your election (*Exercises*, §§ 178–183).

Two more conditions help in discerning God's will. Ignatius stresses that discernment and election should take place within an atmosphere of tranquility: one needs to be able to listen and not be distracted from hearing God's will. Second, one must have made a previous commitment to follow God's will for the greater glory of God, which one scholar calls "the *magis* principle" (Toner 1995b: 6). In other words, one commits to choosing the alternative that offers God the "greater" glory. Finally, and most obviously, such a process is not self-contained: although one uses one's own reason to weigh up pros and cons, this is not a merely internal exercise: it is more like a conversation between the seeker and God. The seeker listens, God communicates, the seeker responds. And God communicates through our thoughts and feelings. To use a metaphor, Ignatian spirituality recognizes that we, ourselves, are written text and text-to-be-written, by us and the Holy Spirit at the same time. The Holy Spirit leads us through our own minds and hearts. God never replaces human effort: He guides our choices but does not substitute for them. And by asking us to seek His will, God invites us to collaborate with Him in building His kingdom (see Toner 1995b: 7). There may be times that God speaks directly, as He did to Paul. But even then, He proposes a choice, not an inexorable command.

Role of the Advisor

Even if we think just about collaborating with Christ, our work in serving God's will is a social one. Of course, most people will be involved in this work with many other people besides Jesus. Because of its sociality and its difficulty, Ignatius emphasizes the importance of not "going it alone" when making spiritual exercises. One should always seek out the guidance of a spiritual director more experienced than oneself (see *Exercises,* § 326). Besides serving a critical role in the discernment process, the spiritual director provides an example for advisors in many other areas of our lives.

Just as God does not jerk human beings about by strings, so too a spiritual director must take care to encourage his pupil to discern and choose in complete liberty, and to find his or her own way. Ignatius explains the spiritual director's careful balancing act this way:

> The one giving the exercises should not urge the one receiving them toward poverty or any other promise more than toward their opposites, or to the one state or manner of living more than to another. Outside the exercises it is lawful and meritorious for us to counsel those who are probably suitable for it to choose continence, virginity, religious life, and all forms of evangelical perfection. But during these spiritual exercises when a person is seeking God's will, it is more appropriate and far better that the Creator and Lord himself should communicate himself to the devout soul, embracing it in love and praise, and disposing it for the way which will enable the soul to serve him better in the future. Accordingly, the one giving the exercises ought not to lean or incline in either direction but rather, while standing by like the pointer of a scale in equilibrium, to allow the Creator to deal immediately with the creature and the creature with its Creator and Lord. (§ 15)

People normally are unbalanced, Ignatius implies. They vacillate from one choice to another, drawn by one aspiration or another. Balanced spiritual directors are not passive or immobile. Quite to the contrary, a spiritual director's neutrality helps neutralize the confusing emotions that obscure most of our choices. Spiritual directors' weight at the center of the scale does not keep their pupils from a decision; rather, they make it more likely that their pupils will perceive and choose the will of God.

Ignatius's advice about the role of a spiritual director reflects once more the view that there are no ready "rules" by which to govern every choice or decision in our lives. If there were, the wise spiritual director could simply enunciate them to the person contemplating a choice. And, it's true, rules—whether Scriptural, civic, or commonsensical—help us navigate many choices. But they cannot cover all scenarios for every individual. Ignatius's advice may make the spiritual exercises look like a special time, exempt from the normal way of proceeding that we take in everyday life. But in fact his advice reflects that there is no such exemption. When someone undergoes the exercises with a balanced and mature spiritual director, he or she actualizes the liberty of finding and choosing God's will that most of us ignore most of the time, as we follow "the rules." If he or she performs the office well, the spiritual director embodies the genius of Ignatian discernment and Ignatius's *Exercises* as a whole.

Using Ignatius Today

Ignatius's model of discernment is not for everyone, but it offers a rich and probing framework for self-discovery and the revelation of God's will. It can help illuminate the daily struggle between right and wrong—in us and the world. And it can be a useful tool in making decisions about money and resources that, we believe, resonate with God.

Although in this chapter we have followed Ignatius in elaborating the steps and conditions of the process, one cannot be too logical about it. In the end, discernment is an art, for it involves more than rational thought. It requires us to understand how to read the signs of God's will.

4 ⟿

Luther

Receiving and Sharing God's Gift

Martin Luther's (1483–1546) effort to discern God's will lacks the calm contemplation of Aquinas, the passionate earnestness of Ignatius, the cool legalism of Calvin, or the joyful philosophizing of Jonathan Edwards. As one recent biographer wrote, Luther "makes the most sense as a wrestler with God," a Jacob in sixteenth-century Germany, and indeed Luther so describes himself at one point. Amid social trauma and his own anxiety, writes Martin Marty, Luther was a "God-obsessed seeker of certainty and assurance" (Marty 2004: xii–xiii). As such, he speaks to the doubts, misgivings, and search for meaning prevalent in our day. Struggle also characterizes Luther's thoughts about giving, making them relevant today as well.

The theme of struggle appears early in Luther's writing, for example in his *Ninety-Five Theses,* which decried the Church's selling of "indulgences" to forgive sins and which Luther, on October 31, 1517, famously nailed to the door of the Wittenberg Castle Church. In the *Theses,* struggle focuses on repentance. "When our Lord and Master Jesus Christ said, 'Repent' (Mt 4:17), he willed the entire life of believers to be one of repentance." By citing "the entire life" of Christians, Luther deftly rebuts the common belief that regularly confessing to a priest and purchasing indulgences could "wash" the soul of sin. Luther replies that forgiveness is never over: the soul always finds itself in sin and must ever struggle against it. Far from flitting by as a momentary emotion, repentance should be a lifelong stance.

Luther's radical view of repentance involved far more than merely longing for forgiveness. Because sin remains with us all our earthly lives, true inner repentance is a form self-hatred, he said, which may even be expressed as self-loathing. Such a notion might seem hopelessly out of sync with our self-help age, but Luther, as we will see, is really calling us to complete honesty with ourselves and an ongoing purification of will and deed. Luther's deeply searching repentance thus pertains to our broader theme, for self-honesty and introspection are qualities that enable us to use wealth properly.

Ultimately, Luther's sense of the Christian struggle is not as mean as it is sometimes depicted. He writes of the Christian wrestling with and even besting God. But how could a sinner conquer God? God, he explains, is not conquered in such a way that God is "subjected" to our will. Instead, God's wrath and fury at our sin "is conquered by us by praying, seeking, and knocking, so that from an angry judge, as He seemed to be previously, He becomes a most loving Father" (Marty 2004: 26–27). God's love gives a silver lining to the torments of doubt or misgiving we experience. They are, says Luther, God's way of stirring up our prayers and appeals and so turning us to the right path. This shift from God as angry judge to God as loving father is the hinge upon which Luther's thought turns. It is the fruit of his meditation on faith, grace, and justification— and why this German monk would have us wrestle with God and ourselves.

The Christian Life: Opening Our Hearts to the Gift

Luther envisioned the end of human life as opening ourselves, through Christian faith, to receive, unmerited, God's gifts of righteousness and love. Through no doing of our own, divine righteousness liberates us from the sin that is the warp and woof of human life. Luther's vision finds expression in various forms. One is that of a spiritual, saving marriage with Jesus Christ, which Luther says is promised all Christians. Putting one's neighbor before oneself and doing other good works are the natural result of this spiritual union and, as such, are another goal of life, according to Luther.

Luther's understanding of ultimate ends is similar in substance to those we have seen but it differs markedly in emphasis. Aquinas describes the end of a faithful life as the virtue of charity, which culminates in friendship with God and, in its most complete form, in sharing in the contemplation of God's beatific vision. Ignatius unfolds a vision of the Christian as God's fellow-worker in the world, changing the world under direction from God's spirit. As we shall see, Edwards depicts the goal of the spiritual life as imitating God's joyous contemplation of the created world and responding to that world with benevolence.

Charity, works, and creation—these are not the main focus in Luther's mind. He places God squarely in the center: people and their works (inasmuch as these express human effort only) are pushed to the periphery. Even faith is not entirely a human work! True faith, Luther teaches, does not spring from pious trust in God or the robust ability of particular people to believe. *Faith is our striking, heart-felt perception of God's grace, given and received.* God gives us grace, we receive it, and we trust in it. God comes first: God acts, and humans react: "the phrase 'through faith' is not to be understood as a means for apprehending grace but as the mode of living by and in the power of God's graciousness" (Dillenberger 1961, xxvi).

Luther's vision of the Christian life also contains a striking element of intimacy and closeness. Faith, he wrote, "unites the soul with Christ as a bride is united with her bridegroom. By this mystery, as the Apostle teaches, Christ and the soul become one flesh [Eph. 5:31–32]" (Luther 1961: 60). The spiritual consequences are profound: "If they are one flesh and there is between them a true marriage—indeed the most perfect of all marriages, since human marriages are but poor examples of this one true marriage—it follows that everything they have they hold in common, the good as well as the evil." The mortal soul experiences a double benefit from this union, Luther writes. On the one hand, it can "glory in whatever Christ has as though it were its own," while, on the other, "Christ claims as his own" whatever the mortal soul has.

Marriage to Christ is a match made in heaven—and as Luther is quick to note by way of comparison, it is unbelievably generous to the sinner.

> Let us compare these and we shall see inestimable benefits. Christ is full of grace, life, and salvation. The soul is full of sins, death, and damnation. Now let faith come between them and sins, death, and damnation will be Christ's, while grace, life, and salvation will be the soul's; for if Christ is a bridegroom, he must take upon himself the things which are his bride's and bestow upon her the things that are his. (Luther 1961: 60)

Luther thus elevates the domestic union, which is understood to involve the community of all things, good as well as bad, to explain justification and salvation. Home economics rises to the very heights of theology.

Luther argues that marriage to Christ provides the only hope of escaping our sinful nature. "Our sins must become Christ's own sin, or else we shall perish for ever" (Luther 1961, 136). Likewise: "This is a singular consolation for all the godly, so to clothe Christ with our sins, and to wrap him in my sins, your sins, and the sins of the whole world, and so to behold him bearing all our iniquities" (Luther 1961, 137). Christ's sacrifice is not limited to a few minutes on Golgotha or even a few days of the Passion. It extends to all times and to every person. It is incomparable itself, but in its immensity it makes all other human sacrifices unnecessary, even sinful.

"Strengthen Faith Alone"

But Luther adds an important caution, one that came to change the course of religious history: we must not let the wonderful benefits, in effect, the "work," of this marriage obscure its meaning. "Since . . . faith can rule only in the inner man . . . and since faith alone justifies, it is clear that the inner man cannot be justified, freed, or saved by any outer work or action at all, and that these works, whatever their character, have nothing to do with this inner man. On the other hand, only ungodliness and unbelief of heart, and no outer work, make him guilty and a damnable servant of sin."

Even trying to prove that we are worthy of marriage to Christ would have this effect. "It ought to be the first concern of every Christian," Luther proposes, "to lay aside all confidence in works and increasingly to strengthen faith alone and, through faith, to grow in the knowledge, not of works, but of Christ Jesus, who suffered and rose for him . . . No other work makes a Christian" (Luther 1961: 56).

That humans can strengthen their faith and grow in love of God posed a dilemma to Luther. If faith is the result of our reaching toward God, Luther reasoned, it cannot be righteous, for the focus then falls on people and their effort, not on God, where it belongs. Early in his career, Luther also agonized over the possibility that self-centeredness would stain the act of confession and contrition.

Could it not be that saying "*I'm* sorry," Luther asked, betrays more concern for oneself than the one wronged? And wouldn't we be more likely to have concern for our own selves when the one wronged is the omnipotent God? For their own safety and salvation, Luther held, sinners are practically compelled to please God, to go along with their sense of what God wants. God thus becomes a tool, something sinners use for their own good. Adopting language from Augustine, Luther sees such sinners as "curved in" upon themselves, "cramped, protective, in no way open for God to break into their souls" (Marty 2004: 15–16).

God's "Imputation" of Righteousness

How then can we love God and receive God into our souls without secretly (or overtly) hoping to "use" God for the benefit of our souls—and hence immediately shutting God out? Luther found the answer in his theory of God's "imputation" of righteousness. God "imputes" righteousness into our hearts in the same way that God imputes faith into the person striving for deeper faith. Here is how Luther explains it:

> By the mercy of God, meditating day and night, I gave heed to the context of the words, "In it the righteousness of God is revealed, as it is written, 'He who through faith is righteous shall live.'" There I began to understand that the righteousness of God is that by which the righteous [person] lives by a gift of God, namely by faith. . . . Here I felt that I was altogether born again and had entered paradise itself through open gates. There a totally other face of the entire Scripture showed itself to me. (Luther 1961: 11)

This discovery—the original Protestant "born again" experience—gave Luther a whole new view of God's righteousness. It became not only divine wrath and justice but also the inner righteousness or "justification" that God mercifully bestows upon sinners. It enabled Luther to see God's work as not only God's action but also the products of that action; God's goodness became not only God's essential and eternal goodness but also the particular, historical good that God works in the world. By underscoring God's saving actions in the world, this belief in grace propelled Luther from fearing judgment to embracing divine benevolence.

Luther held that "righteousness consists in two things: in faith of the heart and in God's imputation." While "faith of the heart" is a sort of righteousness, Luther explains, "[it] is not enough; for after faith there remain certain remnants of sin in our flesh. Our faith is but a little spark of faith, which only begins to render to God his true divinity" (Luther 1961: 127). We need that other part, God's imputation. This gift of grace is perfect and complete at every moment, enough to render us righteous in God's eyes—*but we must first accept it*. We must return to this gift repeatedly, every day in fact, because "the old desires and sins still linger in us, and strive against the spirit" (Luther 1961: 22–23).

For this reason, the struggle of the Christian must continue until the end of life. No person can sit back and relax, as if the threat of sin had vanished. Self-discipline does not exist for its own sake or to produce a weary life of asceticism: imputed to us, God's righteousness invigorates and redirects our living: "This self-discipline is needed in order that we might conform to the death and resurrection of Christ, and also that we might complete the meaning of our baptism; for baptism, too, signifies the death of sin and the new life of grace. The final goal is that we should be entirely liberated from sin, rise again from the body with Christ, and live for ever" (Luther 1961: 29).

Our accepting God's gift does not make us worthy. The gift precedes and establishes, rather than follows, our worthiness. No activity or work prepares us for or initiates us into this righteousness. No ceremony or ritual delivers it. In righteousness, "we work nothing, we render nothing unto God, but only we receive and suffer another to work in us, that is to say, God" (Luther 1961: 101).

When we do otherwise, Luther argued, when we think we can by our own work or efforts "qualify" for this blessing or attain righteousness, we fail. This conviction ultimately led Luther, a Catholic monk and priest, to his historic rejection of the central act of Catholic worship, the liturgy of the Mass. The Mass, under the influence of the medieval Church, evolved over time into an act of sacrifice *by* the priest and the people, Luther believed. People sought to use the Mass to justify themselves. But, Luther asks, if common people or priests can please God through their sacrifices, what purpose did Christ's death and redemption serve? Better to scrap the ritual than God's gift of grace.

Works as a Fruitful Rain

Luther's condemnation of pride and self-centeredness in faith explains why he sometimes exaggerates his condemnation of works. "Every good work is sin," he famously charged. Elsewhere he compares human righteousness to bloody menstrual cloths. In the end, however, Luther does not despise good works but strives mightily not to allow them to distract us from what truly counts: God's gracious love and justification.

When we are taught faith in Christ, says Luther, "then do we teach also good works. . . . Do good to your neighbour and serve him: fulfil your office" (Luther 1961: 111–112). Indeed, Luther allows for the possibility of good works as the action of heavenly righteousness. In that case, the Christian's good work is a means by which God pours "fruitful rain" on, and so replenishes, the world. "When I have this righteousness reigning in my heart, I descend from heaven as the rain making fruitful the earth: that is to say, I come forth into another kingdom, and I do good works, how and whensoever occasion is offered."

Those occasions are offered in manifold ways, Luther tells us: "If I be a minister of the Word, I preach, I comfort the broken-hearted, I administer the Sacraments. If I be an householder, I govern my house and my family, I bring up my children in the knowledge and fear of God. If I be a magistrate, the charge that is given me from above I diligently execute. If I be a servant, I do my master's business faithfully" (Luther 1961: 109). Whether we conceive of ourselves as acting as spouses to Christ, as imitating Christ, or as heavenly rain—this cheerful service to others, in every moment of our everyday lives, is the true end of the Christian life.

The Challenge of Charity

Because of his understanding of God's righteousness and his outrage over the practice of selling indulgences, Luther looks with suspicion on the greatest virtue of the medieval Church, charity. As we saw, Aquinas, using Aristotle's language, describes charity as a virtue, that is, as a settled disposition of the human soul; it is a form of "being-in-action" or activity, and one that makes human beings presumably pleasing to one another and to God. It is beautiful and good.

Luther will have none of this finery. Luther's marriage with Christ displaces Aquinas's friendship with God: "This [belief in Christ] is the beginning of health and salvation. By this means we are delivered from sin, justified and made inheritors of everlasting life; not for our own works and deserts, but for our faith, whereby we lay hold upon Christ." Luther acknowledges a righteousness in the heart of the charitable person; but this quality is to Luther less charity than faith (Luther 1961: 110).

Luther is at pains to make sure that we do not pride ourselves on our charity: "We are justified, not by faith furnished with charity, but by faith only and alone. We must not attribute the power of justifying to that form," meaning charity, but "to faith, which apprehends and possesses in the heart Christ the Savior himself. This faith justifies without and before charity" (Luther 1961: 116). Luther isolates what he sees as the medievals' mistake about charity. "Righteousness is not essentially in us, as the Papists reason out of Aristotle, but without us," he writes. It is "in the grace of God only and in his imputation" (Luther 1961: 131). Greek philosophy, even when adopted in so sublime a form as Aquinas, leads to pride.

Luther denies us the dignity of pride in order to glorify God. Luther's reasoning makes God's decision to give us Christ, or Christ's decision to "marry" us, all the more mysterious: we are so undeserving. Yet it has a fierce logic to it. Were we a thousand times more virtuous, a million times more deserving, we still could never save ourselves. There would be no saving us.

Fulfilling the Law in One's Heart

In his vision of the purposes and ends of the Christian life, Luther maintained a delicate relationship with the role of the law. Luther was no anti-nominian or enemy of law; he accepted some role for the law in human life. But because of his emphasis on God's grace and God's righteousness, the law did pose a tricky theological problem to Luther. If Christians must live in the world, what should they do about these temporal powers, especially if, as Luther claims, God rules over all, and if we have nothing without faith?

Luther begins with some redefinition. Most people, he notes, understand the law to mean the human laws constrained by time and place and, more broadly, the Law of Moses as expressed in the Hebrew Bible (especially the Ten Commandments). He does not deny these meanings but adds another: "You must not understand the term 'law' in its everyday sense as something which explains what acts are permitted or forbidden. This holds for ordinary laws, and you keep them by doing what they enjoin, although you may have no heart in it. But God judges according to your inmost convictions; His law must be fulfilled in your very hearts, and cannot be obeyed if you merely perform certain acts" (Luther 1961: 20). God's law can be fulfilled only in spirit and conscience.

In a commentary on Paul, Luther explains why the apostle called the law spiritual. "If the law were corporeal, our works would meet its demands. Since it is spiritual, however, no one keeps it, unless everything you do springs from your inmost heart. Such a heart is given us only by God's spirit, and this spirit makes us equal to the demands of the law" (Luther 1961: 21). The spirituality of the law reflects its plane of operation: only the soul can meet its demands. Yet Luther reminds us that, paradoxically, the willing heart that enables us to live up to the law is not ours alone: it is also God's spirit imputed to us.

To resolve the conflict between earthly and spiritual law, Luther proposed that we live essentially in parallel worlds, one heavenly and the other earthly.

> The righteousness of [human law] is earthly and has to do with earthly things, and by it we do good works. But as the earth does not bring forth fruit unless it is first watered and made fruitful from above (for the earth cannot judge, renew and rule the heaven, but instead the heaven judges, renews, rules and makes fruitful the earth, that it may do what the Lord has commanded): even so by the righteousness of the law, in doing many things we do nothing, and in fulfilling the law we fulfil it not, unless first, without any merit or work of ours, we are made righteous by the Christian righteousness, which has nothing to do with the righteousness of the law, or to the earthly and active righteousness. (Luther 1961: 104–105)

Luther bases his case in part on Romans 13:7: "Render to every one his dues, tribute to whom tribute is due, custom to whom custom; honor to whom honor; fear to whom fear." Tribute, custom, honor, and fear are aspects of temporal power and obedience. But, citing Paul, Luther observes that the temporal authorities are limited. They can never rule over matters of faith or God's word.

Luther does not claim that the wicked can become good through obeying the law. Only God can save the wicked. The good Christian, Luther continues,

> loses nothing by this, and such service in no way harms him, and yet it is of great profit to the world. If he did not do it, he would be acting not as a Christian but contrary even to love, and would also be setting a bad example to others, who like him would not submit to authority, though they were not Christians. In this way the Gospel would be brought into disrepute, as though it taught rebellion and made self-willed people, unwilling to benefit or serve any one, when in reality it makes a Christian the servant of every one. (Luther 1961: 373)

Concern for others is also the reason why Christians should support the temporal powers that enforce the law. "The reason you should do this is, that in this case you would enter entirely into the service and work of others, which benefited neither yourself nor your property nor your character, but only your neighbor and others; and you would do it not to avenge yourself or to recompense evil for evil, but for the good of your neighbor and for the maintenance of the safety and peace of others" (Luther 1961: 373).

Though expressed in a condensed way, this lesson follows Luther's teaching about grace and righteousness. The earthly law is good in that it directs us toward good works. But we cannot live up to this law completely on our own. We need God's righteousness to set right our hearts, as the earth needs heaven's rain to make it fruitful. God's righteousness directs us in the law of our hearts, which enables us to do the good works earthly law requires.

We can now understand Luther's response to those who claimed that a good Christian needs no earthly law. On the one hand, Luther agrees that a "secular sword" is not needed to compel good works from the righteous. The good Christian does "all and more" the law demands. But he must nevertheless respect the law. Since a true Christian lives not for himself but for his neighbor, "the whole spirit of his life impels him to do even that which he need not do, but which is profitable and necessary for his neighbor" (Luther 1961: 373). Obeying earthly law will not make the good Christian more deserving of salvation. But a Christian life involves service to others. Obeying the law represents an important way to do this.

Luther's stance toward law reflects his understanding of the position of the Christian as a spiritual, unworldly being in the world. In his sermon "On Trade and Usury," Luther said,

> I have often taught thus, that the world ought not and cannot be ruled according to the gospel and Christian love, but by strict laws and with sword and force, because

the world is evil. It accepts neither gospel nor love, but lives and acts according to its own will unless compelled by force. Otherwise, if only love were applied, everyone would eat, drink, and live at ease at someone else's expense, and no one would work. Indeed, everyone would take from another what was his, and we would have such a state of affairs that no one could live because of the others. (Luther 1955b: 45:264, and in Luther 1961: 116)

Lawfulness is not a transcendent end. But it serves more than earthly purposes. It gives the wicked and the just a glimpse of the good works that God's righteousness enables the righteous to do. Obeying the law allows the Christian to serve the needs of his neighbor—benefiting his community but also showing the transcendent goodness of Christianity.

Called to Serve

Luther's thought about the law brings us back to his metaphor for faith, that of a marriage to Christ. This union, as we saw, relieves sinners of sin—but it also delivers them to the "cross" of Christian service, which is expressed through good works. These two—faith and works—are inseparable to Luther. "It is impossible, indeed, to separate works from faith, just as it is impossible to separate heat and light from fire" (Luther 1961: 24). This simile retains the natural primacy in each pair: faith comes before works as fire precedes heat and light.

In speaking of the good Christian, Luther clarifies the demand for service: "He serves the State as he performs all other works of love, which he himself does not need. He visits the sick, not that he may be made well; feeds no one because he himself needs food: so he also serves the State not because he needs it, but because others need it—that they may be protected and that the wicked may not become worse" (Luther 1961: 24).

Luther explains the role of serving others in the Christian life most fully in his *Freedom of a Christian*. He begins this way:

A man does not live for himself alone in this mortal body to work for it alone, but he lives also for all men on earth; rather, he lives only for others and not for himself. To this end he brings his body into subjection that he may the more sincerely and freely serve others . . . Therefore he should be guided in all his works by this thought and contemplate this one thing alone, that he may serve and benefit others in all that he does, considering nothing except the need and the advantage of his neighbor. Accordingly the Apostle commands us to work with our hands so that we may give to the needy, although he might have said that we should work to support ourselves. He says, however, "that he may be able to give to those in need" [Eph. 4:28]. (Luther 1961: 73)

One might worry that Luther is recommending a life of fierce asceticism. But he does not: "This is what makes caring for the body a Christian work; through its health and comfort we may be able to work, to acquire, and lay by funds with which to aid those who are in need, that in this way the strong member may serve the weaker, and we may be sons of God, each caring for and working for the other, bearing one another's burdens and so fulfilling the law of Christ." Because our fundamental orientation should be toward others, we must also take care of ourselves and our own needs.

A key element in service for Luther is the source of our desire to serve, not the outcome or usefulness of the work. The impetus, Luther wrote, must be faith. From faith flows love and joy in the Lord, which in turn create "a joyful, willing, and free mind that serves one's neighbor willingly and takes no account of gratitude or ingratitude, of praise or blame, of gain or loss. For a man does not serve that he may put men under obligations. He does not distinguish between friends and enemies or anticipate their thankfulness or unthankfulness, but he most freely and most willingly spends himself and all that he has, whether he wastes all on the thankless or whether he gains a reward."

We are called, the passage continues, to serve as God does, "distributing all things to all men richly and freely, making 'his sun rise on the evil and on the good' [Matt. 5:45]." Playing on the biblical verse, Luther adds, "So also the son [Christ] does all things and suffers all things . . . freely bestowing joy" on others (Luther 1961: 73–76). The Christian reflects God's generosity on others, radiating, however dimly, the love of God. Having established the primacy of God, and faith in God, over charity, Luther in this way nevertheless returns to the love or charity that Aquinas held so dear.

Common Wealth: Proper and Improper Uses of Resources

Luther writes so much about the state of the soul and one's relation to God that it is easy to imagine him thinking little about material things or human economic relations. Yet he spent much of his life dealing with exactly such matters. Luther came from a well-off family, although his entry into monastic life cut him off from that wealth. His wife, Katherine, had been consigned to a convent after her mother's death; after she fled her order, she, too, had nothing. Luther wrote prodigiously but never earned anything from royalties. In order to support his family, he tried setting up in his house a lathe to turn wood, but his wordsmithing always got in the way of his woodworking. After the Reformation began, local authorities gave Luther an Augustinian monastery as a place to live. An elected official of Wittenberg, Luther's home, gave him a salary and a share in the bounty of his table and wine cellar (see Luther 1961: 227). Katherine turned out to be an energetic wife, not only bearing Luther many children but also setting his home in order and growing or buying much of their food. She became so accomplished at domestic economy that, before his death, Luther broke with custom and appointed Katherine alone as executor of his estate, relying on her to care for herself and their children (see Marty 2004: 110). Luther reveals resources in his own life in the form of faith, friends, and family that far outstripped his earthly wealth.

The life lessons Luther learned from the resources available to him and to others influenced his writings deeply. Noteworthy for our purposes are his thoughts on true and false treasure for the Christian and his argument that belonging to a community deepens one's understanding of riches. We will look at how, in Luther's view, communities should use their riches to benefit those most in need, as well as the worldly and spiritual obstacles that Luther found hedged around material riches.

True and False Treasure

Luther finds true wealth in souls, not in stuff. In his commentary on Paul's "Letter to the Philippians," he says that the apostle urges Christians to devote themselves to others because every Christian "has such abundant riches in his faith that all his other works and his whole life are a surplus" that can be used to "serve and do good to his neighbor." Luther concedes the challenge this poses to people who fear that caring for others will tax their own resources. He replies that caring for others adds to our own faith. In giving to others, we find a surplus for ourselves.

Luther contemplated the nature of "treasure" in his earliest writing, the *Ninety-Five Theses*. He did so in the context of the uproar over the medieval Church's sale of indulgences; believers purchased these tokens of sacramental forgiveness from a priest in order to relieve themselves or their loved ones from a perceived burden of sin. Luther makes clear his view of this trade in Theses 65 and 66: "The treasures of the gospel are nets with which one formerly fished for men of wealth. The treasures of indulgences are nets with which one now fishes for the wealth of men."

Luther here distinguishes true wealth from seeming wealth. The Good News proclaimed in the New Testament, the basis of the Christian faith, is the true treasure. "The true treasure of the Church is the most holy gospel of the glory and grace of God," he writes in Thesis 62. It draws people to God as a net draws fish to the fisherman. Luther writes that Scripture attracts "men of wealth." He may be implying that even those people (or particularly those) with great material possessions have great spiritual needs. But "men of wealth" may also mean those who have the spiritual gift of faith, which draws them to the Gospel message. Their "wealth" is their readiness to receive the true treasure of the Lord's word. Luther contrasts this with indulgences, which he calls a ploy to snag not "men of wealth" but the "wealth of men." The indulgence trade operates not on faith but on fear and selfishness. In giving in to this trick, people lose or forego all types of wealth: their material possessions, the Gospel message, and quite possibly faith itself.

In line with these thoughts, Luther sets himself against the desire for material luxury. He writes that covetousness, which he views as an obstacle to spiritual growth and faith, afflicts his homeland, Germany. A flood of expensive clothing, wool, fur, silk, velvet, and the like has washed over the German nobility and excited the envy of commoners, he says with sadness and disgust. Gilded fancies have swarmed into Germany, sucking its currency abroad. Thus Luther intones, "I believe that, even if the pope did not rob us Germans with his intolerable, fraudulent practices, we should still have had too many of these native robbers, the silk and velvet merchants" (Luther 1961: 481). Given Luther's struggles with the pope, this is no trivial comparison.

Attachment to luxury blocks or obscures the desire for truth, Luther said. The more one thinks of the day's fashion the less one thinks about eternal salvation. Yet Luther, always the wrestler, sees this obstacle as a well-planned one that God allows us a fighting chance to defeat: "It would be impossible to become pure of our attachment to temporal goods, if God did not decree that we should be unjustly injured, and exercised thereby in turning our hearts away from the false temporal goods of the world, letting them go in peace, and setting our hopes on the invisible and eternal goods" (Luther 1955b: 1524). If we did not have to struggle with covetousness, we might not experience true love for the immaterial. What looks like an obstacle is a divinely ordained opportunity.

The Community as the Proper Context for Resources

Luther's trust in God may seem to crowd out any possibility of trusting and working with other people. But his thoughts on money and other resources do not cause him to disparage community. Far from it: the believing community is for Luther one of the Christian's greatest assets. In commenting on the Apostles' Creed, he affirms the Church itself as a community. Luther may have been a renegade who struggled against many institutions of his day, but he would not have his students see the believer as isolated, "an individualist entrepreneur, a virtuoso or hero of courage and faith." Instead, Luther "linked life in community with the life of forgiveness and the hope of the resurrection on the Last Day" (Marty 2004: 126–127). In his attacks on medieval "brotherhoods" or what he calls the "achievement piety" of the Catholic Mass, Luther strives to overcome what he sees as the late medieval Church's individualistic approach to salvation and to reaffirm the Church's original community focus (see Luther 1961: 101).

Attention to community needs determines many of Luther's thoughts on economics, trade, and resources. He argues that when trying to determine the profit of your business or work, you should figure out how much time and work you have put into it, and compare that time and work to the efforts of a day laborer working at some other job; then look to see how much that day laborer gets paid. If your labor and risk are greater, you should get paid more; but if less, then less. Luther calls this "the most accurate, the best, and the most definite advice and direction that can be given in this matter" (Luther 1955b: 1520).

This advice must surely stick in the throats of most professionals, who would hardly be inclined to use the wages of a day laborer as a measuring stick for their own compensation. But beneath the practical computations, Luther's point is that we should look to the least among us, those struggling to earn a day's pay, in order to judge ourselves. In so doing, we are forced to consider someone else's labor, struggles, and needs. We might be led to wonder how a laborer gets by on so much less than we have and how it is that we complain while having so much more. We might also observe that all of us, of whatever station or trade, rely on a power beyond ourselves in order to be able to work and live. All these reflections spring from taking a communal, rather than individualistic, point of view.

Luther takes a similar approach to the often-debated subject of the "just price." This question—how much should craftsmen or merchants mark up their products or wares?—is the other side of the question of compensation for labor. Most people today would answer, "Whatever the market will bear." Luther looks to community in a different way. He urges local authorities to appoint "wise and honest" men to compute the costs of all sorts of wares and to set prices accordingly, which would enable the merchant to get along and provide an adequate living for himself. This is "the best and safest way" to deal with prices and, he adds, was already being done in his day in places "with respect to wine, fish, bread, and the like" (see ibid.).

Today, a recommendation for, in effect, price controls, might sound awful, for it restricts economic freedom. It would probably also deter some people from entering the market or remove from it some energy and innovation. But, if we look closely, we see that Luther recommends price-setting not for all goods but for those requisite for "adequate living," that is, consumer staples. Enacting these controls requires considering the real needs of people within the community; it offers a response to those needs. Luther does not advise wholesale appropriation of wealth, taking from the rich and giving to the poor. He focuses on what people need to live and how they might best get it, with the least harm to others.

Christian Political Economy in Action

In addition to these secular obstacles to a communal approach, Luther identifies Church-sanctioned practices that obscure people's understanding of true needs and true treasure. He rails against guilds or monastic orders that unite their wealth and serve only their members' good. These "brotherhoods" have become so wicked, he said, that even "a sow would not consent to be their patron saint" (Luther 1955a: 35:68; 1:284f). Real brotherhood, in contrast, would gather necessities and offer food to a few tables of poor people, "for the sake of God." Or, he adds, true brothers would put their money into a "common treasury," to be lent to fellow workmen who need a leg up or are starting their careers (Luther 1955a: 34:68–69; 1:285). True brotherhood, Luther concludes, "does not seek its own benefit but that of others, 'above all that of the community'" (Luther 1955a: 35:72; 1:287; see also Luther 1961: 103–104).

Poverty and clerical begging pose other obstacles to a healthy attitude toward material goods. In Luther's time, monks often went from city to city, preaching that money is evil—too evil for holy men to touch—and then demanding that their listeners pay for their support. Luther responds that if money is all that bad, those who vow not to touch it should be praised. But what if money is not truly evil? God creates all things, even gold and silver. And we can use these creations to satisfy our neighbor's needs and to give glory to God. Luther concludes that people who abstain from gold and silver on the grounds that these are evil are foolish and proud: "For gold and silver are not evil, even though they have been subjected to vanity and evil. . . . If God has given you wealth, give thanks to God, and see that you make right use of it" (Luther 1955a: 2:331). It is money's use, not money itself, that is the real problem (see Luther 1961: 111).

Ever concerned for those truly in need, Luther advises cities to distinguish among types of beggars. Itinerant or "professional" beggars, such as mendicant monks, should be turned away at the gates; no one should support those who fool themselves or seek to fool others. But neither should cities tolerate need among their own citizens. Every city should gather support from the rich and the middle class to care for its own poor. Such an obligation helps to identify those who are truly in need and binds the community together in meeting those needs (Luther 1961: 105).

Luther's Ordinance for a Common Chest

Luther's observations about brotherhoods and beggars reveal the direction of his thought on community resources: he favors establishing a sort of common treasury or community chest. In Wittenberg, his advice led the city council to fund a common chest in 1522, creating a sort of welfare program aimed at helping those in need of work, food, or even education (see Marty 2004: 81). While Luther excluded mendicant monks, "the only criterion for distributions of loans or outright gifts" from this common chest "was to be the need of the recipient" (Luther 1961: 119–120).

The provisions of the Wittenberg common chest and an even more robust one enacted with Luther's help in the city of Leisnig reveal the spiritual principles behind Luther's advice. The Leisnig "Ordinance for a Common Chest" begins: "Since by the grace of the Omnipotent God, through the revelation of the Christian and evangelical Scriptures, we have been given not only firmly to believe but also profoundly to know that, according to the ordinance and precept of divine truth and not according to human opinion, all the internal and external possessions of Christian believers are to serve and contribute to the honor of God and the love of the fellow-Christian neighbor . . ." (Luther 1961: 177). The common chest rests on evangelical grounds: the Scriptures, illuminated by grace, disclose what, for Christians, is a common wealth, one possessed in love together. The ordinance uses this spiritual wealth to bind the community together. For example, the actual common chest is kept within the local church, which stands spatially and symbolically at the center of the community; it is where people petition for relief. The chest is provided with four "separate and distinct locks, each having its own key." One key goes to a representative of the nobility, a second to the town council, a third to a representative of the citizenry at large, and the fourth to a member of the rural peasantry (Luther 1961: 183). In typical cities, these classes might see themselves at odds. With Christian love, they work together to steward the common resources.

Once there is value to disburse, the ordinance calls for providing a salary to a pastor and then a sacristan. The needs of the Church come first, not only for transcendent spiritual reasons but also because it facilitates the common good of the community. The trustees of the chest should spend next on schools, both for boys and girls: education is the community's greatest need after the local church. Next, the chest should disburse funds for the poor who are aged and infirm, those who for physical reasons cannot help themselves. After that, they should spend on the homebound poor; that is, people who cannot work at present but who may be able to do so in the future. The chest should then offer loans to industrious newcomers to the city; that the community offers loans instead of gifts reflects the hope that these newcomers will increase the common good rather than only draw from it. Next the trustees should spend money to maintain and construct public buildings, including churches. Finally, imitating Joseph in Egypt, the common chest should spend money during times of plenty to build up stores of grain (see Luther 1961: 186–191).

Much could be said about these provisions of the common treasury, but even a cursory look reveals that six of the eight focus on human beings and their present needs: those of the soul first, then those of the body. Only then do disbursements from the common treasury concern buildings and future needs.

But where, one may well ask, would Wittenberg, Leisnig, or other cities find the means to meet all these needs? How will they fill the common chest? Luther argued that the initial resources should come from church properties, whether abandoned monasteries, foundations created to support specific churches, or trusts established to fund masses or specific church offices. Luther sees these properties or trusts as "horrible dregs which have until now fattened on the wealth of the whole world under the pretense of serving God" (Luther 1955a: 45:169). He does not contradict himself when he would expropriate church property in order to fund a common treasury that itself would fund, in part, church needs. The common chest helps distinguish the proper role of the church from improper excesses. Supporting a reformed pastor contributes, in his view, to the common good. In contrast, setting up a trust to pay for masses so that you might be saved does nothing but oppress those who must work for the trust; your action enslaves them to your perceived good. Consistent with his principles, Luther appropriates property that harms the common good and adds it to that good.

However, Luther also recognizes that seizing badly used Church property will not fund the common chest in perpetuity. (The same could be said today about penalty taxes on mismanaged private foundations or public charities.) Such takings correct a wrong, but they do not secure the right. The Leisnig ordinance also imposes an annual head tax upon every citizen—noble, towns-man, and peasant; man, woman, and child—for the whole of their lives. This tax should not be a burden to those in need. Instead, the ordinance decrees that each person shall pay it "according to his ability and means" (Luther 1955a: 45:192; see also Luther 1961: 125–126).

In making these recommendations, Luther repudiates the medieval insti-tution of almsgiving, a repudiation that reverberates to the present day. Thus he writes in the *Ninety-Five Theses,* "Christians are to be taught that he who gives to the poor or lends to the needy does a better deed than he who buys indulgences" (Thesis 43). In Thesis 45, Luther adds, "he who sees a needy man and passes him by, yet gives his money for indulgences, does not buy papal indulgences but God's wrath." Whereas almsgiving is usually conceived of as a personal expression of charity, Luther stresses the importance of meeting oth-ers' needs in a communal fashion.

In part, Luther mistrusts some almsgivers' apparent attempt to "use" the poor as an opportunity to exercise their virtue. Worse, in Luther's eyes, is the perversion of alms into something that benefits the Church only and the poor not at all. Luther sees this as opposed to the Gospel:

> Not what Christ has commanded, but what men have invented, is called "giving for God's sake"; not what one gives to the needy, the living members of Christ, but what one gives to stone, wood, and paint, is called "alms." And this giving has become so precious and noble that God himself is not enough to recompense it, but has to have the help of others, bulls, parchments, lead, plate, cords large and small, and wax in green, yellow, and white. If it makes no show, it has no value. It is all bought from Rome at great cost "for God's sake," and such great works are rewarded with indulgences here and there, over and above God's reward. But that miserable work of giving to the poor and needy according to God's commandment must be robbed of such splendid reward, and be content simply with the reward that God gives. The latter work is therefore pushed to the rear and the former is placed out in front, and the two when compared shine with unequal light. (Luther 1961: 97)

Giving to the poor should not win one papal bulls, parchment, and all sorts of gewgaws, says Luther; we should cast aside such human distractions or any desire to show our worthiness. Instead, we should rest content in the belief that God alone makes us worthy. We do not give in order to become good; we give because we are good, through the grace of God. It is a lesson relevant to the present, when some people give in order to say that they've given, or just to get their names engraved on sleek new buildings, the modern equivalents of papal parchment.

Luther's approach to resources and the sharing of resources is decidedly communal and ultimately grounded in his doctrine of the "priesthood" of all believers. Among believers, no one is better, more worthy, or closer to God, than anyone else. God offers grace and justification to all baptized believers. All of us start from nothing, and yet all who believe are accepted without reservation or restriction in the believing community. Thus Luther's term for both the universal Church and the local church is *Gemeinde* (assembly or community). It does not seek to separate itself from the state but rather works with the state to serve the same needs (see Luther 1961: 123).

Combining Freedom, Love, and Need in Discernment

In Luther's eyes, as we have seen, human life should be lived as if in marriage to and imitation of Christ. Decisions about resources should take place within a communal context, with attention to the community's needs as a whole. But Luther's criticism of the Church's approach to work and property, and his faith, do not alone yield a finite set of "best" or "better" ways to govern our giving. He opens numerous possibilities for action, including seeing one's vocation as "worldly worship" of God, and he offers certain moral and theological guideposts, such as admitting our lack of true free will and rejecting reason alone in making decisions. Let us turn to Luther's view of that process.

All Work as Vocation

One decision we all must make concerning our resources, broadly considered, is what work we do in the world. Luther challenges the stance of the medieval Church that a religious vocation is more pleasing to God than others; he also condemns the notion that contemplative monks should live without working. To defenders of traditional monastic life Luther replies, "Be not so wicked, my friend, as to say, 'A Christian may not do that which is God's peculiar work, ordinance and creation.' Else you must also say, 'A Christian may not eat, drink, or be married,' for these are also God's work and ordinance." He quotes Paul's statement (1 Timothy 4:4) that nothing, including work, is "to be rejected by the believing and those who know the truth." This applies to "every creature of

God," Luther adds; hence every person "must reckon not simply food and drink, clothes and shoes, but also government, citizenship, protection and administration of justice" (Luther 1961: 377–378). Because everything depends upon God, no person, no worker, is better than any one else. And because we are all equal, each of our occupations contributes something to the common good.

In a passage of evocative images, Luther argues that no occupation can be called closer to or farther away from God:

> God has called men to labor because he labors. He works at common occupations. God is a tailor who makes for the deer a coat that will last for a thousand years. He is a shoe maker who provides boots that the deer will not outlive. God is the best cook, because the heat of the sun supplies all the heat there is for cooking. God is a butler who sets forth a feast for the sparrows and spends on them annually more than the total revenue of the kings of France. Christ worked as a carpenter. (Luther 1961: 181)

In language so powerful as to shock, Luther breaks with the view that a life of constant prayer and self-examination is best. "The mother suckling the baby and washing diapers, the farmer at work, the couple having sex were as likely to be engaged in God-pleasing activities as was any nun engaged in prayer" (Luther 1961: 14:114–115; 31:1, 436–437ff). What pleases God is not selfish supplications or proud abasements, but doing work for the good of others. No one and no moment are exempt from such labor.

Luther goes so far as to call all laborers "masks of God" (see Marty 2004: 104–105). This wonderful image preserves God's mystery: it seeks to depict not the transcendent God but only God's transient masks or faces. It also conveys that human work would be nothing without God's support, that even the humblest occupation holds divine presence and meaning. By being a mask of God, we make divine work in the world possible. Luther makes this clear when speaking about political life, which contemplatives and monks tended to despise:

> Therefore you should cherish the sword or the government, even as the state of matrimony, or husbandry, or any other handiwork which God has instituted. As a man can serve God in the state of matrimony, in husbandry, or at a trade, for the benefit of his fellow man, and must serve Him if necessity demand; just so he can also serve God in the State and should serve Him there, if the necessities of his neighbor demand it; for the State is God's servant and workman to punish the evil and protect the good. Still it may also be omitted if there is no need for it, just as men are free not to marry and not to farm if there should be no need of marrying and farming. (Luther 1961: 378)

To an imaginary questioner who asks why Christ and the apostles did not become kings or husbands, Luther replies: because that is not what was needed from them at the time.

Luther's thoughts on vocation are one with his claims about the security and confidence of the soul. Those who seek to "prove" their worthiness to God will never know if their proofs have succeeded. In contrast, those who do their daily work and serve others as a form of "worldly worship of God" can be certain of their being a "mask" of God, hence dependent on God's will and power. This gives the worker confidence. Luther thus extends the notion of vocation, which means being called by God, beyond monks, priests, or contemplatives. Every Christian has a divinely ordained place in this "worldly worship of God." Being a farmer or a carpenter or a soldier or a politician are all vocations. Luther calls the Christian into the world—in a multitude of ways—not out of it (see Luther 1961: 108–109).

In making such decisions, we may look to the guidance and example of models and authorities as long as we maintain a state of spiritual freedom. Luther's own struggle over whether to marry and have children offers an example. Luther's father, fearing that he would be deprived of grandchildren, did not approve of Luther's decision to become a priest. When Luther left the monastery, his father pressured him to marry, but Luther resisted. Luther's biographer describes his response: "He urged his father to be tolerant about his decision to remain [celibate]. Yes, he agreed, parents had their appropriate authority, but since Christ possessed more, he argued that his father had had to give in to the vocational choice of the son." Luther "thereupon wrapped all human authorities into one package, one line, and rejected them all. Christ alone now, he wrote, was his immediate bishop, abbot, prior, lord, father, and teacher. If this Christ had thus taken one son away, many other sons of fathers, Luther argued, would be saved through his work so long as he remained in the ministry of the Word" (Marty 2004: 75–76).

In Luther's view, Christians should not simply look to established tradition, popular opinion, temporal authority, or even parental dictates when making a decision, major or minor. Their ultimate source of guidance and confidence is the Gospel, which illuminates their deliberations about the particulars. The moment of decision receives more of that light if we remember our lack of power and control.

As seen, the key to Luther's thought is the claim that human beings cannot justify themselves before God; they enjoy at best a "passive righteousness." Luther knows that this must shock his listeners. He imagines someone asking, "What, do we then do nothing? Do we work nothing to obtain this righteousness?" His answer is clear: "Nothing at all. For the nature of this righteousness is, to do nothing, to hear nothing, to know nothing whatsoever of the law or of works, but to know and to believe this only, that Christ is gone to the Father and is not now seen: that he sits in heaven at the right hand of his Father, not as a judge, but . . . that he is our high-priest intreating for us, and reigning over us and in us by grace."

This response reveals the steady, inner calm in Luther's breast. In the end, it is not our part to do anything. Action belongs to God. Paradoxically, this passivity prepares us for true choice and inspires confidence. Our very passivity means that we can accept God's righteousness without fear of falling short: "Here no sin is perceived, no terror or remorse of conscience is felt; for in this heavenly righteousness sin can have no place: for there is no law, and where no law is, there can be no transgression [Rom 4:15]" (Luther 1961: 105). The activity of this righteousness belongs entirely to God; there is no way for us, then, to mess it up.

The Limits of Free Will

For Luther, the belief that we control our own affairs is the biggest obstacle to making wise choices. We must know that any feeling of self-sufficiency or self-mastery is an illusion. To drive home our dependence on God, Luther rails against the notion of free will. He rejects reason as a sovereign guide in discernment. Temptation, depression, even desperation, he argues, better open our minds to God's will. The law, which purports to guide wise choices, can also be an obstacle to discernment. These views may strike some people as shocking, even outrageous, but they make sense within the logic of Luther's beliefs. The struggle against the obstacles, Luther believes, drives us toward Christ's love and the sharing of that love with others.

To understand Luther's view of Christian discernment, we must grapple first with his views of human and divine will. Luther does grant a measure of freedom to humankind, as his own name indicates. He was baptized as Martin Ludher, but, as Marty (2004: 32) relates in his biography, Luther changed his name in a telling way. In 1516, Luther sent a letter on the issue of indulgences to local nobleman and enclosed some of his writings to make his case. In his letter, Luther exalted the count but denigrated himself as being no better than cow dung. As if to mark a turn in his life, he signed it with one word, "Luther," short for "Eleutherius." Like Jacob taking on the name Israel, Luther gave himself a name meaning "the free one" in Latin. (In addition, the Greek gods Dionysus and Eros were sometimes both referred to as "Eleutherios," the liberator.) Luther's playfulness expressed a certain freedom. But how deep does that freedom run?

Let us frame the basics of Luther's world before answering that question. Luther divided human nature into a spiritual, inner realm of the soul and an outer, carnal realm of the body, as in the basic dualism found in Western thought from Plato to Kant. On this Luther turns, again, to Paul (2 Corinthians 4:16) for support: "Though our outer nature is wasting away, our inner nature is being renewed every day." Body-mind dualism typically portrays the soul or mind as less bound by the temporal and physical constraints that chain the body and thus more free. Luther does not quite see it that way, however. The soul, he argued, may not be bound in the same way the body is—but it is bound nonetheless.

He thus rejects the view that humans have free will. What appears to be our freedom is really our ability and disposition "to be caught up by the Spirit and touched by God's grace" (Luther 1961: 187–189). This is what distinguishes men from other animals or plants: our ability to obey God's commands and receive God's righteousness. It is a "freedom" that expresses itself, in the end, in submission to God. We have "free-will" insofar as God bestows that will upon us. We have none of our own accord. Luther's rejection is not only theological but personal:

> I frankly confess that, for myself, even if it could be, I should not want "free-will" to be given me, nor anything to be left in my own hands to enable me to endeavor after salvation; not merely because in face of so many dangers, and adversities, and assaults of devils, I could not stand my ground and hold fast my "free-will" (for one devil is stronger than all men, and on these terms no man could be saved); but because, even were there no dangers, adversities, or devils, I should still be forced to labor with no guarantee of success, and to beat my fists in the air. If I lived and worked to all eternity, my conscience would never reach comfortable certainty as to how much it must do to satisfy God. (Luther 1961: 199)

Luther preferred that no one speak of free will. But if the term must be used, he argued, it should be restricted to the lower bodily realm, such as choices over things such as money and possessions. We may claim a degree of freedom over things that are low or inferior to salvation, he allows. But as far as important things are concerned, we happily resign our fate to God.

If humans do not choose freely, does God possess such freedom? This revives the deeper question of God's justice. Luther pins his entire thought on God's justice and choice to impute righteousness, which makes it all the more pressing to understand his views on divine justice. Luther calls the divine will inscrutable. In his dispute with Erasmus, Luther claims that the Dutch scholar and translator ignores the "distinction between God preached and God hidden, that is, between the Word of God and God Himself." Luther explains:

> God does many things which He does not show us in His Word, and He wills many things which He does not in His Word show us that He wills. Thus, He does not will the death of a sinner—that is, in His Word; but He wills it by His inscrutable will. At present, however, we must keep in view His Word and leave alone His inscrutable will; for it is by His Word, and not by His inscrutable will, that we must be guided. (Luther 1961: 191)

In this sense, Luther's thought is evangelical rather than mystical or contemplative: he appeals ultimately to the Gospel, the word of God, rather than to direct or indirect perception of God's transcendent will. The relation between God's will and word he leaves an open question.

As to the age-old question of why God would create human beings, only to let them sin, Luther replies: "The same reply should be given to those who ask: Why did God let Adam fall, and why did He create us all tainted with the same sin, when He might have kept Adam safe, and might have created us of other material, or of seed that had first been cleansed?" Speaking of God's will, Luther writes: "no cause or ground may be laid down as its rule and standard; for nothing is on a level with it or above it, but it is itself the rule for all things. If any rule or standard, or cause or ground, existed for it, it could no longer be the will of God" (Luther 1961: 195–196). We cannot presume to judge God's justice, according to Luther; rather we must acknowledge our ignorance and humility before God's choices:

> God must be reverenced and held in awe, as being most merciful to those whom He justifies and saves in their own utter unworthiness; and we must show some measure of deference to His Divine wisdom by believing Him just when to us He seems unjust. If His justice were such as could be adjudged just by human reckoning, it clearly would not be Divine; it would in no way differ from human justice. But inasmuch as He is the one true God, wholly incomprehensible and inaccessible to man's understanding, it is reasonable, indeed, inevitable, that His justice also should be incomprehensible . . . (Luther 1961: 200)

Luther insists on the inscrutability of God's will to avert spiritual insecurity or lack of faith. Paradoxically, the freedom that is God's alone is *our* security, Luther teaches. Marty expertly assesses Luther's theological strategy here:

> Luther relied on and stressed scriptural assertions that witnessed to the freedom of God as he circled back to his grand personal question: "What is more miserable than insecurity?" He thought that Erasmus, speaking as if Scripture were unclear, would lead humans to another abyss, that of utter uncertainty. Instead, wrote Luther, the believer takes a leap of faith in a loving God, the God who appears in humility in the suffering and cross of Jesus Christ. "God hidden in his majesty neither deplores nor takes away death, but works life, death, and all in all. For there he has not bound himself by his Word, but has kept himself free over all things." *The Bondage of the Will* became a raucous hymn to the freedom of God. (Marty 2004: 132–133)

Being bound to nothing and free "over all things" leaves God free to keep His promises to man. Were there something superior to God, we could worry whether this "something" loved and cared for us too. That we can take no position above God leaves God's will inscrutable to our mortal gaze.

Luther's thoughts here throw us back onto God's word. Luther does emphasize that even in His revelation through Christ, God remains hidden. As Martin Marty writes of God's incarnation in human form: "Instead of coming only in supreme power, this God thus came in extreme weakness, humility, and suffering. God defied descriptions, definitions, and measures: 'Nothing is so small but God is still smaller, nothing so large but God is still larger'" (Marty 2004: 133). But how can we live for and love this hidden God? Luther says we do so by affirming our faith in God, revealed but still masked in God's word. We are blessed to have the word.

Luther calls knowledge of the limits of free will critical to the life of faith. He writes to Erasmus, "For where they [the truths about 'free-will'] are not known, there can be no faith, nor any worship of God. . . . For if you hesitate to believe, or are too proud to acknowledge, that God foreknows and wills all things, not contingently, but necessarily and immutably, how can you believe, trust and rely on His promises?" (Luther 1961: 184). Luther incorporates knowledge about free will while overcoming the temptation to take free will too seriously. What looks like a snare becomes a step toward salvation.

The Limits of Reason

Luther makes similar comments about reason. Though learned in theology, Luther calls reason a "beast" and "the foundation and headspring of all mischief." The problem, in his view, is that "reason does not fear God, does not love God, does not trust God, but proudly despises God" (Luther 1961: 128). Reason does so when it sets itself up as judge and master of itself. Luther thus recommends that every Christian become a priest who offers up and kills his own reason, "the wisdom of the flesh." By doing so, one gives glory to God. For such priests, "The evening sacrifice is to kill reason; the morning sacrifice is to glorify God" (Luther 1961: 131). In his very last sermon, in 1546, Luther continues this train of abuse, calling reason "the devil's whore," for people seek to use it to reach God on their own and claim to understand God's mysteries (see Marty 2004: 177).

By calling upon us to "kill reason," Luther does not mean that we should become fools. He views the "reason" he denounces as a delusion. While he rejects that we can know all—or even enough to govern ourselves well—Luther allows much room for reflection, thought, and contemplation. For example, he takes the case of a sinner afflicted with fear because he knows God hates sin. Since it is impossible for any human to be without sin, Luther replies, the sinner should not despair over blemishes on his soul, any more than he would despair over wrinkles in his skin: even with these blemishes, he is holy. But, the sinner responds, how can I be holy if I have sin? Luther answers that acknowledging sin is itself a good sign and a reasonable step. Just as someone who knows that he is sick reasonably seeks a doctor, the sinner should seek the only true doctor for sin, Christ. Reason makes the sinner think that he is doomed. Luther concludes that we should "kill reason and believe in Christ" (Luther 1961: 130–131). Luther thus approves of a sort of spiritual reason that operates within the bounds of Christian faithfulness; he rejects reason only when it takes the place of faith.

This faithful use of reason makes sense of some of Luther's other recommendations dealing with obstacles to the Christian life. For example, he counsels his children's tutor about how to deal with depression: "Never be alone. Act foolish and play. Drink a good deal. It would even be a good idea to commit a sin—but not a gross one" (Marty 2004: 181). Reason would tell us never to sin, for God hates sins. Luther recognizes that depression often hides a lurking sense of pride, a pride that isolates the sufferer from human sympathy and compassion. Committing a small sin brings one back to one's sense of humanity and fallibility. The reverse of worldly reason here serves faith.

Luther actually embraces temptations as a kind of guide. He does not do so to show that he can master them. Rather, he sees them as reminders of man's reliance on God and the power of Christ's love. The devil and his tool, the body, are the sources of temptation (see Luther 1961: 100). But these temptations impress on people the need to apply Scripture to their lives. Luther observes that when people feel their flesh battle against their spirit, they may become all the more aware of their spiritual core (see Luther 1961: 148).

Luther describes one of his teachers, Staupitz, who told him that he had sworn a thousand times to become a better man but could never do what he vowed. Staupitz decided never to swear that oath again, since he had come to recognize the empty pride of his vows and his thorough dependence upon God (see Luther 1961: 149). Luther offers himself, too, as an example. He says, "I have suffered many and various passions, and the same also very vehement and great. But so soon as I have laid hold of any place of Scripture, and stayed myself upon it as upon my chief anchor-hold, straightways my temptations did vanish away: which without the Word it had been impossible for me to endure any little space, and much less to overcome them" (Luther 1961: 155).

Deliberation: Others' Needs and Our Own

The imitation of Christ brings with it what Luther calls the law of love: "no better or briefer instruction can be given about this, and about all dealing with temporal goods, than that everyone who is to have dealings with his neighbor set before him these commandments, 'Whatsoever thou wilt that another do to thee, that do thou to him also,' and 'Thou shalt love thy neighbor as thyself'" (Luther 1955b: 1524).

These commandments give rise to three ways for Christians to exchange property: (1) letting people take what they want from you (the best and hardest way); (2) giving freely to anyone who needs it; and (3) lending, but expecting nothing in return (Luther 1955b: 1520). As this hierarchy reveals, the best way is to let others discern their needs and take what they need from you. Second best is to attempt to give others what you think they need. And third is to lend to others what you think they need, hoping for but not expecting a return. This hierarchy does the greatest justice to the Christian's concern with the needs of others.

However, Luther, like Aquinas, does not ignore the giver. "You . . . are not obligated to make a loan," Luther says, "except out of your surplus and what you can spare from your own needs, as Christ says of alms, 'What you have left over, that give in alms, and everything is clean for you.'" If someone wants to borrow a ruinous sum, you are not bound to make the loan. After all, "Your first and greatest obligation is to provide for the needs of your wife and children and servants; you must not divert from them what you owe them." He offers a similar lesson in Thesis 46: "Christians are to be taught that, unless they have more than they need, they must reserve enough for their family needs and by no means squander it on indulgences."

Luther offers what he calls the best rule: "If the amount asked as a loan is too great, just go ahead and give something outright, or else lend as much as you would be willing to give, and take the risk of having to lose it" (Luther 1955b: 1520). It would be better to let the other take what he needs. But as we all have needs, this "best rule" balances them as best we can. Luther is no starry-eyed idealist or fierce ascetic.

Luther uses common sense in attempting to balance the needs of the Church and those of the poor. Although indulgences helped to raise money to build St. Peter's basilica, Luther is no enemy of beautiful churches. He knows that congregations cannot do without churches. Worship "ought rightly be conducted in the finest way." But adornment of churches should be limited. Of the common treasury, "the smaller portion" should go to building churches and the like, and the majority should go toward caring for those in need (Luther 1955b: 1524).

To understand Luther's thoughts on giving, it is important to recall how central giving, in the form of God's gifts to man, is to Luther's whole thinking. Luther begins with the graciousness and generosity of God. His breakthroughs start with recognizing how human beings deserve nothing from this God who gives us righteousness. With this insight, Luther ends his early struggles and embarks upon his reforming path. And giving to community and caring for the community become a response to the primacy of God's generosity in our lives. Because God's gift is totally free, we have to do nothing to deserve it. But, so too, because it is so free, it inspires the free return of giving to others (see Luther 1961: 5, and Thesis 47: "Christians are to be taught that their buying indulgences is a matter of free choice, not commanded").

Another critical principle underlying Luther's thoughts on giving is the importance of vocation. As noted, Luther considers every vocation a mask of God and a "worldly worship of God." It is this divine presence in work that Luther thinks explains why every community is a church, and why the possessions of the church community are common (see Luther 1955a: 45:172–173; 12, 13, 26ff.). Luther's faith leads people to worship through work, and especially in service to one another. His reformation renews both the church and social life (see Luther 1961: 100).

With these principles in mind, Luther offers some simple rules to govern our actual giving. Most simply, do not give only to friends or the powerful. Give to all, including the poor and your enemies. Giving to enemies also requires giving up animosity itself and not just the external signs of animosity (Luther 1955b: 1524). It is hard to overestimate the importance, for Luther, of giving to enemies and the needy: "It is just like His teaching about loving and giving; our lending is to be done without selfishness and without self-seeking. This does not happen unless we lend to our enemies and to the needy; for all that He says is aimed to teach us to do good to everyone, that is, not only to those who do good to us, but also to those who do us evil, or cannot do us good in return" (ibid.).

Luther calls the old teaching that no one is bound to aid the needy unless they are in "extreme want" an excuse *not* to give and a way to circumvent Christian duty. The problem is that everyone reserves the right to determine what counts as extreme need. "We learn that no one is to give or help until the needy are dying of hunger, freezing to death, ruined by poverty, or running away because of debts," Luther writes. "But this knavish gloss and deceitful addition is confounded with a single word which says, 'What thou wilt that another do to thee, that do thou also'" (Luther 1955: 1524).

Luther returns to the law of love and the message of the Ordinance for the Common Chest: "There is no greater service of God than Christian love which helps and serves the needy, as Christ himself will judge and testify at the Last Day, Matthew 25[:31–46]. This is why the possessions of the church were formerly called *bona ecclesiae*, that is, common property, a common chest, as it were, for all who were needy among the Christians" (Luther 1961: 172–173).

Luther does not define the needy only in financial terms. The poor may be those who lack certain resources other than money. The point is to give, even when we think the recipient will not return our gift. As Luther says in *Freedom of a Christian*, those who wish may give to the Church, but they should be careful not to seek some benefit, worldly or heavenly. "Your one care should be that faith may grow, whether it is trained by works or sufferings," Luther writes. "Make your gifts freely and for no consideration, so that others may profit by them and fare well because of you and your goodness" (Luther 1961: 79).

5 ～◦

Calvin

Giving Gratitude to God

John Calvin (1509–1564) was not only a great legislator whose governance of Geneva in the sixteenth century inspired the political aims of John Knox, the English Puritans, and others. His extensive commentary on the Bible recast Christian thought, and Calvin offered much of value to say about humanity's relation to God and to the natural world. But in America today, when we think about Calvin, we usually do so through the lens of New England Puritanism, gloomy Hawthorne stories, or the grim religious fanaticism Arthur Miller portrays in "The Crucible." These associations capture kernels of truth. Even as a boy, young Calvin felt such a calling to shape up his comrades that, according to legend, his peers (who no doubt saw his "shaping up" as nagging) called him "the accusative case" (Harkness 1958: 4).

But our gloomy lenses tend to obscure Calvin's mildness and his reflections about giving. Indeed, Calvin's works abound with fruitful thoughts about money, wealth, and charity, and many of his lessons have to do with the right use of the goods of the world, in relation to God and to fellow human beings.

Calvin begins, as Luther began, with a premise that Aquinas, Ignatius, other Catholic thinkers, and even Aristotle would find outlandish: the depravity of human nature. Calvin's God is so great that all else—natural law, social convention, the authority of kings, parliaments, and bishops—pales in comparison. Yet Calvin's repudiation of the prevailing social order expands the set of potential actions people can take to govern themselves and the fruits of the earth.

It also later made Calvinism more open to economic thought that emerged in the late Middle Ages and flowered in the Renaissance. One precept reigns supreme for Calvin, when it comes to understanding property, wealth, and giving: that we remember that all things come from God. We rely on God for everything. Gratitude for God's generosity should shape all receiving and giving.

Purpose, Amid Joy and Pain

Calvin and Luther

Calvinism's understanding of the goal of life is summarized in the first question of the *Shorter Westminster Catechism,* the defining document of Scottish-English Calvinism, written in 1648: "*Question 1.* What is the chief end of man? *Answer:* Man's chief end is to glorify God, and to enjoy him forever." Calvinism here sounds similar to pre-Reformation Christian thought. Variance begins to emerge in "Question 2," the second article of the catechism: "What rule hath God given to direct us how we may glorify and enjoy him? *Answer:* The Word of God, which is contained in the Scriptures of the Old and New Testaments, is the only rule to direct us how we may glorify and enjoy him."

Here Calvin joins other Reformed thinkers, above all Luther, in emphasizing direct appeal to the Bible. To understand Calvin's view of life's purpose and the framework in which that purpose is pursued, we need to look closely at his thought. After setting Calvin in the context of Luther, we will examine the basic tenets of his theology and then turn to his understanding of good works.

Born in 1509, Calvin came a generation after Luther, who was twenty-six years his elder. When Luther rose to prominence in 1517, as we saw in chapter 4, Calvin was yet a boy in France. Broadly speaking, the theologies of Calvin and Luther widely agree and, on key doctrinal questions, are identical. Each of the great Reformers put God's sovereign power and justification by faith at the heart of Christian belief; each reviled the Roman Church and stressed the Bible as the final authority in faith.

The difference emerges in theological nuance, cultural forms, and matters of emphasis. Like the German-born Luther, Calvin viewed God as a stern and wrathful judge. But where Luther, drawing on his own experience, also saw God as a personal, loving father, Calvin emphasized God's total omnipotence and exercise of will.

Calvin saw God's hand behind any and every motion of the universe. He developed a view of predestination and God's "election" of human souls to salvation that was more radical than Luther's. Before human beings are even knit in the womb, Calvin held, some are destined to be saved and others to be damned. Luther believed in predestination—but not in such a metaphysical or mystical way. Luther saw man's sinful, depraved condition as the consequence of human agency, for example, and he upheld our freedom in matters not essential to salvation. For Calvin, however, the bondage of human will is absolute. God's sovereignty is so great that Calvin believed that God *willed* our fall from grace.

Calvin also differed in his vision of the Church's social role. Rejecting the idea of subordinating the Church to the state, Calvin called for it to be the other way around: the saved or "elect" should Christianize the rule of law and remake society in the image of a religious community. Calvin succeeded in doing precisely that in Geneva, Switzerland, which became the Rome of the Radical Reformation.

The basics tenets of Calvin's theology have been aptly summarized by the acronym TULIP, which, contrary to the cheerful and innocent flower, stands for Total Depravity, Unconditional Election, Limited Atonement, Irresistible Grace, and Perseverance of the Saints.

Total Depravity refers to a primary theological fact for Calvin: Our natural (as opposed to regenerated or saved) state as humans is, strikingly, "depraved" and characterized by original sin. The effects of the Fall infect every part of human personality. Sin infects our minds, our feelings, and our choices. Calvin here relies on Paul's letter to the Romans (5:12): "The unregenerate (unsaved) man is dead in his sins." Without the power of the Holy Spirit, natural man is spiritually dead—blind and deaf to the message of the Gospel.

Though he treats it lightly in the *Institutes,* **Unconditional Election** is perhaps the most famous tenet of Calvin's thought. According to this doctrine, God, before creating the world, chose whom he wished to save. He did not do so based upon merit. Nor did he make it by predicting who would or would not accept the Gospel. God has chosen ("elected") some souls for glory, based solely upon his own will and wisdom—and he has elected others for damnation. Calvin's elect are not identifiable by visible signs or actions. The elect do become able to do good works as a result of their election. But doing good works is an internal indication that God has sown seeds of grace in fertile soil.

Combining human depravity and divine election, Calvin posited his doctrine of **Limited Atonement**, which emphasizes God's justice. All human beings are tainted by original sin. God, being just in nature, would not receive a sinner into heaven. Thus for the elect to enter God's glory, they must be cleansed of that stain. This necessity focuses Calvin on the centrality of Christ: Christ did not die for all people. Christ died for those whom God chooses to save. "The saved" may be many in number, but the number is limited. It does not include all human beings.

Irresistible Grace affirms another central fact for Calvin: God's complete sovereignty. God rules totally and mysteriously over all of creation, including election to salvation. One cannot earn or buy that gift. Likewise, one cannot refuse it. God's grace is irresistible and prompts an inward call that responds to the outward invitations of evangelists or preachers.

Calvin's doctrine of the **Perseverance of the Saints** completes God's sovereignty vis-à-vis human beings. Not only cannot the elect refuse God's grace, they also need not fear that, once gained, they will lose it. God will protect his saints (those whom he has saved) throughout their lives, bringing them to join him in heaven. If the saved could fall from God's grace, it would indicate that God's sovereignty is far from perfect.

These doctrines define all divine-human relations for Calvin. In sum, God will rightly punish sinners, but God is also merciful, choosing to save some individuals. God does this by redeeming sin through substitution: Jesus Christ's suffering and death. By taking on and discharging our debt to God for our sins, Christ returns the fallen to righteousness. In all, God exercises supreme, unquestioned, unobstructed rule. As Calvin explains in the *Institutes:*

> The will of God is the supreme rule of righteousness, so that everything which He wills must be held to be righteous by the mere fact of His willing it. Therefore, when it is asked why the Lord did so, we must answer, Because He pleased. But if you proceed further to ask why He pleased, you ask for something greater and more sublime than the will of God, and nothing such can be found. (*Institutes* 3.23.2)[1]

Critics have called Calvin's view of God's inexplicable rule tyrannical. But as Calvin saw it, God's unfettered command offers people what they expect of God: total freedom.

For Luther, God offers, in addition to supreme rule, love. Calvin emphasizes God's quality of majesty (see Harkness 1958: 74). Calvin does not deny that God is love, but in his estimation such majesty places less of a constraint on God. Essentially, Calvin allows God to hate us for our sins and to punish whom he chooses. But Calvin makes this allowance without opening God to the charge of injustice. As he colorfully explains, "The sun is not evil if its light, falling on putrid flesh, causes foul odors to arise" (Harkness 1958: 74).

Calvin ever exalts God and humbles humans. If we sin, we must look to our fallen nature as the cause. If, on the other hand, we avoid sin and do right, we must not take credit but look to God in thanks and acknowledge God's power and grace. Such dependency may look base, even cruel. But Calvin's commitment to God's sovereignty entails a certain logic. The totality of God's power requires the total inability of people. God is not being cruel; God is being God, and nothing less than God.

Joy in Suffering

In tone, Calvin's writings are redolent of Old Testament stories of retribution and stern justice. Unlike contemporary Christian spiritual writers, Calvin does not don theological slippers and gently invite the reader into a personal "relationship" with Christ. As Harkness suggests (1958: 72), in Calvin's moral

---

1. Translated by Harkness (1958: 70), citing book, chapter, and paragraph of the *Institutes*. All other translations from the *Institutes* are from Henry Beveridge's translation, published in 1599, unless otherwise noted. We use Beveridge not because it is the best translation but because of its extensive influence in the reception and development of Calvinism in the English-speaking world.

teachings, "the Decalogue looms above the Sermon on the Mount." Still, Calvin glorifies Christ as both savior and model of perfect holiness, one we can embrace in our troubled lives.

Calvin contrasts life with Christ to life under the natural law. He points first to "the philosophers," who construct beautiful moral systems only to urge us unhelpfully to live "according to nature." Calvin dismisses this approach as inadequate. God is the one and true standard by which a moral life is achieved. But, as we know too well, people find it hard to live by that standard. Thus God in his mercy set before us Christ, who not only secures salvation but also sets forth a model of living and being "which [all] our lives should express." What, Calvin replies to the philosophers, is "more effectual than this?" (*Institutes* 3.6.3). Christ's life is the proximate goal of our striving.

But what Calvin finds as most exemplary for us in Christ's life is his pain and suffering: "Ever since Christ purified us by the laver of his blood, and communicated this purification by baptism, it would ill become us to be defiled with new pollution" (*Institutes* 3.6.3). Christ's gentleness or kindness, so highly praised today, get scant attention from Calvin.

Paradoxically, for Calvin, Christ's model of suffering reinforces a certain type of joy. In commenting on the words of praise that Paul, in his second letter to the Corinthians, accords the Macedonian Christians who gave beyond their means to help other Christians in need, Calvin calls joy in adversity the proximate goal of Christian life:

> . . . while they [the Macedonians] were tried with adversity, they, nevertheless, did not cease to rejoice in the Lord: nay, this disposition rose so high, as to swallow up sorrow; for the minds of the Macedonians, which must otherwise have been straitened, required to be set free from their restraints, that they might liberally furnish aid to the brethren. (*Commentaries*, on 2 Cor. 8:2)

As Calvin explains, when Paul speaks of joy, "he means that spiritual consolation by which believers are sustained under their afflictions." Affliction opens the believer to the enjoyment of true spiritual consolation—a joy that unbelievers and wicked people miss. They either ignore the affliction and "delude themselves with empty consolations," or they collapse under the pain. Believers welcome affliction and, as Calvin puts it, "seek occasions of *joy* in the affliction itself."

Calvin explains this puzzling claim in his *Commentary on Paul's Epistles* (see Calvin 1981). He reiterates that we creatures are subject to suffering the pain of corruption and depravity not because of our nature but because of God; God allows this to be so. This sounds like a terrible indictment of God, but Calvin intends it as the opposite. If our sufferings were due only to nature, we could not hope for them to cease. We could try to conquer nature, as a Machiavelli or some modern geneticists would have us do, but as conquerors, human beings would tyrannize themselves, other humans, and the whole of nature.[2] If God allows our sufferings, however, we can reasonably hope for their cessation, for God's will is supreme and he has promised to improve our condition.

Calvin follows his observation of our dependency on God for a cessation of evils by explaining Paul's simile in Romans 8:22 that "the whole earth groaneth and travaileth in pain." The earth and its people, writes Calvin, "groan like a woman in travail until they shall be delivered. It is a most suitable similitude; it shows that the groaning of which he speaks will not be in vain and without effect; for it will at length bring forth a joyful and blessed fruit." Like a woman in labor, Calvin says, we are not content to remain in our present state. And yet we are not so beaten down that we should sink into depression without any hope of an end to our suffering. We suffer in the hope of "restoration to a better state." Calvin also picks up on Paul's suggestion that our labor is nearing its conclusion. How terrible it would be, then, for us to give up, right before we reach that end!

Through his own great suffering, Christ gave birth to a new order of existence and to human atonement with God. Even in suffering, Christ was pregnant with great possibility. So too, Calvin suggests, we must suffer our labor pains, looking to Christ as our model. Those pains reflect the end of human life in death. But Calvin argues that the pains of labor also point toward new life and triumph over death. So too, if we have faith, our spiritual pains inspire us with hope, with a conviction that salvation will come. That is why Calvin emphasizes Christ's sufferings as a model and asks us to seek afflictions and press them close.

Giving and Good Works

Even couched in hope, waiting and suffering might sound like spiritually empty ways to live. It is true that, in his sermons and writings, Calvin tends to focus more on human intentions and understanding than on concrete actions. But he does intend that understanding should result in actions: besides being a great preacher and theologian, Calvin was a surpassing legislator, whose decrees ordered every aspect of the lives of his Genevan subjects. The Christian life offers a model not only of suffering but also of acting.

Calvin thus tackled the thorny problem of the relationship of faith and works. Question 86 in *The Heidelberg Catechism,* inspired by Calvin's teaching and published in Germany in 1563, summarizes the problem starkly. "We have been delivered from our misery by God's grace alone through Christ and not because we have earned it: Why then must we still do good?"

---

2. For a book-length treatment of this claim, see Lewis (2001).

His answer summarizes in condensed form the whole of Calvin's understanding of good works. "To be sure, Christ has redeemed us by his blood," *The Heidelberg Catechism* says. "But we do good because Christ by his Spirit is also renewing us to be like himself, so that in all our living we may show that we are thankful to God for all he has done for us, and so that he may be praised through us." The answer continues, "And we do good so that we may be assured of our faith by its fruits, and so that by our godly living our neighbors may be won over to Christ."

According to Calvinism, true faith, which proceeds through the word of God and the Holy Spirit, regenerates sinners, making them new persons, causing them to live a new life, and freeing them from sin's bondage. Although he explains it somewhat differently, Calvin follows Luther in arguing that such faith does not arise from human striving or will. God gives us faith; we do not generate it ourselves.

The saved, then, are not freed from the responsibility to live well. Without faith, human beings would act out of self-love or fear—and "never," Calvin says, out of love of God. It is impossible, he continues, for true Christian faith *not* to produce works that please God. Yet we must still remember that good works do not save. Quite the contrary: "it is by faith in Christ that we are justified, even before we do good works; otherwise they could not be good works, any more than the fruit of a tree can be good before the tree itself is good."

The "tree" in this metaphor is not humanity or human nature but faith in Christ. Human nature can do nothing good on its own, yet faith in Christ turns this fallen nature into something new, something worthy. Good works follow as a natural result. They do not establish a claim upon God. Rather we must thank God that we can do them. Good works are an expression of human gratitude toward God. In this respect, one could say that the attitude and practice of gratitude defines the proximate goal for human acting.

Good works also affect those around us and draw them toward the Christian life. Such conversion will likely improve our lives, spiritually and even materially. Calvin emphasizes this more worldly effect of good works in discussing, in his *Commentary,* Paul's comparison of almsgiving to sowing. On the face of it, Calvin says, sowing seeds looks like throwing them away. They disappear into the dirt and seem lost. But as the farmer gains rather than loses by sowing, so God requites our giving with "large interest."

This double-digit interest that accrues to our acts of goodness is truly a dividend, not principal. Giving to the poor will not affect salvation but it will enrich our enjoyment of salvation. The harvest that the farmer reaps from sowing also refers to "earthly blessings, which God confers upon the beneficent." As Calvin interprets Paul, "The more beneficent you are to your neighbors, you will find the blessing of God so much the more abundantly poured out upon you." Earthly life may be characterized by lack, inability, and suffering. But for the saved, suffering is conditioned and alleviated by some blessings, which confirm their election.

It is worth briefly comparing Calvin and Luther on good works. Though Luther saw liberality as important and necessary, he made spiritual witness the chief means by which to distinguish the saved from the lost. Calvin accepts this criterion but emphasizes righteousness and moral activity as a sign of salvation. As Harkness writes in her life of Calvin, "Luther was a mystic; Calvin a man of action. Luther looked upon the saved man primarily as the vessel or receptacle of the Holy Spirit; Calvin regarded him as the instrument or tool by which God's will is wrought." Paraphrasing Calvin's own words, Harkness concludes (1958: 79–80), "Faith must be an effectual faith, revealing itself in outward deeds."

Such a faith, and thus good works, stand for Calvin as the goal for human action, even if it is a goal humans cannot reach by their own efforts. For this reason, Calvin's model Christians cannot be only people of action; they must be mystics of a sort as well. Calvin demands that we prepare ourselves to receive the gift of grace by acknowledging God's majesty and total sovereignty. This brings us to a state of humiliation that people today, inheritors of modernity's pride, find uncomfortable. Calvin's doctrine of election, while hardly democratic, awakens us to the hope that suffering is not an endless torment but the labor preceding birth and regeneration into new worlds.

Dealing Gratefully with the World

God's Ownership

The Calvinist *Heidelberg Catechism* (1563) opens by posing this question: "What is your only comfort in life and in death?" The correct reply is: "That I am not my own, but belong—body and soul, in life and in death—to my faithful Savior Jesus Christ." As this text suggests, Calvinism finds comfort and security in a kind of spiritual ownership. Where English empiricism posed that modern human beings ultimately are their own property (Locke), stock and barrel, the Calvinist locates the title to their life in God.

Calvin's understanding of property and wealth is much debated. Although Max Weber's claim is much criticized—that a Calvinist "Protestant work ethic" inspires an attachment to the world and pursuit of material things—it still resonates a century after Weber made it. In this section, we consider, briefly, the theological underpinnings of Calvin's views on property and wealth, then turn to Calvin's illuminating comments on prosperity, morals, and usury. We will conclude by reconsidering Weber's thesis in light of Calvin's teaching about wealth and property.

Calvin infuses his understanding of God's sovereignty with more common Christian sources to develop his view of property. Like many Christian thinkers, Calvin begins with the belief that all things belong to God. God's complete ownership stems from his role as the Creator. But for Calvin, the work of creation does not provide God title to all things. Calvin sees that such a claim could degenerate into the argument that God's labor vests ownership of the product. But God labors not. Nor does God create with any means of production other than divine will.

Instead, Calvin emphasizes the free nature of creation (see *Institutes* 3.7.4). Because God's sovereignty is complete, because he is omnipotent and mysterious, no one can state *why* God created. The creation must stand as a completely free and spontaneous act. To speak of the freedom of creation is a positive way of saying that God's creation does not depend upon anything else. Nothing hinders or helps God in creating. This inexplicable freedom, and not the resulting "product," vests God with ownership in the whole of things. It also highlights God's liberality, or free giving. God is primarily the ultimate giver, not just the ultimate creator.

But Calvin does not look only to creation as proving God's ownership of the cosmos and all its inhabitants. Calvin's emphasis on God's sovereignty could reduce creation to an ultimately insignificant object of interest when compared with God himself. But the stories of the Old and New Testaments, and above all Christ's life, death, and resurrection, transform the relationship between God and the created world and so transform our understanding of God's ownership.

Christ lifts creation—or one part of creation—above insignificance. Christ singles out humankind for a new, special relation to God. In speaking of property, Calvin emphasizes that through the incarnation and resurrection, human beings become part of a new body, the body of Christ. As he warns in *Institutes,* "Ever since he engrafted us into his body, we, who are his members, should anxiously beware of contracting any stain or taint" (3.6.3). Calvin's point is that human beings, or more precisely the saved, no longer belong to themselves alone. No one does, besides God. The saved become organic elements in the divine who in a vital way advance the divine activity.

Calvin suggests that membership in Christ's body should instill a certain detachment toward the rest of the created world. When Christ reconciled humanity to God, attachment to the world's good might have been understandable. After all, God told our forebears to work in the garden and tend it. But after his metaphor about becoming part of Christ's body, Calvin continues, "Ever since he who is our head ascended to heaven, it is befitting in us to withdraw our affections from the earth, and with our whole soul aspire to heaven" (*Institutes* 3.6.3). Because of the intercession of Christ, we are no longer truly of this world, nor is it our home.

Being members of the divine body and agents of the divine work should, in Calvin's view, change our understanding of property in other ways as well (see Harkness 1958: 176–177). Since God freely created everything, and then deposited special trust in human beings (in Eden and through Christ), all possessions are held in a sort of sacred trust from God. "No man can be deprived of his possessions by criminal methods, without an injury being done to the Divine dispenser of them" (*Institutes* 3.8.45, quoted in Harkness 1958). Theft and fraud are not only crimes against natural law. Much more importantly, they offend God, for they upset that trust.

Nor does greed pertain only to taking another's material possessions. Calvin teaches that to fail to serve one's neighbor, whether by paid labor or simple kindness, is to rob our fellow being and offend God. Such injury, he said, "relates not only to money, or to goods, or to lands, but to whatever each individual is justly entitled to; for we defraud our neighbors of their property, if we deny them those kind offices, which it is our duty to perform to them . . . [likewise] if . . . a master inhumanely oppress his family, God holds him guilty of theft" (*Institutes* 3.8.45, quoted in Harkness 1958).

Calvin's understanding of property is as expansive as his understanding of God. Human beings tend to regard as property moveable material goods, land, and perhaps the products of their intellect and art. Such definitions reveal our intellectual, imaginative, and moral limitations, in Calvin's view. Everything belongs to and is due God, including our service to one another. Such goodness becomes all the more obligatory as we conceive of ourselves as members in the body of Christ.

Asceticism and Moderation

Calvinists are often associated with a perceived asceticism and even an extreme form of it. Such views are not wholly without basis. Some residents of Calvin's Geneva agitated to ban church bells as tokens of popery. And the New England Puritans, Calvin's spiritual heirs, took a harsh view of theater, singing, dancing, wearing finery, and eating fine foods. The prohibitions of Puritan Boston do bear a general resemblance to the dictates by which Calvin governed Geneva.

Nonetheless, to call Calvin an ascetic with regard to worldly goods is to perpetuate a misunderstanding. Calvin understood the dangers of excessive attachment to goods. But he also recognized that asceticism, taken to extremes, could become a kind of religion in itself—in other words, a form of idolatry.

Following an ancient formula, Calvin divided the worldly things into three classes: the obviously good, the obviously harmful, and the indifferent—those which could be good or bad depending upon the use and context. God, being beneficent, wants us to pursue the good and avoid the harmful. But what about the indifferent, which comprise a large number of things, including many foods and drinks? Calvin exercises his judgment and, again in the manner of Luther, affirms human liberty: "We are bound by no obligation before God respecting external things, which in themselves are indifferent. . . . And the knowledge of this liberty also is very necessary for us; for without it we shall have no tranquility of conscience, nor will there be any end of superstitions" (*Institutes* 3.19.7).

Calvin's reference to superstitions is critical, for it points to the spiritual danger of asceticism. Superstition, enhanced by extreme asceticism, wreaked havoc on Salem, Massachusetts, in the early 1690s.

Not that Calvin would have his followers become libertines: "Many in the present age think it a folly to raise any dispute concerning the free use of meats, of days, and of habits, and similar subjects, considering these things as frivolous and nugatory; but they are of greater importance than is generally believed." People should not, however, devote more attention to dietary laws and the like than such things deserve. "Once fallen into the snare," the human conscience "enters a long and inextricable labyrinth, from which it is afterwards difficult to escape" (*Institutes* 3.19.7). Once people proclaim that God does not want us to drink wine, they soon find themselves arguing (and perhaps killing each other) over whether they can drink anything besides water.

Calvin doubts that divine law speaks with precision about such things. For political purposes, he once made an ill-starred effort to restrict alcohol sales in Geneva. But he never attempted prohibition, and he never defends asceticism. His judgment rests upon an appreciation of human liberty directed at gratitude for the divine gift of worldly things. He does counsel that the saved, as members of the body of Christ, separate themselves as much as possible from the world. But that separation need not extend to despising a moderate enjoyment of the pleasures and good things of this earth.

That qualification, moderate enjoyment, was of great concern to Calvin. He knew that human beings have never had an easy time reconciling freedom with moderation: "All things that are connected with the enjoyment of the present life are sacred gifts of God, but we pollute them when we abuse them." His concern for abuse and pollution explains why Calvin sought legislation to restrict outward expressions of enjoyment, such as theater, games, and luxurious clothing. Permitting such things, he feared, would lead to their abuse. Calvin also feared that outward expressions of pleasure might draw people's hearts toward worldly goods and away from their source, God. Finally, Calvin's conviction that those who are saved long for release from this world also weighed in his pursuit of restrictions. The issue was not simply our use of the worldly things, but how that use affects our relation to God. These beliefs do not make Calvin an unrelenting ascetic. The body of Christ enjoys pleasures too. But its members should not forget preparation for a life following this one:

> He who commands us to use this world as though we used it not, prohibits not only all intemperance in eating and drinking, and excessive delicacy, ambition, pride, haughtiness, and fastidiousness in our furniture, our habitations, and our apparel, but every care and affection which would either seduce or disturb us from thoughts of that heavenly life, and attention to the improvement of our souls. (*Institutes* 3.10.4)

Calvin asks less for asceticism than for moderation. But unlike the form of moderation extolled by ancient philosophers or modern environmentalists, Calvin's moderation does not find its standard in our "natural state." It is intended, in fact, to free our thoughts from nature as we make our ascent to heaven.

Calvin and Prosperity

Far from being a booster of consumer capitalism, Calvin expresses a lively concern for the perils of prosperity. In this respect his thought jars with secular opinions today. From America's birth as a nation up through the mid-twentieth century, most people have held an unquestioning faith in the goodness of prosperity. Calvin holds a different view.

In Calvin's eyes, scarcity is not something to complain about. All things come from God, and when God sends us abundance we tend to misuse his gifts. If people have a lot to drink, they get drunk and begin to make trouble. Even worse, they have a tendency to swear oaths and speak scandalously about God. In the same way, if people have a lot of any other earthly goods, they become drunk with prosperity. That fountain of sin, pride, wells up in their hearts, and they will suffer neither instruction nor correction. In addition, when stuffed with pride, they act cruelly toward each other, and whoever has the most often ends up lording it over his neighbors. This is what people do when times are "good," and so God changes his policy and send us scarcity, in order to bring about true humility. Scarcity is not God's fault, but our own.[3]

Calvin's God has other reasons to send or withhold prosperity. For example, when God sends prosperity, "the affluence of our blessings is to try our frugality." God gives us an opportunity to practice the virtue of moderation, to keep ourselves back from excess and abuse. Likewise, when God gives us more than we need, he tests our gratitude, to reveal what we will do toward others. As Calvin explains, God takes pleasure when we pursue moderation in abundance, for it shows our gratitude (*Commentaries*, on Zech. 9:15). A much degenerated form of Calvin's virtue lives on today in the proverbial rich Yankees who wear moth-eaten sweaters, keep the heat at 50 through the New England winter, and refuse to give more than a few dollars to charity each year, though in each case they could afford much more.

Such are the tests posed by prosperity, in Calvin's view, but no one should race to embrace them. They are difficult, and few pass. For these reasons, Calvin looks upon prosperity with a wary eye. He warns the wealthy that God has given them a dubious blessing: "Dangers attend both poor and rich, but the poor are safer. A small boat on a streamlet may strike a tree along the bank, but it is safer than a ship on a tempestuous sea." Calvin continues, "The rich are like those who skate on ice and are apt to fall, or like those who walk among

---

3. See *Commentaries*, Sermon on Deuteronomy 28:46–50, and Lecture on Jeremiah 42:13–17.

thorns and must walk carefully lest they be pricked" (*Commentaries,* Sermon on Job 2:2–5).

But, we must be clear, Calvin does not warn the rich to be frugal and careful for various earthly reasons (e.g., fear of natural disasters, political turmoil, or the vicissitudes of chance). His admonitions rest, ultimately, on Calvin's view that God exercises total control over earthly property and we are to live accordingly:

> As the Psalmist shows, it is in vain to rise up early in the morning, and go to bed late, and drink water and eat only half enough bread; that will advance one not at all unless God extends His hand and bounty. On the contrary, goods sometimes come to His children as they sleep. And this shows that men err if they think they enrich themselves by their own merit. (*Commentaries,* Sermon on Deuteronomy 8:14–20, ref. to Psalm 127:2)

Likewise, Calvin here is not preaching fatalism or a total withdrawal from the world. If they withdraw from the world, the saved cannot perform good works.

But production or preservation of material wealth can never be foremost in the minds of the saved. In the end, production and preservation depend not on human beings but upon God. The ownership that results remains ever an opportunity for gratitude:

> Let us walk always in the fear of God, rendering gratitude and homage to God for the goods we possess, knowing we cannot enjoy them unless it pleases Him to continue his grace toward us. Then riches will be a blessing, and like honors, delicacies, and the like, will not intoxicate men or put them to sleep, but rather will make them more vigilant in placing everything in God's hands. (*Commentaries,* Sermon on Job 22:18–22)

Owning something should not make us want merely to preserve it or to own more. Rather, it should make us remember God's generosity and seek to devote with gratitude what we have (above all our time and our labor) to God's ends.

Calvin's Defense of Usury

Calvin's view of God as the source of all property leads to his demand that we use God's gifts to promote the public good. This demand in turn helps to wreak a major economic development in European history: the removal of the ban on usury, or charging interest on loans of money. This development reveals the change in the understanding of property that Calvin's beliefs created.

Prior to Calvin, the Roman Church and most secular authorities banned usury on two grounds. Philosophically, usury violates Aristotelian precepts, which hold that making money on money is a base and unnatural form of profit. Scripturally, many interpreters read Luke 6:35 ("Lend, hoping for nothing again") as outlawing usury. As we saw in the chapter on Aquinas, people in medieval times found various ways around these prohibitions, especially when lending commodities (e.g., wine or grain). But markets in money itself were severely restricted.

Calvin attacks both grounds. He argues that, in Luke, Jesus really means that one should give rather than lend—to the poor. Jesus's comments expand our options, rather than limit them. In his own legislation, Calvin outlawed charging interest to the poor; but he allowed interest to be charged in other transactions. Calvin also argues that other passages in the Bible held to outlaw interest (such as Deuteronomy 23:19) are meant either to apply to particular political situations or to target fraud rather than usury (see Harkness 1958: 205).

Calvin also knocks over the Aristotelian prohibition, which claims to rest on natural law. In response to the charge that it would be "unnatural" for money to give birth to money, he replies,

> What does the sea beget? What does the land? I receive income from the rental of a house. Is it because the money grows there? The earth produces things from which money is made, and the use of a house can be bought for money. And is not money more fruitful in trade than in any other form of possession one can mention? Is it lawful to rent a farm, requiring a payment in return, and unlawful to receive any profit from the use of money? (*Letter to Sachinus,* 7 Nov. 1545, cited in Baumer 1978: 231)

Here Calvin attacks a caricature of Aristotle's argument rather than the argument itself. As we saw, Aristotle condemns usury not for lacking the fertility of the sea or land but rather because fishing, farming, and usury all instill specific ways of life, and in Aristotle's judgment these have different degrees of moral worth. Calvin's response does not reflect Aristotle's understanding as much as Calvin's own assumptions about nature and human occupations. Because God is supreme, and nature lacks any force of its own, arguments about what is natural (for human beings or anything else) mean little to Calvin.

Calvin concludes with guidelines governing usury: First, one must not take interest from the poor. Second, one must do right and not only seek gain. In other words, the lender must exercise care not only for the principal lent but for the good of the borrower. Third, one must obey the equity demanded by the Golden Rule. Fourth, the borrower must earn more on the money than the lender—a rule Calvin includes to ensure that usury promotes more than the good of lenders. Fifth, one should obey the word of God in such transactions, not local custom or law. If local law allows exorbitant interest rates, one must not take advantage of that allowance. Sixth, each party to the transaction must contribute to a public good.

The Spirit of Capitalism

This embrace of usury appears to prove Weber's claim that Calvin inevitably fosters the "spirit" of productive capitalism. Capitalism is the ownership of the means of production by those who do not contribute labor to production—and the corresponding reduction of those who do labor to wage-laborers. By the "spirit of capitalism," however, Weber meant something larger, which may exist without capitalism proper. This "spirit" is a felt obligation to make the goods of the earth as productive as possible. Allowing money to make money amidst restricted consumption would almost seem to define that spirit.

Weber links Calvinism, and specifically Puritanism, to the spirit of capitalism by means of the Calvinist view that everything in this life and the next depends on election (Weber 1950: 110–111). Under this view, it is of the greatest importance to know whether you have been elected. Calvin teaches that good works stem from election. But—and this is crucial—Calvin himself did not teach that election was manifested by visible signs. However as Calvinism mutated and spread, as Weber shows, good works did come to be seen as a convincing, visible sign of election (Weber 1950: 115, 121).[4] Since God's election is eternal, it results in not a few good works, but a constant, thoughtful lifetime of them (117–118). This constant do-gooding, coupled with the Calvinist doctrine of human depravity, gives the Calvinist worldview an anti-sensual or ascetic form (103, 119). The individualism instilled by predestination also takes the form of an individual quest to better the world through one's work or vocation, ostensibly for the glory of God (104–106). Finally, in Weber's view, such betterment over time rationalizes social arrangements for the good of people, not God (108–109).

Scholars have attacked Weber's argument, and on good grounds. Most troubling is his deduction of this argument from Calvinists who might have distorted their master's teaching rather than from Calvin himself. Troubling, too, is the effect that Weber's argument has had on the understanding of Calvin's thought. Many have taken it to mean that Calvin thought that if you are rich, you are saved: that possessing wealth indicates salvation. This clumsy claim contradicts Calvin's own testimony: "The elect differ externally in this life in no way from the damned . . ." (*Letter to Bucer,* cited in Weber 1950: 110). Also, Calvin explains, faith may be subject to various doubts, but in the elect these resolve into an inner—an unseen—tranquility (*Institutes* 3.2.37). Finally, Calvin argues that no external signs reveal election. "God does not always declare his love to those on whom he bestows uninterrupted prosperity, nor his hatred against those whom he afflicts" (*Institutes* 3.2.38). The elect form a "church invisible."

Weber was nevertheless on to something. Calvin's denunciation of nature as depraved makes Calvinism receptive to capitalism, which reduces labor and different occupations (with their accordingly different lives and manners) to

---

4. A significant departure from Calvin's views, but present even in the great Calvinist confessions of faith, e.g., *Belgic Confession* 29. See Weber (1950: 237n88). These were reproduced in pamphlets throughout the Reformed Churches.

an undifferentiated "capital," devoid of any nature besides productivity. Calvin does not actually take this step, but his principles are vulnerable to it. Capitalism and its "spirit" existed before Calvin; Machiavelli is especially important in its development (see Harkness 1958: 173 and 188). It would be safer to say that Calvinism became a powerful "carrier" of the spirit of capitalism rather than its source.

But that amounts to saying that, in carrying the "spirit of capitalism," Calvinism broke with its founder. It is not quite so black and white as that. Calvin's thoughts about property and wealth are more nuanced than usually supposed. As we have seen, Calvin ascribes ownership of all things to God, and membership in the body of Christ to the saved. It is hard to imagine reducing the body of Christ to capital. Calvin's beliefs bring with them the duty for us to use our sacred trust (tangible property and our talents) to further God's ends on earth. He does not promote asceticism, but he warns us that to be moderate about prosperity is a test that, more than likely, few pass. Nature or arguments about nature should not restrict our use of God's goods (e.g., through usury), but our ultimate duties toward God and our neighbors must do so.

In the end, then, it seems fair to say that, in Calvin's view, wealth depends not on possession but on attitude, and above all, on the belief that you depend upon God for all things. Without that attitude, possessions do you no good; in fact, they more likely will harm you. You must distinguish, then, between possessions (goods) and wealth broadly considered. You may come into possession of things many ways: through hard work, luck, or theft, or even while sleeping. Such possessions signify nothing about your soul or merit. These things become wealth, that sacred trust, when you recognize your dependence upon God (and membership in Christ's body) and carry out the vocation to use possessions for the good of the Church and humanity. Once more, we see that the right understanding of property and wealth depends, for Calvin, on gratitude.

Discernment: Finding Ourselves in Others

The Ambiguities of Command

The bedrock of Calvinist theology as described above—the taint of Adam's sin on human nature, a total commitment to God through justifying faith, God's election of some to salvation, the good works that the elect perform to praise God—gives rise to several choices about the use of resources couched in different contexts. To do good works (such as give) we must repudiate our natural inclinations (especially self-love): we must deny our (natural) selves. The saved embrace this step not as individuals but as members in Christ's body, the Church—and this body forms the obvious primary recipient of their giving. Likewise, as everything belongs to God, nothing is ours, and nothing we possess will do any good unless we devote it to others or God.

Discernment concerning resources begins, for Calvin, with commands, not those of human law but of God. For example, God commands us to give to those who need—and loves for us to obey willingly (not under duress, guilt, or any other "carnal" motive, as Calvin says). But he does not specify amounts or recipients.

This element of Calvin's thought is expressed in his *Commentaries* as he discusses Paul's second letter to the Corinthians. After describing the generosity of the Macedonian Christians (2 Cor. 8:8), Paul says, "I speak not according to commandment." Calvin explains the meaning of Paul's words this way: "He qualifies his exhortation, by declaring that he did not at all intend to compel them, as if he were imposing any necessity upon them, for that is to *speak according to commandment,* when we enjoin any thing definite, and peremptorily require that it shall be done." Then Calvin imagines someone asking in return, "Was it not lawful for him to prescribe what he had by commandment of the Lord?"

Calvin replies, "The answer is easy—that God, it is true, everywhere charges us to help the necessities of our brethren, but he nowhere specifies the sum." Calvin offers a qualification: "after making a calculation, we . . . divide between ourselves and the poor." However, even this specification remains vague: "[Paul] nowhere binds us to circumstances of times, or persons, but calls us to take the rule of love as our guide."

Calvin here is not justifying our giving less to other people. Quite the contrary. He intends his discussion to open wider our choices for giving: "True, indeed, it is certain, that we owe to God, not merely a part, but all that we are, and all that we have." But he would protect his followers from asceticism or a fanaticism that demands depriving themselves of all things: "In His kindness [God] spares us thus far, that He is satisfied with that participation of which the Apostle here speaks." And he also intends to affirm that Christians need not feel bound by the exact precepts of the Mosaic code, as distilled from the Pentateuch: "What he teaches here you must understand to mean an abatement from the rigor of law" (*Commentaries,* on 2 Cor. 8:8).

Calvin is often viewed as a strict legalist. But he cared about the spirit of the legislation he proposed and its impact. As his remarks on Corinthians show, his trust in legislation extends only to its ability to meet particular needs in particular places at particular times. As far as giving generally is concerned, he looks to no law. True, he begins with the precept that we "divide" what we have between ourselves and the poor. But he does not make even this division (which would demand more than the Old Testament tithe) an inflexible rule. One suspects that he offers it less to guide actual giving than as a reminder of the importance to apply the principles of God's ownership and care for others in our plans and projects concerning wealth.

The Law of Love

Calvin's foremost concern is not with law but with love. The first step in making choices about giving, then, is not external but interior: one must purify one's love. This is no small task, and to understand it we must go to the heart of Calvin's teaching about human motivations.

Calvin begins by focusing on what the Bible emphasizes, care for others: "Let us therefore hold that our life will be framed in best accordance with the will of God, and the requirements of his Law, when it is, in every respect, most advantageous to our brethren." He then calls for judgment in applying this law to oneself and others. "In the whole Law, there is not one syllable which lays down a rule as to what man is to do or avoid for the advantage of his own carnal nature." That omission is due, Calvin explains, to the natural inclinations of the human heart: "And, indeed, since men are naturally prone to excessive self-love, which they always retain, [however] great their departure from the truth may be, there was no need of a law to inflame a love already existing in excess" (*Institutes* 2.8.54).

Calvin concludes about the law: "Hence it is perfectly plain, that the observance of the Commandments consists not in the love of ourselves, but in the love of God and our neighbor; and that he leads the best and holiest life who as little as may be studies and lives for himself; and that none lives worse and more unrighteously than he who studies and lives only for himself, and seeks and thinks only of his own" (*Institutes* 2.8.54).

As many theologians did before him, Calvin looks to Mosaic law not only for precepts for action but also for seeds of understanding. What he finds is care for others and disregard for self. This form of care is the earthly reflection of our supreme gratitude toward God. We give because God has given to us.

As we have seen, Calvin is not an ascetic when it comes to enjoying the goods of the earth. But he does regard an attitude of self-disregard as the starting point of deliberation about resources: "Self-denial gives us the right attitude toward our fellow men. Moreover . . . self-denial has respect partly to men and partly (more especially) to God." What he has in mind here is a sort of contest, into which God plunges us and our nature. He explains it this way: "when Scripture enjoins us, in regard to our fellow men, to prefer them in honor to ourselves, and sincerely labor to promote their advantages . . . [God] gives us commands which our mind is utterly incapable of obeying until its natural feelings are suppressed." Why? Because "so blindly do we all rush in the direction of self-love, that every one thinks he has a good reason for exalting himself and despising all others in comparison." Calvin adds thoughts that are familiar to us from his words on property: "If God has bestowed on us something not to be repented of, trusting to it, we immediately become elated, and not only swell, but almost burst with pride." Because of this pervasive self-love, though we may hide it for a time, "The poor man yields to the rich, the plebeian to the noble, the servant to the master, the unlearned to the learned, and yet every one inwardly cherishes some idea of his own superiority" (*Institutes* 3.7.4).

The antidote to this natural depravity is Scripture—not the rules and precepts of law in it but rather the spirit and attitude behind them. "This the doctrine of Scripture does," Calvin says: "It teaches us to remember, that the endowments which God has bestowed upon us are not our own, but His free gifts, and that those who plume themselves upon them betray their ingratitude." Interior introspection, he notes, can also help restrain this destructive self-love: "By a diligent examination of our faults let us keep ourselves humble. Thus while nothing will remain to swell our pride, there will be much to subdue it."

It is also important for us to remember the source of all good things when we see them in others' hands; doing so helps dispel envy and self-love: "We are enjoined, whenever we behold the gifts of God in others, so to reverence and respect the gifts, as also to honor those in whom they reside. God having been pleased to bestow honor upon them, it would ill become us to deprive them of it." This attitude brings with a corresponding social and even psychic improvement: "The only way by which you can ever attain to true meekness, is to have your heart imbued with a humble opinion of yourself and respect for others" (*Institutes* 3.7.4).

Calvin does not ignore how difficult it is for us to attain this self-denying attitude, but neither does he back away from the radicalism of his demand: "Unless you leave off all thought of yourself and in a manner cease to be yourself, you will never accomplish it. How can you exhibit those works of charity which Paul describes unless you renounce yourself, and become wholly devoted to others?" He also emphasizes how impossibly it conflicts with our nature: "Were it the only thing required of us to seek not our own, nature would not have the least power to comply: she so inclines us to love ourselves only" (*Institutes* 3.7.5).

The key to practical action, however, is to remember that all that we have "is granted on the condition of our employing it for the common good of the Church." Likewise, we must remember that we, or at least the saved, are all members of a single body: "No member has its function for itself, or applies it for its own private use, but transfers it to its fellow-members; nor does it derive any other advantage from it than that which it receives in common with the whole body." Thus, Calvin adds, "whatever the pious man can do, he is bound to do for his brethren, not consulting his own interest in any other way than by striving earnestly for the common edification of the Church" (*Institutes* 3.7.5).

Neighbors

As these passages make clear, Calvin largely equates "the neighbor" of Paul's letters or of other Scripture passages with "the Church." He demands erasing, as much as possible, boundaries between yourself and others, your family and other families. Calvin's demand localizes care and concern in the Church; the Church and its members should be our first, and sometimes only, concern.

Why, one may ask, does the Church, the body of Christ, needs such attention? After all, God is self-sufficient, and Calvin repudiates the Mosaic laws concerning temple offerings and the like. Calvin responds this way: "It is in vain to contend that you cannot enrich the Lord by your offerings. Though, as the Psalmist says 'Thou art my Lord: my goodness extendeth not unto thee,' yet you can extend it 'to the saints that are in the earth'" (*Institutes* 3.7.5). God will provide for the Church, and no member of the body of Christ will be lost. But God will also test the saints and put them through trials. While undergoing these trials, one follows the model of Christ, and shows one's own gratitude to God, by alleviating the suffering of one's fellows in the Church.

While Calvin points to the Church as the foremost recipient of our giving, he does not shut the door on other people: "The Lord enjoins us to do good to all without exception, though the greater part, if estimated by their own merit, are most unworthy of it." The Bible "tells us that we are not to look to what men in themselves deserve, but to attend to the image of God, which exists in all, and to which we owe all honor and love." Therefore, to whomever is presented to us as needing our assistance we must give help—and we have no ground for not doing so:

> Say he is a stranger. The Lord has given him a mark which ought to be familiar to you: for which reason he forbids you to despise your own flesh, (Gal. 6:10.) Say he is mean and of no consideration. The Lord points him out as one whom he has distinguished by the luster of his own image, (Isaiah 58:7.) Say that you are bound to him by no ties of duty. The Lord has substituted him as it were into his own place, that in him you may recognize the many great obligations under which the Lord has laid you to himself. Say that he is unworthy of your least exertion on his account; but the image of God, by which he is recommended to you, is worthy of yourself and all your exertions. But if he not only merits no good, but has provoked you by injury and mischief, still this is no good reason why you should not embrace him in love, and visit him with offices of love. He has deserved very differently from me, you will say. But what has the Lord deserved? Whatever injury he has done you, when he enjoins you to forgive him, he certainly means that it should be imputed to himself.

To act this way would be a triumph, for it is not only "difficult but altogether against nature." Nevertheless, we must live the words of the Gospel, "to love those that hate us, render good for evil, and blessing for cursing, remembering that we are not to reflect on the wickedness of men, but look to the image of God in them, an image which, covering and obliterating their faults, should by its beauty and dignity allure us to love and embrace them" (*Institutes* 3.7.6).

Calvin's words about our all being made in the image of God do not undermine his demand that we give primarily to the Church and "the saints." For the saints have been made and reborn, in their natural and spiritual forms, in God's image. Calvin thus extends the reaches of our beneficence. He understands that beneficence is due to sympathy, compassion, and identification with all members of the body. All such "carnal" motives would pale in comparison with loving and caring for others, not as human beings, but as images of God. Regarding pity, Calvin says: "First, they [givers] should put themselves in the place of him whom they see in need of their assistance, and pity his misfortune as if they felt and bore it, so that a feeling of pity and humanity should incline them to assist him just as they would themselves" (*Institutes* 3.7.3). But such thoughts form only the beginning of a truly Christian attitude toward giving.

The Christian attitude will bring great social benefits: we will treat the objects of our beneficence well, "just as we do not insult a diseased member when the rest of the body labors for its recovery, nor think it under special obligation to the other members, because it has required more exertion than it has returned." Not to do so, or to refuse to give without a servile return, would be, for Calvin, "monstrous." All the members of the body depend upon one another. Thus we should remember not only our dependence on God, but also upon each other: "Every one should rather consider, that however great he is, he owes himself to his neighbors." This consideration should also affect our giving, showing that there is no real line to be drawn between our own and others' goods. A true body lives in a state of complete communism of property: "the only limit to [the giver's] beneficence is the failure of his means. The extent of these should regulate that of his charity" (*Institutes* 3.7.7).

Calvin begins his true teaching on choices regarding property and giving by focusing not on law but on love. Such choices must proceed from an attitude in which self-love finds itself restricted. The fifth question of the *Heidelberg Catechism* reveals what a mighty task this is: "Question. Can you live up to all this [that is, God's law] perfectly? Answer. No. I have a natural tendency to hate God and my neighbor." Calvin is grimly set against human nature, which he sees as dominated by self-love. Good giving must begin, in his view, with self-denial. We also see here the striking reliance he puts on Scripture and its lessons in meeting this challenge. It is a reliance that leads him to envision, if only in theory and not in practice, a complete communism of the goods of the body of Christ, and universality of human care. More practically, it is a reliance that causes him to identify the Church as the primary recipient of whatever beneficence we struggling beings can muster.

Liberality

As noted, Calvin repudiates specific laws concerning giving. General precepts are fine: we should keep the poor and their needs before our eyes, as much as we do our own. We should give to the Church, to sustain the saints and our fellow members in the body of Christ. We should give to other people, for they too were created in the image of God. But he does not refine these generalities into specific rules to govern our beneficence. Calvin thus takes a somewhat unusual (for him) stance on liberality.

In Aristotle, this virtue requires a great deal of thought and practical judgment. In Calvin, liberality comes to be characterized almost by a lack of planning, for planning might imply self-concern and self-love. "What makes us more close-handed than we ought to be is when we look too carefully, and too far forward, in contemplating the dangers that may occur." When we contemplate such dangers, Calvin continues, we become "excessively cautious and careful" and "we calculate too narrowly what we will require during our whole life" (*Institutes* 3.7.7). Such thoughts reveal our carnality, sinfulness, and, ultimately, our lack of gratitude toward God.

But though he would have the giver not think at all (or as little as possible) about himself, Calvin does not make liberality a thoughtless virtue. One should think about the recipient. These thoughts provide a sort of balance to any possible enthusiasm. He explains, commenting on 2 Corinthians 8:13: "This doctrine . . . is needful in opposition to fanatics, who think that you have done nothing, unless you have stripped yourself of every thing, so as to make every thing common . . ." Communism might be the ideal in theory (for the body of Christ), but it has terrible effects in practice. Such fanatics cause such a frenzy that "no one can give alms with a quiet conscience." Calvin praises Paul's "mildness" and "moderation," for Paul asks only that "we relieve the necessity of our brethren from our abundance, not in such a way that they are at ease, and we are in want; but so that we may, from what belongs to us, distribute, so far as our resources allow, and that with a cheerful mind." Again, Calvin avoids inflexible rules. His "mild" teaching may require much more giving than the Old Testament tithe, or much less. It eschews material comfort, for the giver or the receiver—which makes sense for people who set their minds not on earth but on heaven.

Calvin helps clarify these precepts about giving through further commentary on 2 Corinthians 8:14. He considers what Paul means by saying that we should give "equally" to one another. Calvin does not take it to mean that we should give each other equal amounts (either a set figure or a set percentage, such as 10 percent of income). Rather, he looks to "equality" as demanding "a proper adjustment." Here he for once follows Aristotle to take "equality" as meaning "proportional right" (see *Nicomachean Ethics*, book V). For instance, masters owe their servants a kind of humanity and kindness, and servants owe their masters dutifulness and attention. Calvin asks that we apply such proportional thoughts to the realm of giving: "Thus the Lord recommends to us a proportion of this nature, that we may, in so far as every one's resources admit, afford help to the indigent, that there may not be some in affluence, and others in indigence." "The true rule of equity," Calvin concludes, does not require that we destroy ourself in order to help others. We give according to what we have and what the recipients need.

Because of Calvin's similarity here to Aristotle, it is tempting to interpret what Calvin calls "proportional right" as what Aristotle calls "natural right" (cf. Aristotle 2002: V.4 and V.7). But this would warp Calvin's argument. Natural right takes its standard from nature. It demands that one give to others in accordance with their natural desert, without regard to conventional law. The one who owns a horse but cannot ride it should give it to someone who knows how to use the horse well. Classical natural right teaches that knowers rightly direct all things and even all other people, for the knowers know best how to use them. As Socrates explains in Plato's *Republic,* book IX, classical natural right finds its summit not in the rule of the wise but in the withdrawal of the wise from politics in order to take up the happy care of their own individual soul.

Calvin takes issue with the very foundations of natural right. In his view no one has anything—wisdom, knowledge, skill, not to speak of a body or other material possessions—without God. God, not nature, ordains what we deserve. It makes no sense for us to find in ourself or our nature the justification for our claiming to own anything. Nor would it make any sense for us to withdraw from caring for others in order to care for our own soul. Calvin's proportional right demands recognizing from the start that the proportional differences between us, our abilities, and our properties derive ultimately from the mysterious choices of God. Once we accept that premise, we can care for one another (and, to a degree, for ourselves), in gratitude to God.

Calvin's Legacy

Though he looks to the Bible as an authority in all things, and established what some have called a "bibliocracy" in Geneva, Calvin does not produce fixed rules to govern our use of resources, in particular our giving. Instead he demands that we bow to the rule of love, which, for him, requires first humbling ourselves.

But self-denial would make a poor form of giving. Thus Calvin directs our attention to the needs of the Church and, more broadly, needy people in general, all of whom share the image of God. This universalism may seem to threaten the livelihood of the giver. Wouldn't the demand easily outstrip one's resources? It would. But God does not wish givers to destroy themselves. Calvin asks that we give with a view to what we have and what our recipients have, seeking a "proportional equality" based not on comfort but need. Such an approach expresses in more complicated terms his basic injunction, that we "divide" our goods (our attention, our care) between ourselves and the poor.

The self-denial that looms so large in Calvin's account of giving stands as the other side of one of his most important tenets: that we show gratitude toward God. God's act of creating the world can be called an act of great liberality, though in its mystery we cannot understand its essence by squeezing it into a human virtue. Still, the proper response for us is to feel gratitude. When people today explain their philanthropy by saying that they felt an obligation to "give back," they do not necessarily identify themselves as Calvinists. But in his own determined way, Calvin shows quite clearly what this attitude of "giving back," when taken to its theological and moral limits, might mean: a grateful response to unmerited gifts from God.

6 ~ᴖ

Jonathan Edwards

Awakenings to Benevolence

American theologian Jonathan Edwards will be our last interlocutor as we explore the nature and purpose of wealth in a life of faith. Although the great evangelical Puritan divine is last, he returns us to our first thinker. For Edwards, as for our Aristotle, the core question about the use of wealth is, how can we apply practical judgment to our equipment (or resources) in such a way as to achieve happiness?

Edwards lived from 1703 to 1758. As a fiery Calvinist preacher in Northhampton, Massachusetts, he helped to spark the first Great Awakening, which focused on personal salvation and so challenged the somber and increasingly intellectual tone of Puritan piety. Edwards, who displayed a mystical sensitivity to nature, was also a theologian of great significance.

Edwards teaches that human beings fall into three groups, according to their relation to God: the fallen or depraved, the awakened, and the saved or regenerate. Because human nature is depraved, all of us start in the darkness of the fallen state. Yet some individuals are awakened to the light of divinity; within them, Edwards held, a struggle ensues between the light and the darkness. The saved are those persons in whom the light conquers the darkness and so reconciles them to God.

While all people live and work with the earthly goods that come from God, only those who have awakened become truly cognizant of their source. The awakened then seek to discern what they have and what they should do with it. Edwards offers a model of discernment that emphasizes human weakness, spiritual growth, and reliance on God.

While Edwards had a strong metaphysical bent, he also continued the efforts of Calvin and other Reformation leaders to sanctify aspects of daily life, including our calling in work and our wealth. As Hall explains, quoting Edwards,

The millennial virtues [Edwards] celebrate[s] as incentives for prayer are preeminently social ones. They include the sanctification of commerce, i.e., "*holiness should be as it were inscribed on everything, on all men's common business and employments*," and of politics, i.e., "*vital piety shall take possession of thrones and places*"; church union, i.e., "*the church of God shall not be rent with a variety of jarring opinions*"; and, above all, international accord, i.e., "*the most universal peace, love and sweet harmony*," for in the millennium, "*the whole earth shall be united as one holy city, one heavenly family*." (Hall 1990: 104; emphasis added)

Edwards indeed provides a model for connecting lofty aspirations and heavenly visions with practical living.

Aspiring to True Ends

Edwards recognizes a single worthy goal in life: to be saved and spend eternity with God. But all people start this journey in the total depravity of human fallenness. This does not mean for Edwards that people are wicked or vicious. The totality of this Calvinist doctrine refers to the *extent* of human sin—not its intensity. In the unregenerate (those who remain in the fallen state), every faculty—thought, emotions, and will—is fouled by sin. Unaided by God, such people cannot live well.

The Fallen

SELF-SUFFICIENCY AND DEPRAVITY

Invoking the Old Testament, Edwards uses the generic term "Old Man" to signify the fallen. As Edwards understood it, the fallen find themselves in a struggle between their Scriptural duties and free will—the former painfully constraining the latter. This struggle reflects a deeper condition: in Old Man, the will succumbs to a self-love. The fallen cannot see and choose the true good for themselves. They cannot make or act upon estimations of true worth. They live under the sway of private appetites and passions. They hope worriedly for a personal "reward" from God, while they make claims on personal property. It is only with difficulty (and under the dictates of Scripture) that such people give "their own" goods to those who are in need.

In his account of the Fall, Edwards does not stress the corrupting influence of sin. Sin is not chiefly a product of free will for Edwards. We are rather born to sin. Our nature, as humans, is inherently deficient: We were never meant to stand on our own; we were made to be in union with God. Our deluded passion for "self-sufficiency" reflects our depravity.

God created human beings as wondrous and able appendages of Himself, and originally humans were united with God. Human nature and divine nature coexisted: the divine to govern, and the human to serve. But God did not intervene and prevent our forebears from rebelling against this role. (Edwards reasoned that God forces no person to sin or not to sin.) As a result, God withdrew His divine nature from the human, as a "light ceases in a room, when the candle is withdrawn" (Edwards 1970: 382). This withdrawal was a just and natural consequence of our rebellion: the superior nature could not coexist with an inferior one that did not know its place.

From that point on, we have been left to our own devices and subject to our own human powers, such as self-love, carnal appetites, and private affections. But these powers were not designed to rule. Like fire and money, they make good servants but bad masters. And so the sins that human beings commit flow from the sad liberation and blindness of our essential nature. The result, says Edwards, is a "fatal catastrophe" (1970: 383).

NATURE AND "FREE WILL"

One particular consequence, he continues, is the human propensity or disposition toward moral evil, which forms part of our very "make-up." In this view Edwards disagrees with devotees of "free will," who in his day were known as "Arminians" (after the Latin name of one of Calvin's main disputants, Jacob Arminius). The Arminians taught that sin springs from human will, and that no one is born predisposed to sin or not to sin. Indeed, the Arminians saw any predisposition as negating the idea of sin. They reasoned that if people sin no matter what because they are predisposed to do so, then they are not freely *choosing* to sin and thus not truly sinning. If, for example, I am naturally disposed to drink and I become a drunk, well, then, I could not help myself. And so why should I be blamed as a sinner?

Edwards rejects this attempt to locate sin (or its absence) in the freedom or unfreedom of an action. He looks to the principles governing the action, not the action itself or its conditions. Sinful deeds possess a sinful character or nature. Sinful choices may proceed from unchosen antecedents in our own nature, but these unchosen antecedents do not negate our responsibility and our sinfulness. Likewise, virtuous deeds may be virtuous even if forced. The virtue resides in the character of the choice, not its freedom or necessity.

To Edwards, the real issue is not will but human depravity. What difference does free choice make if all your choices are bad? Fallen humanity is characterized for Edwards by a mistaken fascination with completely "free" will, which denies the fundamental fact: our proper place as subordinate to God. The first step in recognizing that fact lies in understanding the true meaning of "natural depravity."

Edwards also saw the Arminian "free will" stance as a source of proud, unhealthy individualism. If sin is solely a matter of choice, the Arminians held, what we need most of all is to get a handle on our choices. We need self-control, self-mastery. (Think of the "self-help" section of a bookstore, and you have pretty much a library of Arminian thought.) The problem for Edwards is not a lack of human control but our rebellion against divine sovereignty. No amount of self-control will make up for our rejection of God. Proudly attempting to rule ourselves may only make the matter worse (see Marsden 2003: 439).

Sin may be each person's starting point, but depravity is not our fate. Edwards here disagrees with those at the other extreme, whom he calls "fatalists." They held that everything has been determined prior to our births (or particular choices we face) and that our lives follow inexorable laws that determine all possible outcomes. For them, fate has ordained our "destiny" long before we have a chance to choose. As a result, they argued that reasonable people should accept this fate and gather what enjoyment falls to them. We should not complain about "what should have been." There is plenty of fatalism under different names—cynicism, relativism, Epicureanism—in modern American spirituality that Edwards would still combat.

Edwards sees fatalism as self-contradictory. When fatalists propose accepting their conviction as a way to be happier, they imply that being happy versus miserable is within our choice. But if everything in life were fated, it would not be up to our choices and so impossible for us to influence such an outcome.

Edwards's conviction that the moral quality of an action resides in its nature, character, or principle, rather than in choice, leaves him vulnerable to the charge that he reduced human beings to nothing more than machines. Contemporary psychobiologists, who argue that our choices are "hardwired" by our genes, for example, might argue that Edwards's stance turns people into automatons, and everyone knows that a machine cannot sin. Edwards rejects this criticism. People, unlike machines, he noted, can to some degree form themselves through understanding and will. Human effort may not determine whether my actions are good or bad, but it very well may determine what kind of person I become.

In summary, the fallen state denotes humanity without God. It is a state in which people withdraw into themselves, into self-love. Delusion afflicts this state: it causes us to see ourselves as equals to God, as wise, and as possessed of wondrous free will and majestic self-control. Left to himself, Old Man is doomed to choose poorly.

But it is not a hopeless state, whose inhabitants must live like animals or automatons, because human beings do possess a limited ability to reform themselves. And they may receive something that no machine can hope for: a grace that transforms our lives and restores our ability to recognize and serve God. While denying the supremacy of unfettered choice, Edwards allows the fallen, like any good servant, to possess *some* freedom, choice, and ability to reform. The fallen state is not less than human—it is merely human. That is its wonder—and its problem.

The Awakening

In awakening, the divine light returns for a moment, perhaps for a lifetime, to the darkened prison of Old Man. As it returns, the soul awakens from its depraved slumber and begins to try to reorient itself toward God. As Edwards learned during what became known as the first Great Awakening, terrible struggles and psychological trials usually accompany the soul's awakening.

Struggle is the primary characteristic of this state. Awakening human beings are torn between two poles. Human nature tells them to look primarily to their self-interest, while the divine light draws them outside themselves, toward true virtue and holiness. It is an uphill path, for they must carry the heavy burden of human nature upon their backs.

Edwards uses struggle as a means of determining the progress of an awakening. Awakened people still live in the kingdom of darkness and sin. For this reason, their condition is marked by a "lack of relish" for holiness. The awakened pursue the light of virtue but do so painfully, and anything done with pain cannot be wholly relished. As a result, Edwards preaches, sin consists not only of that which is immoral and wrong but also of a lack of desire for that which is virtuous and good. Awakening indicates the human potential for growth, improvement, and (ultimately) salvation. We have a potential, a freedom that other animals or inanimate objects will never have. But the awakened state is still beset by the shadow of sin. Human potential does not equal holy actions or choices, and even less does it equal virtue.

For these reasons, Edwards emphasizes the importance of Scriptural duties in the awakened state. Awakening often begins with a painful recognition that we have shirked these duties. Edwards insists that the awakening soul pay strict attention to them, for they provide guidance and support. The awakened soul must, after all, not only struggle *against* sin but also *for* something positive, and Scriptural duties provide that direction. This is true even if the awakened soul experiences fulfilling these duties as a painful obedience to external constraint.

Especially at the beginning of its awakening, the soul worries anxiously about its own good; it focuses selfishly on its own reward or punishment, to the exclusion of caring about most anything else. Awakened people will weep and beg at the thought of suffering eternal punishment for their sins. The awakened human struggles to obey, experiencing Scriptural duties as external impositions rather than freely chosen ends. Struggle characterizes the awakened soul in every aspect of its life, including giving.

The Saved

REMANATION AND RELISH

Salvation stands for Edwards as the highest human aspiration. During mortal life, the saved state reunites the human and divine natures. Human nature takes its rightful place as servant and looks to the divine for guidance. This guidance may come through the word of God, but its demands are no longer seen as external constraints and obedience flows from internal motivations. To the outward glance, saved people may look and act much like people who have only begun to awaken. The differences reside inside.

In contrast to Old Man, Edwards calls the condition of being saved "New Man." New Man "remanates" or reflects, in a necessary but still virtuous fashion, God's "emanations" of goodness; in doing so, the New Man no more struggles than does a jewel that reflects the sun. The minds of saved people are shaped by the divine principle of holiness. Instead of setting up their will and other faculties as masters, they make these powers serve their divine understanding.

Understanding that true good is found in God, they recognize a true register of worth, with God at its top. They do not struggle with holiness, but come to "relish" it. Their private affections lose themselves in true virtue or benevolence. Such benevolence is the participation in the divine mind that Edwards called "being in general." They find their true happiness in union with God; they come to see all things as belonging to God, all men as members of Christ's body, and to love all creatures as God does, for God's own glory.

The saved both enter and reflect back God's own existence as far as humanly possible. In the saved, God's self-love becomes complete devotion. God emanates His goodness to the world as creation and providence, and the saved remanate it back as good works. God is being in its completeness. As God loves Himself, so the saved seek union with this complete being. For Edwards, this benevolence governs the life of the saved.

GOD'S NECESSARY RELATEDNESS

It is worth taking a moment to look closely at Edwards's understanding of God's existence, for it bears on his understanding of the saved. As a Trinitarian, Edwards attaches great importance to God's three persons (Father, Son, and Holy Ghost). God's "basic disposition" is to love Himself, in all His persons, and this interpersonal love causes God to seek to extend Himself. One form of that extension is God's creation of external reality. By creating a world, God enlarges His own being, creates further relationships, and multiplies His delight (see McDermott 1992: 97–98). As Marsden puts it, for Edwards, creation itself is a "a quintessential explosion of light from the sun of God's intertrinitarian love" (2003: 443).

Reality, in Edwards's view, therefore possesses a dynamic and divinely charged essence. It is God's disposition to love Himself that flows into creation.

This disposition extends to human beings, as we are part of reality and created in God's image. Our inclination to create relationships with others is due to our origin in God. The saved are disposed to relate to others even more, for they have returned to an awareness of God's sovereignty (see McDermott 1992: 100).

In this emphasis on relatedness, Edwards presents a contrast with Aristotle. For Aristotle, it is a fine thing to have friends, and a necessary thing to rely upon other people (e.g., for food and shelter), but at our best we exercise our souls in solitary contemplation. Aristotle's intellectual God spends eternity contemplating himself. Edwards's virtuous person and his personal God are quite different.

As we have seen, Edwards locates sin not in choices or decisions but in human nature. A choice may be dictated by our predisposition for evil and yet also be sinful. So too, the saved may exercise true virtue or benevolence on the basis of unchosen antecedents, that is, without completely free will or choice. In these thoughts Edwards's emphasis differs significantly from that of Calvin. Edwards's emphasis on human nature rather than choice also extends to his thoughts on God, and further distinguishes him from the great Reformer.

Edwards goes so far as to argue that God does not exercise choice or free will, as we understand it, but loves Himself and creation "necessarily," and that God emanates His goodness in the same way. And, once again, the saved do not live by choice or free will alone; instead, they love others and feel benevolence in a necessary manner. For Edwards, for something to be moral and necessary is not a contradiction. This combination characterizes the best state (see Marsden 2003: 441–442).

As a result, between the depraved states (the fallen and the awakened) and the saved state yawns an immense gulf—one which people cannot bridge by their own efforts. We can improve ourselves and further our awakening. But to attain true virtue and salvation requires an effort that goes beyond anything human nature can attain. It requires God's grace. Human beings can attain salvation only through God's agency, not their own. Human agency is to be aligned to God's agency.

This is what Edwards and other reformed preachers (including Calvin and Luther) mean when they echo Paul's teaching that salvation comes "through faith alone." Faith here does not mean some human striving to believe. Faith is a gift from God; that gift takes the form of belief, but its essence is grace. Grace acts as the affective core of faith, which establishes the reformed sinner in the saved state.

In Edwards's case, his doctrine of grace reflects his teaching about the origin of sin. When divine nature withdrew from rebellious human nature, human nature became mired in sin. Left to itself, it will remain there. It simply follows that people require a divine aid to stand upright; that aid is grace. Edwards's teaching here also bears echoes of Aristotle's view of the act of wishing. Aristotle taught that human beings can choose the means to their wished-for ends, but they cannot choose the ends themselves. Those ends appear to them in a moral vision not of their own choosing, and for which they rely on what he called *nous,* or intellect, the divine in man. In the same way, human salvation for Edwards depends upon entrance into God through grace.

COMMUNITY AND FRIENDSHIP

However, it is critical for Edwards that the saved state is not a solitary condition of lonely, intellectual perfection. It involves community, the coming together of human beings with each other and with God. The affection and love that characterizes saintliness reaches not only for God but also for our fellow human beings, for they are made in God's image.

Unity is a feature of the community of the saved for Edwards. He "extols social union in prayer as beautiful because 'union is one of the most amiable things, which pertains to human society; yea, 'tis one of the most beautiful and happy things on earth, which indeed makes earth most like heaven.' And it is especially so in the church. Edwards cites Scripture to the effect that unity is 'the particular beauty of the church of Christ'" (Hall 1990: 83).

He also distinguishes the importance of this interpersonal union by speaking emphatically about friendship and the conversations that support it: "For Edwards, significantly, 'the well-being and happiness of society is friendship. It is the highest happiness of all moral agents'" (Hall 1990: 119). Edwards explains further, "The need of conversation in order properly to support and carry on the concerns of *society,* may well appear, by considering the need of it for answering all the purposes of *friendship,* which is one of the main concerns of society, in some respects the main social concern, and the end of all the rest" (Hall 1990: 119). This conversation and friendship may take the form of everything from organized meetings to silent prayer. It exists among human beings alone, between human beings and God, and within God Himself. It thoroughly characterizes the saved state and provides a standard for judging the health or sickness of depraved communities.

Edwards's distinction between "pious" and "civil" conditions characterizes his social thought in general, as Hall points out:

> There are fundamentally two types of social order—the pious and the civil. The social bond distinctive and constitutive of pious society is cordial [or heartfelt] consent *qua* love, and that of civil society is cordial consent *qua* choice and natural consent. Pious society is essentially an affective and benevolent union of persons founded on the disinterested love of its members wherein they, as the objects of bonding benevolent love, have primacy as ends in themselves. By contrast, civil society is essentially a rationalist and functionalist union of persons founded on the self-love of its members. . . . The end of pious society is communion with God, and that of civil society is the expeditious realization of political and economic ends. (1990: 131–132)

Just as Aristotle teaches that the contemplative soul must practice various moral virtues in order to get along with others, Edwards accepts the necessity, in this life, of both civil and pious society. Since we live in a fallen world, we must pursue and realize political and economic ends. When faced with our depraved passions and ignorance, we must make choices and follow natural consent, that is, self-interest. But in the best state we will obey divine wisdom, live in communion with God, and love one another.

Again, the state of salvation is one best understood as an immersion in divinity itself. The saved live as God lives: loving God, loving creation, seeking union with God above all. If the fallen state reveals people withdrawn into themselves, the saved state shows humankind returned, as much as possible, into the divine embrace, and so embracing one another.

Wealth and Earthly Goods

Wealth as the Crown of the Wise

Having considered Edwards's sense of purpose, we can now examine the role that wealth plays in the pursuit of it. Given Edwards's view of the world as a fallen and shadowy realm, one might expect him to condemn its goods as tainted with sin. Edwards does criticize those made indolent by possessing riches, but he affirms the goodness of the physical world as a sign and creation of God. In Edwards's view, one's spiritual state will determine one's views of wealth, and, predictably, those views differ among the fallen, the awakened, and the saved. While these categories matter, the most important one with regard to material possessions is an individual's relationship to God. For Edwards, one's stance toward God determines all else.

Edwards's view of wealth is in general positive, but he is vigilant in condemning its misuse. The "rich" waste their time and treasure on an "indolent and useless way of living . . . in eating and drinking, and sleeping, and visiting, and taking their ease, and pleasures," according to Edwards. "They by their idleness cease to be beneficial members to human society." Edwards also has harsh words for the market economy, which he sees as threatening "the cement of any society and its happiness," and he imagines the market may lead men to act "like wolves one to another" (quoted in Valeri 1991: 42).

But Edwards recognizes that commerce and profits are human activities and thus ambivalent, and are not always beneficial as are the goods of the earth, including wealth. This recognition is based on his dual foundational premises: (1) God is the source of all, and (2) God is good. Therefore the fruits of the earth and all created things are good. This position had ample precedent in Calvinist thought. A century earlier, Thomas Manton, an English Puritan, wrote, "Riches in themselves are God's blessings that come within a promise." Citing Psalm 112 that "wealth and riches" shall accrue to him "who fears the Lord," as well as Proverbs that riches are the "crown of the wise," Manton wrote that, "from being a hindrance to grace" riches "are an ornament to it." A person who is rich and wise, he observed, "hath an advantage to discover himself which others have not." On the other hand, "a fool is a fool still, as an ape is an ape though tied with a golden chain." Manton concludes that riches are as men use them. They "are blessings promiscuously dispensed—to the good, lest they should be thought altogether evil; to the bad, lest they should be thought only good."[1]

Likewise, at the end of the sixteenth century, Puritan William Perkins wrote, "These earthly things are the good gifts of God, which no man can simply condemn, without injury to God's disposing hand and providence, who hath ordained them for natural life." Considering these passages, Leland Ryken, a scholar of the literary dimension of the Bible, asks: "Why were the Puritans so sure that money was a good thing?" His answer is simply that "they believed that money and wealth were gifts from God." "The more we explore Puritan attitudes," Ryken writes, "the more apparent it becomes that the key to everything they said on the topic was their conviction that *money is a social good, not a private possession*. Its main purpose is the welfare of everyone in society, not the personal pleasure of the person who happens to have control over it."

This is clearly Edwards's position, as Valeri attests:

> Edwards . . . took great pains to teach his people that wealth belonged ultimately to the community, not to individuals. From the mid-1730s through the early-1740s, he often preached on the Christian duty of charity to the poor, a theme occasioned by a growing number of indigents in the town. He grounded his exhortations on the primacy of the "body social" over private property; individuals were stewards of the common wealth. Giving freely to the poor, he argued in 1733, was mandated by biblical law and by "nature." Mankind had "like needs, like aversion to misery, and . . . one blood." Individuals were but "members of the natural body. One cannot subsist alone, without union with and help of the rest." Again, Edwards characterized [pure] economic self-interest as sheer brutality: "he who is all for himself, and none for his neighbors, deserves to be cut off from the benefit of human society, and to be turned out among wild beasts." Any refusal to give charity, Edwards continued, implied a perverse insistence on an individual's property rights over the rights of God. "You have no absolute right to [your goods]," he told his people, "only a subordinate right." The one who kept his wealth for himself "is guilty of robbing his master and embezzling his substance." (1991: 45)

---

1. This section relies extensively on Leland Ryken, *Worldly Saints: The Puritans as They Really Were* (Grand Rapids, Mich.: Zondervan, 1986), 57–71. Some quotations also derive from Ryken, *Redeeming the Time: A Christian Approach to Work and Leisure* (Grand Rapids, Mich.: Baker Books, 1995), 95–112.

Edwards practiced what he preached. According to his disciple and first biographer, Samuel Hopkins, he had an "uncommon regard" for the practice of liberality and urged everyone to do likewise. Edwards often spoke of how the New Testament urgently recommends charity and that the church should keep a large fund for the deacons to distribute to those in need. Edwards gave extensively to the poor, even though he had a large family and a need to buy books. According to Hopkins, Edwards always tried to give anonymously and in private (McDermott 1992: 115).

For Edwards, then, wealth, even money (which Aristotle calls "unnatural" wealth), holds power for good. Used properly, wealth is the treasury of God's earthly gifts to us. For all the sinful desires they may stir in the human heart, how much worse life would be without wealth and money!

Prosperity, Poverty, and Merit

Because the Puritans held that wealth is a sign not of individual effort but rather of God's blessing, they tended to view prosperity as a gift from God—perhaps a challenging gift, a testing gift, but a gift nonetheless. In effect, they disassociated it from the idea of human merit. After all, if prosperity is an inexplicable divine gift, what point is there to debating whether the recipient merited it? As Ryken explains, this viewpoint extended to their ideas about the absence of wealth in a person's life. Neither was poverty a sign of damnation.

The Puritan mindset drew heavily on the biblical story of the Israelites, Ryken continues, a result of which is that personal suffering and material want were actually sometimes associated with godliness. "The Puritans claimed that poverty may well be God's way of spiritually blessing or teaching a person," he writes. "In dealing with biblical passages that promise God's blessing to believers, Samuel Bolton wrote: 'But shall we judge nothing to have the nature of blessing but the enjoyment of temporal and outward good things? May not losses be blessings as well as enjoyments?'" If wealth is all that God gives us, then by this way of thinking perhaps we should total up even our losses in accounting for our wealth! These can serve as our teachers and improvers, and thereby can be counted among our riches.

In line with this thinking, reformed preachers such as Edwards do not agitate for equality in the distribution of wealth. God gives different people different abilities and different needs. Thus Perkins preaches, "We must not make one measure of sufficiency of goods necessary for all persons, for it varies according to the diverse conditions of persons, and according to the time and place. More things are necessary to a public person than to a private; and more to him that has a charge than to a single man" (Ryken 1986: 57–71).

Edwards even makes inequality in wealth an element in God's plan: "God gave some the skills, energies, and means to wealth, and did not give those means to others, so that society would be knit together in mutual dependence and Christian service" (Valeri 1991: 45). Wealth inequality prods the poor to ask and the rich to give. It occasions solidarity and friendship, two of the most important elements in Edwards's social thought. Of course, along the same line of reasoning, Edwards teaches that if there are people in a community suffering "pinching" want, then the Christians in that community have not done enough (McDermott 1992: 114).

Stewardship versus Ownership

The goods of the earth are wealth. But the proper use of wealth takes more than mere ownership. Edwards and other Puritans teach that the proper attitude toward wealth is stewardship: we should take care of, rather than simply take, these goods. We should apply them to the best end possible. When human beings cease to see themselves as stewards and conceive of themselves as possessors, sinful or carnal attitudes take control and pervert our wealth.

For example, Edwards rails against merchants' profiting through price gouging. He coaxes merchants to see such seemingly "economic" issues as pricing in a broader moral and social context, and so woos them to a higher path. Edwards regarded prices as a moral issue because they were set by people, not by impersonal market forces, as Valeri points out. Edwards, Valeri writes,

> described inflated prices and deflated currency as part of a pattern of narrow self-interest; he emphasized *"men's* raising the price of commodities." In his estimation, "a greedy sp[irit]," evident in those who would "advance their private interests on the great loss and damage of the public society," was the real cause of inflation. With moral fervor, then, Edwards condemned inflation as socially ruinous, as it "tends very much to the hurt of public society in general, to throw things in confusion; it tends to excite and provoke others to also raise [the price of] their commodities or labors. [This] issues in the great depreciating of the public medium of trade; and that is a public loss." Aware of the immediate effects of the currency crisis, Edwards also pointed out that "it tends greatly to distress the poorer part of society." (Valeri 1991: 50)

Edwards here attacks selfish pricing as a sin not only against purchasers and the poor, but also society. He does so because it promotes inflation, which undermines the social good of money. Much of what Edwards teaches about giving seeks to counteract this sinful fall into property and possessiveness. As an earlier Puritan teacher colorfully explains, in referring to the bag of money a merchant might possess, "We teach you not to cast away the bag, but covetousness."

Discernment in the States of the Soul

For Edwards, discernment plays a progressively larger role within each of the three primary states of the soul—damned, awakened, and saved—as the character of human giving moves from compulsion to choice to happy necessity.

On the first level, that of Old Man, Edwards sees a narrow selfishness and grasping attitude toward material goods, which generates the delusion of private property. At this level, little discernment occurs. Discernment begins slowly in awakening, which changes a sinner's attitude toward owning and sharing. The awakened move from dutiful, even shame-bound, handouts toward cheerful and bountiful giving. In the third stage, charity becomes effortless. And since the saved possess a maximum of liberty, their giving takes no predetermined form.

At this third level, of the saved, giving reflects not only love of other human beings but also benevolence or union with God, that blissful state Edwards calls "being in general." God, the highest being, is our being, our true source and home. Paradoxically, benevolence excites our souls because it returns us to our true home and what is truly most "our own." On this point, Edwards differs from those who praise disinterested giving, both in his day and ours.

Giving by Decree

OLD MAN'S DELUSIONS

If one is to understand Edwards on discernment, one must begin with the fallen state. The Fall, in Edwards's view, is the source of personal property. Originally, God the creator was the sole "possessor" of all things. However the earth's goods, being emanations of God's being, are possessions in only an equivocal sense. Indeed, they *are* God. God's "possession" does not dispossess anyone else, but rather serves as the most striking example of generosity.

The case is different with human beings. In Edwards's view, taking property as one's own is a hallmark of the fallen state, from Adam and Eve taking fig leaves to clothe their bodies to the piles of wealth in walled cities. The confusion in Old Man between what is inferior and superior, between mastery and service, underlies the fallen soul's notion of property as private and personal. Having fallen from grace into depravity, people no longer saw themselves as subject to the divine nature. Human self-understanding shrank, as it were, and withdrew to the walls of the body and human nature. Locked in this shaky fortress, the fallen soul deludes itself as though it were autonomous, without need of God. This view leads to appropriating property and all sinful selfishness.

As a consequence, Old Man blunders into thinking that more "ownership" of things can fortify and secure one's condition. Property claims grow from this delusion. They also reflect a human sense of inability after our rebellion, which caused the divine nature to depart from us. As we have seen, the total depravity of the fallen amounts to total inability. As a sign of this, the fallen soul believes that acquiring things will fill the void. Far from spiritualizing the earth's goods, fallen human beings terrestrialize the spiritual.

This delusion leads to ever more insistent claims of ownership, the division of the earth itself, and often, shortages and inequities in distributing its goods.

In this sense, human sin and depravity are the cause of material want and poverty in the world. But they are not the only cause, says Edwards. In His providence, God sometimes uses disasters and catastrophes to leave people, even His chosen people, poor and hungry—not to torture them, but to test, strengthen, and relieve them of temptation or perhaps to better them in other ways.

EDWARDS'S RESPONSES

Today, extreme proponents of a market economy view acquisitiveness as good: producers' selfish pursuit of profit, they say, can drive them to produce goods that meet the wants and needs of others, turning selfishness (a "private vice," to Edwards) into a public virtue. Edwards saw such an economy emerge in his day. He didn't approve of its effects, on producers or society as a whole, nor did he sanction passing off profit-oriented production as a form of charity:

> Probing [his fellow citizens'] acquisitiveness, he found bad faith. It is a shameful cover for materialism when people "plead for their covetousness" by saying that "they have a good end in their caring for the world. They call it by the name of frugality, and prudence, and diligence; they say if they have good estates they shall be under better advantages to serve G[od] and their generation; they say it's their duty." Edwards probed deeper. He took his text from Isaiah ("Woe unto them who call evil, good, and good, evil") to pose an ethical question about the improper use of commercial energies: "Put it to your own conscience whether you have been forced to use a great deal of industry and art to quiet your conscience in the liberties you take . . . to advance your own gain to the diminishing of your neighbor's." (Valeri 1991: 41)

Thus Edwards urges farmers and merchants to place their businesses "in the service of the community." As his career progressed, Edwards became more and more suspicious of the spirit of commercial life. As Valeri notes (1991: 53), Edwards goes so far as to suggest allowing enlightened rulers to oversee and regulate people's "bad tempers," which result in bad economic choices. Today, the frugal, diligent, grasping pursuit of earthly wealth is sometimes called "the Puritan ethic." Yet in this faithful Puritan one hardly finds praise of that misbegotten stance!

Edwards does not try to coax the fallen to "choose" a better course. His strategy is not to extol the goodness of benevolence—and hope that the better angels of human nature will lead them hither. Instead, he emphasizes giving by decree—our duty and obligation to give one's "own" goods to others. How does he accomplish this? Edwards takes a threefold approach.

First he reiterates that the goods of the earth belong to God, not human beings, which goes to the heart of fallen human beings' confusion about themself, material goods, and what each one "owns." Second, he points to the many biblical passages that command and praise giving as a duty. Among Scriptural duties, giving to the poor and needy, he observes, ranks as high as congregational worship or praying. And noting that Jesus never repudiates Old Testament injunctions on giving, Edwards uses these passages from the Hebrew Bible and New Testament. Third, Edwards appeals to shame and fear in order to overcome human laziness. He demands us not to expect that others will always help the needy. Others' action—or their inaction—will never excuse our own inaction. When the day of judgment comes, God will examine each one of us, to see what we did or did not do.

Edwards also puts the Church at the center of this type of discernment. He urges the Church to take an active role in discerning the proper uses of wealth, especially to provide guidance to the fallen.

> Edwards . . . pushed his church beyond private acts of virtue to institutionalized benevolence. He worked to strengthen the position and extend the activities of deacons. He explained that "the main business of a deacon" was not to care for the meetinghouse and the Lord's Table—as commonly held—but to care for the needy. In order to do this, he proposed that the church establish a "public stock . . . as it were, a bank" that would enable deacons to distribute charity quickly and expansively. . . . Benevolence, Edwards held, was most effective and consistent when channeled and organized through the church: "let private persons do their duty, but [let] the deacons be the officers to take care and see that the thing is done." . . . As Edwards put it, "when the Apostle James [in James 1:27] declares what is pure religion, he doesn't say it is to pray." (Valeri 1991: 46)

Giving by decree, through the institution of the church, is then the most basic form of giving in Edwards's moral world. Giving's enforced character may not always loom so large for sinners, but this is how it must begin. Decreed giving suits the narrow perspective of fallen man; it allows for little of the reflection and discernment enjoyed by the awakened and the saved. At the same time, giving by decree is not something that one "grows out of" through spiritual growth. We should all engage in it, Edwards believes, for it promotes the most heavenly virtue (benevolence) and the most heavenly community, the friendship and solidarity of believers and God. As Edwards explains, "in most cases an honest heart, and sincere respect to the commands of God, and an aim at the public good . . . will be sufficient to direct us" (see Valeri 1991: 53).

Discernment and Giving during Awakening

SHAME, REWARD, AND GRACE

In the awakening soul, a desire to give and an active choice to do so begin to displace giving by decree; giving emerges into a realm of liberty. Nevertheless, at least at the outset, shame plays a part in this process. The awakening soul feels shame on many fronts, and Edwards capitalizes on this to spur gifts that will benefit the poor and needy. An analogy might be the charitable work of those in our society who recognized that they had gained wealth through "bad means"—whether from trade or investment in tobacco, oil, or the sale of weapons. Giving serves as an expiation.

Shame-propelled giving tends to fixate on the hope of rewards for the giver, such as personal salvation. Initially, awakened givers give because they think it will redound to their benefit. As did pagans in their propitiatory sacrifices, they give in order to get. But shame animates giving in this state only for a limited time. The awakened soul quickly moves to hopefulness.

The reason is that while a sharp consciousness of duty and sorrow for having sinned can spark this process of conversion, neither dutifulness nor shame can take the process to completion. As Edwards emphasizes over and over, one needs the gift of faith, which comes through the grace of God, and the sinner must be born again. A conversion experience can begin humbly, as the result of a spoken word or a particular sight, or it may begin in terror. For example, as a boy Edwards nearly died from disease. This brush with death led him directly to his first joyous vision of God's sovereignty.

AWAKENED CHOICES

While it is not within our means alone to bring conversion to completion, our choices and attitudes can prepare us for it and foster the process. In his study of Great Awakening conversion experiences, Edwards offers examples of such choices and reflections. For example, awakened people reflect upon the smallness of "their own," whether that is their personal (natural) lives or their personal possessions. The awakened souls put others' good before their own, in as disinterested a manner as possible. Awakened sinners come to see humanity itself as a rather small thing: they don't love human beings for merely parochial or tribal reasons. Awakening fosters in the heart feelings of repentance, humility, and sorrow. But at the very same time it can inspire the soul with great effusions of joy and union.

To advance discernment, Edwards recommends that awakening sinners attend to examples of others' conversions. These stories show us what it is that we can hope for, and also that it is possible for us to attain it. Such attention will also create envy and thus a desire for conversion in the hearts of sinners. While this outward attention is helpful, the main action, says Edwards, is within our own souls. We must become conscious of our own wickedness, whether by listening to others' views of our own behavior, by self-examination, or by studying and meditating on Scripture and sermons.

Edwards also recommends that we withdraw from our usual routines—for example, to put aside all business except the strictly necessary and the religious. He also demands that we come to see that we cannot help ourselves solely by our efforts. He cites his young friend David Brainerd as an example. Brainerd found himself on the path to awakening, but kept slipping back into sin and despair. Finally he realized that all the while he had been secretly hoping to attain salvation *by* himself, that his prayers were laced with this selfish goal. This recognition humbled him, and he saw that he could never achieve saintliness without God's miraculous intervention. By recognizing his weakness, he found the path toward accepting God's strength, and in that strength he eventually found his greatest support.

As this example reveals, the path of awakened discernment can be a bumpy one. The sinner may progress one day, and retreat into despair or anger at God the next. Such tribulations teach us to put ourselves into God's hands, according to Edwards. Edwards found true encouragement in the doctrine of God's absolute sovereignty. In his own life and conversion, he found that fear turns into humiliation, and humiliation turns into calm.

Lest those in the process of awakening become complacent with their progress, Edwards recommends that sinners undergo tests of their faith. These examinations should be conducted orally, in order to disclose our spontaneous thoughts, by ministers or by the sinner's friends or family. We can imagine them as something in between catechism and personal therapy. Edwards's recommendation of these tests demonstrates that awakening has a communal dimension and can grow into its fullness only through the shared efforts of many people.

Finally, Edwards advises the awakening to reflect that they are not completely whole or truly independent, but are members of a larger whole. At first that whole looks like a family: Edwards uses terms of affection to draw awakened givers toward their "brothers" or "sisters" in Christ. Next that whole is seen more broadly: we should care for one another not only as though family members but even more so as fellow human beings. But even this natural union is but a stand-in for an even truer union. That most powerful and encompassing whole is the body of Christ.

In and through Christ, Edwards argues, we are all interrelated members. And so we should "give" to one another the way that our bodily members "share" nutrients and other goods with each other. Such "giving" never causes loss for some members and gain for others but rather results in wellness for the whole body. Edwards even argues at one point that none of us can be understood as truly converted unless we confess "a general benevolence to mankind" as a whole (McDermott 1992: 113).

Edwards sees this recognition of membership in the body of Christ as central to awakening. "By 1738, Edwards had come to envision a millennial future in which the church was 'one orderly, regular, beautiful society,' blessed by travel and commerce with 'temporal' as well as spiritual prosperity" (Valeri 1991: 44–45). Awakening delivers the true prosperity—material as well as spiritual—that the depraved economy vainly promises.

Edwards's advice for awakened givers is to continue to focus on Christ, to recognize that our hope for salvation and true happiness relies on God's grace embodied in Christ's sacrifice. Imitating Christ, we should acknowledge our gracious existence and give to those in need all the more. Though such giving may look proud—as though we could emulate Christ!—in truth it should inculcate a spirit of humility in our giving. As fallen beings, we give not because we can save ourselves or even less because we can glorify ourselves, but in humble recognition of how much we have been given. A spirit of humble gratitude—giving because we have received—marks this stage in the awakened person's development.

In the end, we should see Christ in both the giver and the recipient. We should give to the poor above all, for they are Christ's representatives on earth. People can testify all they like about marvelous visions and "illuminations," but Edwards would not state that they bore the true signs of being saved unless they also gave to the poor (McDermott 1992: 113). In any poor person, Edwards said, we may see not merely an *image* of Christ but, for all we know, the actual Christ. Christ also serves as the model, as the greatest philanthropist of all. Thus we should imitate his giving. We should give as much as we can, bountifully and cheerfully. In this way, the giving of the awakened blossoms into the benevolent practice of the saved.

Discernment, the Saved, and Benevolence

NECESSARY AND YET FREE

Giving by the saved remains necessary, as it is in the fallen and awakened states, and yet it is also free. The struggle ceases. The saved soul gives necessarily, effortlessly, as the sun sheds its light upon the earth. Yet this necessity does not negate the virtue of the generosity of the saved. If anything, the absence of moral struggle and choice reveals how true and wholehearted their benevolence is. The importance of benevolence to Edwards cannot be understated: "while [Edwards holds that] other forms of piety 'cost us nothing,' giving to charity was [for him] one of the few truly reliable, visible signs of sainthood" (Valeri 1991: 46).

The saved imitate God: God loves all human beings, and so the saved love all human beings. Theirs is the most comprehensive philanthropy. The saved do not love their fellow human beings simply as human, but as the lofty work and fruit of God's benevolent being. As in Aquinas's vision of charity, the saved love human beings for the sake of God, and, in truth, love themself.

Edwards here addresses those persons today who would claim to care deeply for their fellow human beings but take no interest in God. In Edwards's view, it is not enough to love only humankind; true benevolence must "chiefly consist in love to God," as the "sum and comprehension of all existence" (McDermott 1992: 102).

Similarly, since God is complete goodness, the saved seek God as the fulfillment of their own happiness. This wholehearted devotion distinguishes them from the fallen and even from the awakened, who struggle with their piety. The saved savor holiness: their devotions are passionate and joyful. Edwards experienced such piety himself, moving from a merely dutiful and even frightened believer as a child into someone whose heart overflowed with emotion and joy when he thought about God's total sovereignty.

PASSION AND INTEREST

Edwards's benevolence was not simply goodwill or compassion. Compassion is a feeling, an emotion in which we take on the pain or suffering of others, as when we grimace or feel sad when we see a dog struck by a car or a sickly, starving child on the television screen. Edwards's benevolence is not a feeling, it is not rooted in a natural sympathy with other living beings (see McDermott 1992: 105), and it is not bound up with pain. It is rooted in the supernatural, in the love of God. And we may exercise benevolence toward beings who are not suffering (such as God). What we understand today as compassion or sympathy is but a dim reflection of benevolence.

Edwards's understanding of benevolence differs even from that of his successors, notably Samuel Hopkins (1721–1803), his student and disciple, who later advanced Edwards's views from pulpits in Massachusetts and Rhode Island. A theologian in his own right, Hopkins held that benevolence must be "disinterested." Any element of personal interest in it he saw as damning evidence of depravity. Hopkins thus felt that Edwards's effusions about the soul's pleasure at participating in "being in general" showed self-interest and had to be shed.

Edwards had in fact argued that the joy of uniting with God is so overwhelming and so true that no one would willingly forego it. He did not believe that this joyous desire is selfish or narrow; it is simply the spiritual response of the saved as they recognize that they will find their true selves, and hence their true happiness, only in God. In a sense, the joy at participating in "being in general" transcends merely personal concerns. But in another sense, Hopkins did understand Edwards correctly: Edwards's vision of salvation promises complete self-fulfillment in the most secure and comprehensive vision of the self possible: in God.

GRATITUDE AND CONSCIENCE

Today many people preach that we should give out of gratitude, in return for all we have received. Edwards recognizes gratitude as a motive, as we saw with the awakening. But gratitude does not govern the giving of the saved, in Edwards's view. The saved are thankful, but they give primarily out of benevolence. After all, God created the world from his overflowing love—love for Himself, or "being in general." Similarly, Edwards explains, we respond to beauty not out of gratitude for it but because we love it as an end in itself. In the saved state, gratitude is important, but as a positive virtue benevolence comes first: we give from our immersion in God's overflowing generative love.

A similar line of thought reveals the place of conscience in the discernment of the saved. As we saw, the exercise of conscience, which may produce shame, influences the giving of the newly awakened. But like compassion, conscience is a dim reflection of the true virtue of benevolence. To Edwards, conscience provides the way to free benevolence when it is crammed into the tiny box of the personal self. True benevolence always acts with a view toward complete selfhood in God. Conscience leads self-absorbed minds, afflicted with malevolent desires, in the general direction of benevolence.

THE RANGE OF BENEVOLENCE

Edwards does not describe the benevolent work of the saved only as caring for the poor or tithing to the Church and the like. In his view, the saved possess greater freedom than the awakened or fallen human beings. Their giving reflects the ultimate freedom possessed by God. Thus Edwards does not limit the forms of the benevolence of the saved.

While most people give when coaxed by others, the saved give as leaders and so incite more giving. Edwards writes that such benevolent givers include wise and pious rulers and statesmen, and he says that they benefit the public in two ways. "First, they contribute to the public's material well-being: 'Their influence has a tendency to promote wealth, and cause temporal possessions and blessings to abound.' Second, they foster the public's moral well-being and cultivate good citizenship among their people. Thus, the influence of good rulers tends 'to promote virtue amongst them, and so to unite them one to another in peace and mutual benevolence, and make them happy in society, each one the instrument of his neighbor's quietness, comfort, and prosperity'" (Hall 1990: 196).

As such, Edwards says, the saints perform a specialized form of benevolence toward the living: offering us a taste of the union or love that characterizes heaven itself. "Besides that general benevolence or charity which the saints have to mankind," he writes, "there is a *peculiar* and very *distinguishing* kind of affection, that every true Christian *experiences* toward those whom he looks upon as truly *gracious* persons. The soul, at least at times, is very sensibly and sweetly knit to such persons, and there is an ineffable *oneness of heart* with them" (cited in Hall 1990: 249; emphasis in original).

As these examples show, the benevolence of the saved extends to the whole human being—indeed, the whole cosmos, including God, or "being in general"—and does its best to develop what good is needed. Thus when speaking of giving, Edwards focuses on the interior state or condition of the soul rather than outward acts. Whether benevolence takes the form of giving to this poor man or that poor woman, or giving time or advice instead of property, or something else entirely, we know that it must look to the good of others, spend itself as freely as possible, and reach as comprehensively as possible, in imitation of the divine emanation of benevolence. In Edwards's account, the metaphysical more than the moral impulse governs the giving of the saved. But allied to these metaphysical "reasons" are highly charged states of joy.

"Always Devise Liberal Things"

Edwards summarized his view of philanthropic discernment in one phrase in a sermon on charity: "Always devise liberal things," he preached. What matters for Edwards is not just the form that the devising takes but also the interior state of the soul that conceives the giving.

The giving that Edwards and other Puritan ministers preached had the virtue of moral exactitude, simplicity, and a crystal-clear sense of the purposes to which wealth should be put. "The genius of Puritanism was its clear-sightedness about what things are for, and that genius did not desert them in money matters," Ryken writes. "Everything depends on how a person uses his or her money." And there was no righter course than to use it for God and in union with God.

In the Puritan mind, there were many worthy ways to spend wealth, including the relief of "needy brethren," the promotion of good works, and other uses "for the glory of God and the good of others." (As Ryken wryly observes, this does not convey the impression that "income is something people have a right to spend on themselves simply because they have earned it.")

A Puritan thinker quoted earlier, William Perkins, synthesized these ways in a hierarchy of ends to which to direct our wealth: "We must so use and possess the goods we have, that the use and possession of them may tend to God's glory, and the salvation of our souls. . . . Our riches must be employed to necessary uses. These are first, the maintenance of our own good estate and condition. Secondly, the good of others, specially those that are of our family or kindred. . . . Thirdly, the relief of the poor. . . . Fourthly, the maintenance of the church of God, and true religion. . . . Fifth, the maintenance of the Commonwealth." Given Edwards's belief in the freedom of the benevolence of the saved, he may well have allowed some reshuffling of these ends. But all of them would reside within his universe of options.

And the Puritans believed that giving was an occasion for spiritual growth, as Thomas Manton put it. Watch for opportunities "to distribute and dispense your estate [rather] than to increase it; for nothing will free us from this sin so much as the continual exercise of charity," Manton wrote. Addressing his congregants, he said, "Your office is not that of a treasurer, but of a steward." Therefore possess riches "in your hands, not in your hearts; otherwise not you, but your chest, is rich."

Conclusion

Classical Wisdom and Contemporary Decisions

*The Contribution of Western Christianity
to Discernment about Wealth*

> O Wisdom, O holy Word of God, you govern
> all creation with your strong yet tender care.
> Come and show your people the way to salvation.
>
> —LITURGICAL TRADITION OF EARLY CHURCH

> I like the dreams of the future better
> than the history of the past.
>
> —THOMAS JEFFERSON

Almost every pulpit sermon on the topic of wealth and God recommends some dogma that the preachers derive from their Scripture text or denominational tradition. They translate this heritage into instructions for their congregants about how to live a godly life of wealth. So much of what we find in the myriad books, sermons, and workshops on religion and giving turns out to be quite pre-Reformation, in part because it is pre-modern in content, even in the midst of a modern market economy. When applied to our time, these financial duties appear from a storehouse of obligations framed in or in view of a previous era when wealth was plundered, stolen, or expropriated from others. Gathering a compendium of canons to be applied to the contemporary world is not enough. What is needed is instruction about a process of decision-making relevant to economic life that expands rather than confiscates wealth, raises standards of living, and reflects a concentration of private wealth in the hands of a growing but proportionately still low percentage of the population. There needs to be more attention to the spirituality of accumulation and its consequences. So here we turn to the wisdom of Aristotle and various Western Christian denominational traditions to discover a forward-looking rather than a backward-looking financial spirituality of allocation.

We pursue this fresh approach in two ways. First we have read each author in the light of the contemporary theory of agency, especially that of Anthony Giddens. Second, rather than seeking to identify or derive prescriptions for practical living, we seek to focus on the dynamic aspects of deliberation and discernment. In our view, this is where each of the six founders has the most to offer contemporary people who are faced with figuring out rather than receiving their choices in this age of wealth. More of the practical vocation of wealth needs to be discovered instead of received from tradition. This does not mean that the insights, spirituality, and exhortations from the past are hollow. It is just the opposite. They frame and direct the process of decision-making and instill values and a spiritual outlook. But the more practical, personalized, specific, and contemporary are the decisions we make about wealth and the will of God, the more we best make these decisions through deliberation about how the light offered from the past helps us clarify the path going forward.

To arrive at a new spirituality of allocation that is related to the wisdom of religious heritage, the bulk of the book inquired of the six authors their views on

- Ultimate reality;
- Penultimate reality, or the profoundest way to approach ultimate reality in daily life;
- The meaning of wealth;
- The place of material care for others; and
- The process of discernment whereby individuals deliberate how to live properly in accord with their personal circumstances.

In the remainder of this concluding chapter, we first situate our endeavors within contemporary understandings of agency. Second, we provide a synthesis of what we have discovered according to this framework of agency. We shift from covering the central topics by author to reviewing the authors by topic. In the best sense of an ecumenical effort, we offer readers the way we compare, contrast, and synthesize the teachings we have learned. Moreover, we encourage readers to formulate their own views and to set their own course in discerning riches in the service of care.

Organizing Principle of Agency

Significant strides have been made in understanding agency as the activity carried out by deliberating conscious human beings. Many writers have worked on this issue, but the key figures are Giddens (1979, 1984) and then Sewell (1992) and Emirbayer and Mische (1998). The latter authors have provided constructive contributions to clarify and improve upon Giddens's ideas.

Drawing together the work of these authors, we suggest that agency is a reflective practice of individuals by which they mobilize their capacities to accomplish purposes, desires, and aspirations. Agency reflectively takes what is at hand, introduces purposes that are partly new and partly a continuation of the past, and implements the purposes as best as possible by carrying out strategies of action. Within the framework of this book's concerns, agency takes what is latent, namely wealth, and activates it according to purposes, desires, aspirations, and values. Agency is the realm of deliberation by which individuals activate their capacity, say wealth, in the light of their ultimate goals and their more immediate purposes, desires, and aspirations in order to implement a valued earthly activity.

This can be clarified more by looking at the work of Emirbayer and Mische (1998). They recast Giddens's notion of agency into a *"chordal triad."* Their triad explains how people arrive at their practices by considering elements of the past, present, and future. This is not unlike Giddens's triad of existing conditions, agency, and desired outcomes. Emirbayer and Mische define agency as *"the engagement by actors ... in ... response to the problems posed by changing historical situations"* (1998: 970; emphasis in original in this and the following quotes). For instance, wealth holders are responding to the existing historical situation of great individual wealth.

According to Emirbayer and Mische the first aspect of agency refers to the *"reactivation by actors of past patterns of thought and action"* (1998: 971). The second aspect is the projective element, akin to what we speak about as the desire to achieve one's ultimate goal and the relevant proximate goals that are defined by desires, purposes, aspirations, and so forth. This projectivity, say the authors, encompasses *"the imaginative generation by actors of possible future trajectories of action ... [shaped by] actors' hopes, fears, and desires for the future"* (1998: 971). The final aspect of agency relates to deciding in the present what action to take. It is the practical evaluative element by which agents choose from *"among alternative possible trajectories of action"* by deciding what arrays of capacity they wish to mobilize by just what desires for future outcomes.

Drawing on Giddens and Emirbayer and Mische, our understanding of agency is that it is the array of discerned deliberations and strategic practices by which actors seek to close the gap between the existing past and a desired future. This is what all six of our authors have in common. They offer ways of life—some more imposing, others more emancipated. They suggest a theology of religious dogma and ethical tenets to their adherents about what to do or not do in regard to their material, spiritual, and moral storehouses of resources. These writers propose a general destiny for all their adherents and indicate the extent to which particular characteristics and circumstances of the agent allow for individual vocational variation within the fold. They suggest, too, a method of deliberation that purifies, frees, inspires, and fortifies the soul to discover and live out properly its personal version of wealth and the will of God.

Agency, then, is the set of practices that implement the possible choices facing agents and that constitute a perpetual migration from genesis to telesis, from history to aspiration. Making wise choices is the central practice of moral agency. A wise choice activates capacity as a means to achieve a proper goal. Notice that we do not give any particular content to what constitutes wisdom or a wise choice. But if wisdom is understood as a sensitized or conscientious normative orientation, the term is akin to what Emile Durkheim means by *morally* oriented behavior. For Durkheim and others, sociology was not the study of action; it was the study of action and its social or moral foundations and aspirations. By moral, they did not mean a particular theological or secular ethic. *Moral* was a neutral term derived from the Latin *mores,* meaning the customs, traditions, or value-laden normative currents. These mores provide the frameworks of consciousness and cultural understandings that served as starting points for meaning-infused activity of individual agents.

Our six authors from Aristotle to Edwards offer to their adherents and potential adherents a spirituality. This involves a particular understanding of individuals' worldly capacities in the light of their ultimate origin and destiny. The authors offer particular mores, values, aspirations, and purposes according to which people should put their capacities into action. And they give broader or narrower leeway for personal choice and, hence, for how far individuals are free to deliberate about putting their morally activated capacities into daily practice. Still, all their spiritualities provide teachings for a broad band of adherents and, by implication, for a universal audience. Thus the authors must come to grips with how their teachings can speak to a broad array of individual circumstances, including family, talents, education, inheritance of jobs and class, and so forth. So we find in each author a particular form of deliberation or discernment. This is the process by which the general becomes the particular for each individual. It is the process by which adherents properly apply the given theology, dogma, spirituality, and ethics to the particulars of their daily life. It is a process for figuring out and then choosing to carry out a calling in the world. It is this process of discernment that remains vital for every Western Christian tradition as the eras change. And this is the reason for this book and the following synthetic summary: namely, to guide today's wealth holders to take the religious heritage they cherish and move more wisely from the general to the particular in doing the will of God in the twenty-first century.

In our thinking, then, agency is the implementation of practical-evaluative choices in the light of historical conditions and directed toward a projectivity of aspiration. Agency revolves around genesis, telesis, and choice—what Emirbayer and Mische call routine, purpose, and judgment (1998: 963). In regard to the past, agency is situated in what is given. It occurs within the conditions comprised of normative and existential frameworks of thinking, feeling, and acting. It is composed of human and material resources (Giddens 1984; Sewell 1992). In turn, agency is directed toward accomplishing one's normative and utopian frameworks, and toward creating new distributions or orders of human and material resources. Agency is the realm of human causal practice of choice that draws on starting conditions (personal and social) of capacity and moral foundations in order to generate purposeful outcomes (personal and social) which, in turn, create new starting conditions of capacity and purpose.

Agency, to reiterate, is not just acting. Agents are deliberating actors—conscientiously drawing on and directing what Giddens calls the "enablements and constraints" of their domains of capacity. For the religious and spiritual person, these enablements and constraints are not just material, but philosophical and theological. It is to the five philosophical and theological elements of agency in regard to wealth allocation that we turn, synthesizing by element rather than by author.

Ultimate Realities

The moral aspirations or purposes which our thinkers discuss range a wide gamut, from Aristotle's thoughts on happiness to Edwards's ecstatic praise of remanation. All connect the aspirant with the spiritual, though within very different frames.

For Aristotle, the ultimate purpose of human life is happiness, understood as an activity of the soul in accordance with virtue. This happiness takes the form of "being-in-action," a full energizing of human potential that comes through excellent habits and thought. Aristotle's highest virtues can be most neatly summarized as wisdom (excellence in thought) and friendship (excellence toward others).

These virtues resemble with significant differences the virtues that Aquinas unfolds. But the end differs as well. For Aquinas, our ultimate purpose is not only human or natural happiness but above all supernatural happiness. This happiness is found through the virtue of charity, which quite consciously points toward spiritual union with God. This charity reflects God's own love for humankind, thereby distinguishing itself both from mercy (which looks down rather than up) and gratitude (which returns a thanks rather than originating a blessing).

Ignatius further explores ultimate purpose and its relation to God. For him, the highest end is to praise and serve God, particularly through companionship with Christ. His *Spiritual Exercises* prepare Christ's knightly comrades both imaginatively and actively. Of particular importance is the development of a stance of indifference toward anything except the inspiration induced by God's love.

Just as Aquinas resembles and differs from Aristotle, so does Luther with Ignatius, though they are so often contrasted. If Ignatius would have us become true companions of Christ, Luther enthusiastically endorses a spiritual marriage. This marriage is the active expression of the fundamental spiritual goal for Luther: opening the heart to the strength of faith, which comes from God alone.

Calvin offers a similar emphasis on God's preeminent role in bringing about the ultimate end for human beings: salvation, which comes through faith alone. This election by God brings about, necessarily, good works, just as clouds bring rain. And while it does not guarantee that the saved will live a life of comfort—indeed, more likely is a life of hard work—Calvin extols the saved state as one that lives with joy and gratitude in suffering, much as a women in childbirth.

Jonathan Edwards writes within the same faith-based tradition as Luther and Calvin, but his expression of ultimate purpose takes on an even more spiritual tone. For Edwards, the goal is to "remanate" divine love in the way that a clear jewel reflects back and outward the rays of the sun. This remanation brings with it union with God as well as social union with those saved among us.

As even this extremely brief survey indicates, all these thinkers locate the ultimate end or purpose of human life within a particular relation to reality, whether that is understood as wisdom, charity, companionship, marriage, or "remanation." Each relation may bring pleasure or riches or good works, but the quality of the relation transcends these lesser goods.

This survey also indicates how differently these different thinkers understand the ultimate end of human life. Even those who identify the end in a certain relation to God differ on the character or content of that relation. The diversity of their views underscores how little we can speak of only one "tradition," even within Christianity, and it responds well to our desire to discern our own path rather than receive one from "the" tradition.

Penultimate Reality

Accompanying each writer's expression of ultimate reality and the ultimate end of life is also a formulation of the penultimate earthly existence by which human beings best align themselves and enter into ultimate reality. Penultimate reality is the intermediate end carried out through daily activity in time and space. As an intermediate end it is, at the same time, the means that brings a soul closest to fulfilling its ultimate end. None of the authors suggests a narrow set of particular behaviors that constitute penultimate undertakings. Each does, however, formulate a broad category of activity that best represents the way of life that corresponds most fully to the ultimate purpose of life.

For Aristotle, as we have seen, the ultimate goal of life is an informed happiness. The penultimate goal of daily living that best brings us to happiness is friendship (*philia*) informed by wise choices (*phronesis*). These are means to happiness and indicate how the daily rounds of individuals exist at their best. Friendship is mutual nourishment, and is enacted throughout a range of relationships from the intimate to the instrumental. To be truly nourishing for both parties, friendship finds its content through the virtue of wise choices. Each situation of friendship requires that the parties possess an insight about what is truly nourishing and the disposition to carry it out.

As we have noted, Aquinas moves Aristotle to a supernatural plane. Aquinas joins Aristotle in speaking about love in practice as friendship, but explicitly includes God in the relationship of mutual nourishment. For Aquinas daily life best intends its ultimate purpose as the emotions and practices by which we carry out the unity of love of God, love of neighbor, and love of self. None of the loves is true without the existence of the others. In fact, Aquinas takes pains to affirm his argument that love of self is an essential ingredient in this triad of love. It is not merely an acceptable love, a by-product of the love of God or love of neighbor. It is a necessary cause and effect without which love of God and love of neighbor are imperfect.

The penultimate purpose for Ignatius is congruent with that of Aristotle and Aquinas, except that Ignatius personalizes the purpose. Earthly purpose is the *imitatio Christi* (imitation of Christ), not so much following His example as being Christ, and bearing Him and His mission into the world. The ultimate goal is to know, love, and serve God as companions of Christ and to live for eternity alongside Christ in active union with the Divine Majesty. The penultimate goal for Ignatius is finding God in all things or contemplation in action. It is an orientation and practice by which we would wend our way through life bearing Christ's standard in the earthly war against evil by becoming a heartfelt companion and imitator of Christ. At each step along the way, we are invited to a deeper interior knowledge of God, a greater personal love for Christ, and an alignment as companion, follower, and presence of Christ. Our daily call is to go where God is and to act in personal alliance with Christ as he would act given our contemporary circumstances. The more specific aspects of this, Ignatius leaves for the individual to decide by becoming emotionally indifferent to everything except the will of God, and then finding that will by feeling oneself in union with God and following the inspiration felt by the soul.

Luther is akin to Ignatius in advocating a set of conditions, rather than specific actions, that set one on the course of salvation. In fact, both authors broke with their antecedent traditions by doing much of the legwork for, respectively, the Protestant and Catholic reformations. For Luther it is not the absence of works but the absence of the works of the law that kills the potential for a deeper encounter with God and, hence, with our personal vocation for salvation and service of others. What is to be done as earthly penultimate purpose is not the mandates of externally imposed works that become rote. Work and service are the "fruitful rain" of grace and faith. Our vocation is to accept the saving grace of God, which instills the desire and ability to discover going forward the will of God for daily life. The penultimate purpose, then, is to receive, recognize, and dwell in the saving grace of Christ's redemption. Once captured and freed by grace, good and faithful servants will find that their activities emerge according to what is important to do, what they are able to do, and what brings them the joy of God.

Calvin is often misread as bringing a dour and heartless earthly purpose to his followers. On the contrary, Calvin is smitten by the graciousness of God in saving us poor souls from the devastating eternal fate we deserve. We are fallen as a community of humans; we are saved as a community. By entering into a community that recognizes and receives the gracious salvation of Christ, we too become smitten with gratitude and saved. This gratitude for the utterly unmerited blessing of salvation animates a desire to "give back" to God through good works, both material and spiritual. Such good works of gratitude enable us to be to others as God is to us, purveyors of blessing. Not surprisingly, such an interconnected life of blessing and gratitude is consoling, reassuring, rewarding, and joyful.

Turning finally to Jonathan Edwards, we find again that the penultimate purpose is to enter a process by which the relation of God to us becomes the relation of us to each other. For Edwards, God is benevolent and offers an entry into the benevolence of his kingdom for those who have devoted themselves to conversion. As God communicates blessing to those who welcome it, the saved communicate blessing to others through the intercourse (conversational and practical) of daily life. The key to living amid and internalizing this flow of blessing and benevolence is to expand its existence through community and friendship. This makes the presence of God on earth as it is in heaven.

Clearly none of the penultimate purposes expressed by our authors dictates a specific action. The authors do suggest, however, a broad category of activities and dispositions that are to be the highest calling of life on earth, the means to enter more fully into ultimate reality. More specific than the broad directives for the character of earthly life on the path to eternal life, but still leaving room for individual variation, is what the authors say about the nature of resources and how they are to be used for material care of others.

Resources and Material Care

A similar variety underlies these six thinkers' treatment of resources and material care for others. Aristotle divides human resources into three parts: psychic, bodily, and external goods, the last of which he calls "equipment." Wealth is one of these external goods, and it can be divided into natural wealth (e.g., food and drink) and unnatural wealth (money). The standard, for Aristotle, of what counts as wealth is the "good life," the happy life. And he identifies two virtues—liberality and magnificence—that help the happy person direct wealth toward the ultimate reality, happiness.

Aquinas also keeps the ultimate reality of spiritual happiness in mind when putting his finger on the danger posed by "unnatural wealth": that it encourages a sort of "virtual happiness," in which one imagines all the things one can possess through wealth without "being-in-action" with regard to any of them or toward others. This virtual happiness enables the vice of covetousness, which draws us away from others and God and toward things. Thus Aquinas asks us to consider two penultimate virtues—liberality, which for him involves indifference toward external things, and magnificence, which he derives as a sort of courage in overcoming the desire for wealth. Armed with these two virtues, the good person can pursue the ultimate purpose of charity as expressed through the tithe and other such practices.

Ignatius takes this focus on spirituality to another level in his teaching on "spiritual poverty." Ignatius neither embraces nor disdains riches. They are a tool to an end. But for him, the end, God's will, is so encompassing that it should leave room for nothing else. Put positively, everything else derives its proper meaning from God's will. Spiritual poverty involves emptying oneself of the desire for anything else but fulfillment of God's will. The objectives of *Spiritual Exercises* themselves, especially knowing, loving, and following Christ, help one shed all inordinate desires (including riches) and fill one's life with a dedication to pursing God's will, discovered through discernment.

Luther lived and wrote in a time when material riches and luxuries were becoming much more widespread and desired, both in secular communities and in the Church. He accordingly distinguishes between "true treasure"—the Gospel—and the "false treasures" of luxuries. He also lived at a time when individual vocations and even entrepreneurship were beginning to take the place of the guild or brotherhood mentality. And yet he encourages individuals to look to the community's good and community standards in determining how to value their own activities or products. The desire to live ultimately by "faith alone" does not lead Luther into individualism, but instead inspires him to repudiate individual almsgiving and advocate communal resources to support those in need.

Thanks to Weber, many people see Calvin as the father of the "Protestant work ethic" and the "spirit" of capitalism. But Calvin himself teaches something much different about material resources and penultimate realities. All material resources, including our labors, belong to God, as the free creator of this world. Even material prosperity comes from God, not as a gift but as a test. Calvin does buck long tradition in allowing for taking interest on money lent, but he puts strict limits upon usury in order to make sure it fosters the community's good, not just the lender's. The penultimate reality or compass that Calvin asks us to look toward in moving toward God is gratitude: everything we do or have depends upon Him.

Edwards takes a kinder view toward creation than many of Calvin's followers, seeing it as reflective of God's goodness and therefore good itself. Money too is good, as emanating ultimately from God. But, critically, it is a social good, not an individual possession, in Edwards's eyes. The penultimate virtues of charity and almsgiving help us live rightly toward this good. So too Edwards preaches the importance of maintaining the value of money and combating inflation, as it devalues this social good and especially harms the poor.

Again, all six of our thinkers unite in evaluating material resources not simply in themselves but from the point of view of the attitude one brings to them. This attitude depends upon the ultimate reality that each thinker points toward. It also takes shape from the penultimate virtues or purposes that each describes. These purposes range from personal virtues (liberality or magnificence) to social standards or economic policies. But all six see material goods as deriving their meaning from these attitudes and the ends of care to which they are directed.

Discernment

As we described above, agency is the realm of choice in which people draw upon starting conditions in order to generate purposeful actions. The starting conditions for each of our six thinkers we have described above, in their understanding of material resources and spiritual capacities. We have also surveyed their ultimate purposes or realities. What holds the two together is choice and, in the language of this volume, discernment. Once more, we can discern common themes and much variety in our six thinkers' views on this topic.

For Aristotle, the realm of choice finds perfection in the virtue of practical judgment. This virtue connects deliberation with intellect—the varying with the unchanging—based upon reflection on yourself and the world around you. It culminates in wise choices in the moment. Practical judgment requires experience in making choices and also clear "moral lenses" through which to see ultimate realities. At the center of the required experience lies personal reflection and questioning.

Aquinas describes a much different vision of discernment, one that depends ultimately on the "order of charity," which describes a ladder of love from God, to oneself, to one's neighbors. This ladder also translates into an order of almsgiving, involving both spiritual and material alms. But these lists are not rigid hierarchies. Aquinas asks us to deliberate in making choices about giving and to factor in considerations of our own needs and our own "station" as well as the needs and station of recipients. Love doesn't operate from a list of "to do's," for Aquinas.

In Ignatius, discernment finds its purest form, for discernment forms the center of his thoughts. Ignatius identifies two forms of discernment: discernment of spirits, clarifying motives or aspirations leading to choice in order to make an "election" or vocational decision about what practical path to take, and subsequent discernment of God's will. Again, there is no rote method for discerning these directives. The book *Spiritual Exercises* involves imagination, reflection, and dialogue in order to promote discernment. Ignatius also emphasizes the role of a spiritual director, who can guide the inclinations of the aspirant without interfering with God's direction or individuals' liberty to follow the inspiration of their heart.

Luther offers a challenge to discernment: our will is not our own and our reason is feeble and weak. We cannot hope to justify ourselves based on our "wise choices." Nor can we simply hold fast to tradition. We must trust in God. This challenge is also liberating. For Luther, each vocation is a "mask" or manifestation of God, and we reveal God's will in our every daily act. Also, because God gives so freely to us, we have a model for giving freely to each other, including the needy and our enemies. Discernment has a place here, for Luther does not ask us to ruin ourselves to give to others, but it is secondary to the great commandment to love others as ourselves.

As one might expect, Calvin begins with what is commanded in the Scriptures, but he quickly moves to a more discerning approaching to care for others. Calvin suggests a rule of dividing material resources equally between oneself and those in need. But he does not command this division. Instead the "law of love"—to love your neighbor as yourself—must find its expression within the needs of both parties. One guide that Calvin offers is to meet first the needs of the body of Christ, the Church, within which each believer is a member. But even this direction does not exclude treating the needs of others, who after all are also made in the image of God. Liberality for Calvin becomes less a rational exercise, as for Aristotle, and more an expression of heartfelt concern for your fellow members of this divine body.

Edwards locates his teaching about choice and discernment within his three-part understanding of the state of this world: that some are damned, some are awakening, and some are saved. When living in the damned state, one should follow the decrees of the Church, including those around tithing, since one's own judgment is hopelessly false. When awakening, choice rises to its fullest. One must struggle with shame and selfish desires as well as generous impulses. Examples of other awakening souls can help greatly in this time of discernment. But when one is fully awakened to the saved state, discernment falls once more into the background. Here one possesses perfect freedom, like God, and one "remanates" God's goodness to others. This remanation begins with caring for the public material well-being and moral goodness. But it also takes particular forms in benevolence toward members of the community.

Remanation and benevolence are very different from self-reflection and practical judgment. A central fixation on discernment is very different from living the law of love. Once more, we see a wide range among our six thinkers, one that keeps us from simply pointing to a "tradition" that could dictate our own choices. But we do still find a constant theme, in each one's attention to the importance of choice and the need for some process of reflection, deliberation, or discernment that connects foundation with aspiration in order to follow God's will for daily life.

Closing the Ring

We began this journey with an ancient tale, the tale of the ring, bequeathed from father to son, which would open the "door to wealth." As we saw, the "true" ring was eventually lost and the children turned to quarreling. But seekers discovered that the treasury remained open to all those who could approach it with indifference toward the value of the ring and merely trace its outline on the door.

In the preceding chapters, we too have offered traces. They are traces of the thoughts of each of these six authors. We could not detail their thoughts here; we could not even flesh out substantial pieces of them. The most we could do was offer an outline, based upon our theory of agency—a trace of each one's ideas.

These chapters offer traces in a different sense too, the sense implied in the story of the ring. The door to the wise use of wealth and the will of God stands open in every age and place. It can be found through the thought of Christians, Jews, Muslims, and even ancient pagans. Within each thoughtful author there lies a trace of its key. The key does not belong to any one tradition or history. Each of these supplies a foundation for moving forward and making choices in the present toward the future. Nor is the key, the trace, a single thing, a single theme, persisting unchanged through these different authors. The magical trace differs for each one of us, depending upon our history, our capacities, our resources, and our aspirations. That is why the thoughts of Aristotle, Aquinas, Ignatius, Luther, Calvin, and Edwards can differ so radically and yet serve us so well. We are all different listeners and different seekers. They—and many other authors—can help each of us find the trace that we need for our time and place. And their thoughts and this inquiry can provide a model for continuing to seek the Wisdom that governs all creation.

Selected Readings

Alcorn, Randy. 2003. *Money, Possessions, and Eternity.* Wheaton, Ill.: Tyndale.

Aquinas, Thomas. 1945. *Summa Contra Gentiles.* In *Basic Writings of Saint Thomas Aquinas,* trans. Anton Pegis. New York: Random House.

———. 1947. *Summa Theologica.* Trans. Fathers of the English Dominican Province. New York: Benziger Brothers.

———. 1988a. *Commentary on the Politics.* In *St. Thomas Aquinas on Politics and Ethics,* trans. and ed. Paul E. Sigmund. New York: W.W. Norton.

———. 1988b. *De Regimine Principuum.* In *St. Thomas Aquinas on Politics and Ethics,* trans. and ed. Paul E. Sigmund. New York: W.W. Norton.

Aristotle. 1985. *Eudemian Ethics.* Trans. J. Solomon. In *The Complete Works of Aristotle,* ed. Jonathan Barnes. Princeton, N.J.: Princeton University Press.

———. 1995. *Metaphysics.* Trans. J. Sachs. New York: Rutgers University Press.

———. 1998. *Politics.* Trans. C. D. C. Reeve. Indianapolis: Hackett.

———. 2001. *On the Soul.* Trans. J. Sachs. Santa Fe: Green Lion.

———. 2002. *Nicomachean Ethics.* Trans. J. Sachs. Newburyport, Mass.: Focus.

———. 2006. *Topics.* Trans. W. A. Pickard-Cambridge. New York: Oxford.

Bainton, Roland H. 1950. *Here I Stand: A Life of Martin Luther.* New York: New American Library.

Barth, Karl. 1995. *The Theology of John Calvin.* Trans. Geoffrey W. Bromiley. Grand Rapids, Mich.: Eerdmans.

Baumer, Franklin le Van. *Main Currents of Western Thought.* 4th ed. New Haven, Conn.: Yale University Press, 1978.

Bremner, Robert H. 1994. *Giving: Charity and Philanthropy in History.* New Brunswick, N.J.: Transaction.

Buckley, Michael J. 1973. "The Structure of the Rules for Discernment of Spirits." *The Way,* Supplement 20: 19–37.

Calvin, John. 1957. *Institutes of the Christian Religion.* Trans. Henry Beveridge. Grand Rapids, Mich.: Eerdmans.

———. 1981. *Commentaries.* Trans. and ed. John King et al. Grand Rapids, Mich.: Baker Book House.

Carson, D. A. 1999. *For the Love of God.* New York: Crossway.

Conforti, Joseph A. 1981. *Samuel Hopkins and the New Divinity Movement.* Grand Rapids, Mich.: Christian University Press.

Dabney, Robert Louis. 1985. *Systematic Theology.* Carlisle, Pa.: Banner of Truth.

Dempsey, B. W. 1947a. "Money, Price, and Credit." In Aquinas, *Summa Theologica*. New York: Benziger Brothers. 3366–3375.

———. 1947b. "Property Rights." In Aquinas, *Summa Theologica*. New York: Benziger Brothers. 3357–3365.

Dillenberger, John. 1961. Introduction to *Martin Luther: Selections from His Writings*, ed. John Dillenberger. New York: Doubleday.

Edwards, Jonathan. 1959. *A Treatise Concerning Religious Affections*. Ed. John E. Smith. New Haven, Conn.: Yale University Press.

———. 1966. *Basic Writings*. Ed. Ola Elizabeth Winslow. New York: New American Library.

———. 1969. *Freedom of the Will*. Ed. Arnold S. Kaufman and William K. Frankena. New York: Library of Liberal Arts.

———. 1970. *Original Sin*. Ed. Clyde A. Holbrook. New Haven, Conn.: Yale University Press.

———. 1972. *A Faithful Narrative*. In *The Great Awakening*, ed. C. C. Goen. New Haven, Conn.: Yale University Press.

———. 1989a. *Charity and Its Fruits*. In *Ethical Writings*, ed. Paul Ramsey. New Haven, Conn.: Yale University Press.

———. 1989b. *Two Dissertations: Dissertation I. Concerning the End for Which God Created the World. Dissertation II. The Nature of True Virtue* (1755). In *Ethical Writings*, ed. Paul Ramsey. New Haven, Conn.: Yale University Press.

Emirbayer, Mustafa, and Ann Mische. 1998. "What Is Agency?" *American Journal of Sociology* 103(4): 962–1023.

Flynn, Frederick E. 1942. "Wealth and Money in the Economic Philosophy of St. Thomas." Ph.D. diss., University of Notre Dame.

Ganss, George E., S.J. 1992. "Introduction to Ignatius of Loyola." In *The Spiritual Exercises of Saint Ignatius*, trans. George E. Ganss. Chicago: Loyola University Press.

Giddens, Anthony. 1979. *Central Problems in Social Theory*. Berkeley: University of California Press.

———. 1984. *The Constitution of Society*. Berkeley: University of California Press.

Gray, Howard J., S.J. 2001. "Ignatian Spirituality." In *As Leaven in the World: Catholic Perspectives on Faith, Vocation, and the Intellectual Life*, ed. Thomas M. Landy. Franklin, Wisc.: Sheed and Ward.

Griswold, A. Whitney. 1934. "Three Puritans on Prosperity." *The New England Quarterly* 7(3): 475–493.

Hall, Richard A. S. 1990. *The Neglected Northampton Texts of Jonathan Edwards: Edwards on Society and Politics*. Lewiston, N.Y.: Edwin Mellen.

Harkness, Georgia. 1958. *John Calvin: The Man and His Ethics*. New York: Abingdon.

Ignatius of Loyola. 1922. *The Spiritual Exercises of Saint Ignatius of Loyola*. Trans. W. H. Longridge. London: Robert Scott Roxburghe House.

———. 1992. *The Spiritual Exercises of Saint Ignatius*. Trans. George E. Ganss, S.J. Chicago: Loyola University Press.

———. 1996. *Personal Writings*. Trans. Joseph A. Munitiz and Philip Endean. New York: Penguin.

Ivens, Michael, S.J. 1998. *Understanding the Spiritual Exercises*. Trowbridge, UK: Cromwell.

James, William. 1929 [1902]. *The Varieties of Religious Experience: A Study in Human Nature*. New York: Modern Library.

Jodock, Darrell. 2001. "Vocational Discernment—A Comprehensive College Program." In *The Vocation of a Lutheran College*. ECLA Conference Proceedings, Gustavus Adolphus College, August 3.

Kass, Amy. 2002. *The Perfect Gift: The Philanthropic Imagination in Poetry and Prose*. Bloomington: Indiana University Press.

Keynes, John Maynard. 1933. *Essays in Persuasion*. London: Macmillan.

Lesser, M. X. 1981. *Jonathan Edwards: A Reference Guide*. Boston: G. K. Hall.

———. 1994. *Jonathan Edwards: An Annotated Bibliography 1979–1993*. Westport, Conn.: Greenwood.

Lewis, Clive S. 2001 [1944]. *The Abolition of Man*. New York: HarperCollins.

Lindberg, Carter. 1993. *Beyond Charity: Reform Initiatives for the Poor*. Minneapolis: Fortress.

Luther, Martin. 1955a. *Preface to Ordinance of a Common Chest*. In *Luther's Works*, vol. 45:2, gen. ed., Helmut T. Lehmann. Philadelphia: Muhlenberg.

———. 1955b. "Trade and Usury." In *Luther's Works*, vol. 45:2, gen. ed., Helmut T. Lehmann. Philadelphia: Muhlenberg.

———. 1961. *Martin Luther: Selections from His Writings*. Ed. John Dillenberger. New York: Doubleday.

MacLaren, Drostan. 1948. *Private Property and the Natural Law*. London: Aquinas Society of London.

Manton, Thomas. 2002. *The Works of Thomas Manton*. Lafayette, Ind.: Sovereign Grace.

Marsden, George M. 2003. *Jonathan Edwards: A Life*. New Haven, Conn.: Yale University Press.

Marty, Martin. 2004. *Martin Luther*. New York: Viking.

McDermott, Gerald R. 1992. *One Holy and Happy Society: The Public Theology of Jonathan Edwards*. University Park: Pennsylvania State University Press.

Muench, Aloisus J. 1947. "Social Charity." In Aquinas, *Summa Theologica*. New York: Benziger Brothers. 3326–3336.

O'Brien, George. 1920. *An Essay on Mediaeval Economic Teaching*. London: Longmans, Green.

O'Malley, John W. 1993. *The First Jesuits*. Cambridge, Mass.: Harvard University Press.

Otto, Rudolf. 1923. *The Idea of the Holy*. New York: Oxford University Press.

Pelikan, Jaroslav. 2003. *Credo: Historical and Theological Guide to Creeds and Confessions of Faith in the Christian Tradition*. New Haven, Conn.: Yale University Press.

Pink, A. W. 2001. *Practical Christianity*. Lafayette, Ind.: Sovereign Grace.

Rahner, Karl. 1980. "Christmas in the Light of the Ignatian *Exercises*." In *Theological Investigations, vol. 17: Jesus, Man, and the Church*, trans. Margaret Kohl. New York: Crossroad.

Richey, Sr. Francis Augustine. 1940. *Character Control of Wealth according to Saint Thomas Aquinas*. Washington, D.C.: Catholic University of America Press.

Ryken, Leland. 1986. *Worldly Saints: The Puritans as They Really Were.* Grand Rapids, Mich.: Zondervan.

———. 1995. *Redeeming the Time: A Christian Approach to Work and Leisure.* Grand Rapids, Mich.: Baker Books.

Schumacher, Leo S. 1949. "The Philosophy of the Equitable Distribution of Wealth: A Study in Economic Philosophy." Ph.D. diss., Catholic University.

Sewell, William H. 1992. "A Theory of Structure: Duality Agency and Transformation." *American Journal of Sociology* 98(1): 1–29.

Shah, Idries. 1970. *Tales of the Dervishes.* New York: E. F. Dutton.

———. 1971. *The Sufis.* New York: Anchor Books.

Spinks, Bryan D. 1999. *Two Faces of Elizabethan Anglican Theology.* Lanham, Md.: Scarecrow.

Spohn, William C. 1996. "Finding God in All Things: Jonathan Edwards and Ignatius Loyola." In *Finding God in All Things: Essays in Honor of Michael J. Buckley, S.J.,* ed. Michael J. Himes and Stephen J. Pope. New York: Crossroad. 244–261.

———. 2003. "Spirituality and Its Discontents: Practices in Jonathan Edwards's *Charity and Its Fruits.*" In *Journal of Religious Ethics* 31(2): 253–276.

Tetlow, Joseph A., S.J. 1989. *The Fundamentum: Creation in the Principle and Foun dation.* Studies in the Spirituality of Jesuits 21(4). St. Louis: Seminar on Jesuit Spirituality.

Toner, Jules J., S.J. 1982. *A Commentary on Saint Ignatius' Rules for the Discernment of Spirits.* St. Louis: Institute of Jesuit Sources.

———. 1995a. *Spirit of Light or Darkness: A Casebook for Studying Discernment of Spirits.* St. Louis: Institute of Jesuit Sources.

———. 1995b. *What Is Your Will, O God? A Casebook for Studying Discernment of God's Will.* St. Louis: Institute of Jesuit Sources.

Valeri, Mark. 1991. "The Economic Thought of Jonathan Edwards." *Church History* 60(1): 37–54.

Walker, Williston. 1991. *The Creeds and Platforms of Congregationalism.* New York: Pilgrim.

Weber, Max. 1950. *The Protestant Ethic and the Spirit of Capitalism.* Trans. T. Parsons. New York: Scribner.

Wood, Diana. 2002. *Medieval Economic Thought.* New York: Cambridge University Press.

Youngs, J. William T. 1990. *The Congregationalists.* New York: Greenwood.

Index

Abrahamic faiths, xi, xiii
actions, voluntary vs. prescribed, 68–69
advisor role, 9–10, 80–81, 85, 88, 95–96
affluence. *See* prosperity
agency: hyper-, 7–8; and moral biography,
    4–5; as organizing principle, 170–73, 180
Alexander the Great, 22
allocation, new spirituality of, 170–80
almsgiving: and charitable love, 64, 73–74,
    178; definitions of, 65–67; discernment
    on, 69–73; rules for, 86–88; spirituality
    and, 67–69; for wrong ends, 112–13
Ambrose of Milan, 46, 55, 60, 72
Aquinas, Thomas, xi; and Aristotle, 40,
    46–47, 53, 72; on charity, 40–45; and dis-
    cernment, 15, 63–74, 178; on economics,
    52–55; on happiness, 40, 177; on liberal-
    ity, 53–57; and Luther, 98; and mate-
    rial care, 177; on penultimate purpose,
    64–73, 175; on trade, 50, 60; on ultimate
    purpose, 40–42, 173; on usury, 50–52; on
    wealth, 46–63
Aristotle, xi; and Aquinas, 40, 46–47, 53, 72;
    and discernment, 15–16, 178; on friend-
    ship, 6, 19–21; and God, 36–37; on good
    life, 3–4, 23–27; on happiness, 15–20; and
    material care, 176–77; on natural right,
    145; on penultimate purpose, 19–21,
    175; on *philia*, 6–7, 19–21; on practical
    wisdom/judgment, 4, 19, 29–36; and
    proportional right, 144–46; on ultimate
    purpose, 15–21, 173; on use of resources,
    21–29; on usury, 135; on virtue, 1; on
    wealth, 21–24, 177

Arminians, the, 149–50
asceticism, 105–106, 132–34, 140
atonement, limited, 125
Augustine, Saint, 62
awakened, the, 151, 161–64, 179

being-in-action, 16–17, 26, 29, 173, 177
benevolence: as disinterested, 165; God's,
    160–61; human participation in, 160–67,
    179–80
bequests, 8
Bible, the: direct appeal to, 124; Good News
    in, 107; Law of Moses in, 103; tithing in,
    62–63; usury in, 50–51, 135–36
biography: moral, 1–6; spiritual, 5–6; of
    wealth, ix
body-mind dualism, 116–17
born again experience, 100
Brainerd, David, 162–63

Calvin, John, xi; on asceticism, 132–34;
    on depravity, 123; and discernment, 15,
    138–46, 179; as legislator, 128, 136, 139; on
    liberality, 143–45; life of, 123–25; and Lu-
    ther, 124–26, 130; and material care, 177;
    on penultimate purpose, 130–38, 176; and
    proportional right, 144–46;
    on prosperity, 134–35; on spiritual own-
    ership, 130–38; on suffering, 126–28;
    TULIP formula of, 125–26; on ultimate
    purpose, 124–30, 174; on usury, 135–38;
    on wealth and gratitude, 130–38; on
    works, 128–30
capacity: clarified, 11; as focus, xii–xiii;

mobilized by agency, 171–80; and moral biography, 4–5; and purpose, 6–7, 14; resources as, 2

capitalism, 136–38, 177

care: for church community, 111, 112–13, 120–22, 142; for family, 69–71, 120–22; material, 176–78; moral citizenship of, 6–7; for others, 15, 145–46; of things, 61–62

Carnegie, Andrew, 24

charity: Aquinas on, 40–45, 173; Edwards on, 167; order of, 64–65, 178

choice: agency and, 4–5, 172, 179; Aristotle on, 1, 175; awakened, 162–64; and indifference, 81; and practical judgment, 35–36, 178; and quality, 13

Christ: and the awakened, 163–64; collaborating with, 95, 173; imitation of, 78, 102, 175; marriage to, 99–100, 102, 105; membership in body of, 131–34, 138, 163; and reason, 119–20; service under, 75–76; suffering of, 126–28; sympathy with, 78–79, 92

Christian tradition, xiii, 172

Chrysostom, John, 46

church/state relations, 124–25

Cicero, 59

Commentary on Paul's Epistles (Calvin), 127–28, 129–30, 139

community: Calvin on, 144; as church, 121; as context for resources, 108–109; and friendship, 154–55; Luther on, 110–13

community chest, 110–12

conspicuous consumption, 27–29

Corinthians, Paul's second letter to, 127, 139

covetousness, 46–50

deliberation, 30–33

depravity of humans, 123, 125, 137–38, 149

desires, 33–34, 48, 179

discernment: and agency, 171–80; on almsgiving, 69–73; Aquinas on, 15, 63–74, 178; Aristotle on, 10–16, 178; Calvin on, 138–46, 179; defined, 15; Edwards on, 15, 147–48, 158–67, 179–80; as focus, xii–xiii; and free will, 116–19; of God's will, 75, 88, 94–96; Ignatius on, 75, 83–96, 179;

Luther on, 113–16, 179; and moral biography, 9–10; obstacles to, 116–17; and philanthropy, 10–14, 29; and practical judgment/wisdom, 29–36; of spiritual influences, 75, 89–90, 92–93; and spiritual poverty, 83–88; and states of the soul, 158–67; as term, 9; and vocation, 113–16

"The Economic Possibilities for Our Grandchildren" (Keynes), 13–14

economics, 52–55, 106–13, 160, 168

Edwards, Jonathan, xi; and Aristotle, 147, 153–54; on the awakened, 151, 161–64; on benevolence, 160–67; and discernment, 15, 158–67; on the fallen, 148–53, 159–61; on grace, 153–54; life of, 147, 157; and Luther, 98; and material care, 178; on penultimate purpose, 160–67, 176; on prosperity, 157–58, on the saved, 152–54, 164–67; on Scriptural duties, 148, 150; on three categories of salvation, 147–53, 158–59; as Trinitarian, 152–53; on ultimate purpose, 148–55, 174; on wealth, 155–58

elect, the, 124, 138

Emirbayer, Mustafa, and Ann Mische, 171–73

equality, 144–45

Erasmus, 117, 119

Ethics (Aristotle), xii, 24, 32, 36–37

excellent activity (*energeia*), 16

Exodus, book of, 2

faith: and grace, 153–54; Luther on, 45, 98–108, 174; and reason, 119–20; and resources, 106; tests of, 163; as ultimate purpose, 98–103; and works, 44, 105, 128–30

fallen, the, 148–53, 159–61, 179

fatalism, 150

"fitting" expense, 28–29

foresight, 55

Franciscan order, 52

free will, 116–19, 148–53

freedom, 4, 9, 83, 117, 126, 131, 166, 179

Freedom of a Christian (Luther), 105

friendship (*philia*), 6–7, 19–21, 26–27, 41–43, 57, 154–55, 175

Paul G. Schervish is Professor of Sociology and Director of the Center on Wealth and Philanthropy at Boston College. Schervish has published in the areas of philanthropy and on the sociology of money, wealth, biographical narrative, and religion. He is author of *Gospels of Wealth: How the Rich Portray Their Lives* among other books.

Keith Whitaker is a research fellow at Boston College's Center on Wealth and Philanthropy and Managing Director, Family Dynamics, at Wells Fargo Family Wealth. Prior to these roles, Whitaker was a philosophy professor at Boston College, focusing on political philosophy and ethics. His work has appeared in *Philanthropy Magazine, The Journal of Financial Planning,* and *The Wall Street Journal.*